BEYOND THE FRONTIER

BEYOND THE FRONTIER
AFRICAN AMERICAN POETRY
FOR THE 21ST CENTURY

EDITED BY

E. ETHELBERT MILLER

BLACK CLASSIC PRESS
BALTIMORE, MD

Copyright © 2002 by E. Ethelbert Miller
Published by Black Classic Press 2002
All rights reserved
Library of Congress Card Catalog Number:

ISBN1-57478-017-4
LCCN: 2002105792

Cover Art: Watcher One
by Edgar H. Sorrells-Adewale
Cover Design: Ron Crognale

Printed ON DEMAND by
BCP Digital Printing
A division of Black Classic Press

This book is dedicated to the memory of Leon Damas, Lance Jeffers, Larry Neal, Stephen Henderson, Sterling A. Brown, C.L.R. James, Walter Rodney and Julian Mayfield. These men helped chart the waters of blackness. We are their children, fighting to survive and live in this world. Our dreams carry us beyond the frontier.

Sea green birds, hungry after their flight,
peck at the new morning in me,
and the nine syllables of Egyptian desire
        spell my ancient name.
I must learn the dialectic of love's form
in the call that came with the light,
and live with the three-petaled rose of my new name,
        here, in this new world.

                Jay Wright

Acknowledgements

"Memory of Wings", *Shooting Star Review*, 1991; "Set Piece", *Passing Over*, Lotus Press; "Tar Baby on the Soapbox", *Callaloo*, Vol. 14. No. 4, 1991; "From the Mouth of the Gxara", *The Tar Baby on the Soapbox*, 1999; "Pretty White Girls", *Drum Voices Revue*, Vol. 6. Nos. 1 and 2, 1996, 1997; "Bird", *Obsidian II*, Vol. 11. Nos. 1 and 2, 1996; "April 19—: A Sonnet", *Duke University Libraries Forum*, Fall 1997, *Graffito*, Spring 1995; "American Sonnet #45", *Bathwater Wine*, Black Sparrow Press, 1998; "Brown Bomber", "Love Song of a Red Cap", "Something Terrible Something", and "Mississippi on the Doorstep" *Folks Like Me*, Zoland Books; "High School', "Exits from Elmina Castle: Cape Coast, Ghana", "Boy at Patterson Falls", "Christmas Eve; My Mother Dressing", and "Black Bottom", *Captivity*, University of Pittsburg Press, 1989, *Tender*, University of Pittsburg Press, 1998; "Refugee", *Black American Literature Forum*, Vol. 20-3. No. 3, Modern Language Association, Indiana State University, Fall 1986; "The Plea", *Prairie Schooner*, Vol. 51. No. 2, Summer 1977; "Concerning Violence" *River Styx*, 1996; "Another Ode to Salt", *The Caribbean Writer*, 1995; "Memorial", *Voices 1 An Anthology of Barbadian Writing*, 1997, *First Impressions*, HomeGrown Press, 1999; "hazing" and "coming to the net (for arthur ashe)", *Spirit and Flame*, Syracuse University Press, 1997; "The Museum Cashier", *Indigo*, Vol. 20-21, September, 1996; "Midnight" and "What I Am", Musculon Music, 1999; "Annuals and Perennials", *Fertile Ground*, Runnagate Press, 1996; "Memorial Drive", "Cross Burning Black" and "Paralyzed", *Pudding Magazine*, 1996; "The Love of Travellers", Callaloo, 1988; "Moment", Columbia Poetry Review, 1992; "1619. Virginia" and "1619. Tituba of Salem", *Bridge Suite: Narrative Poems Based on the Lives of African American Women in the Early History of These New Nations*" Storm Imprints, 1998; "After the 200th White Person Locks Her Car Door at Me", "Vivian, Take 57", "Friendly Skies", "Lost", "Black On Black", and "It's A Dog's Life", *Speaking Through My Skin*, Michigan University Press, 1997, "Friendly Skies", *African American Review*, "Lost", *The Pearl*, "Black On Black" *Obsidian II*, 1995; "What is There for Us", *A Gathering of Mother Tongues*, 1998, "Saudades", *A Gathering of Mother Tongues*, 1998, *Eyeball*, 1998; "At the Jackson Pollock Retrospective in L.A.", *Fireweed: Poetry of Western Oregon*, April, 1991; "The Names of Summer", *Fireweed: Poetry of Western Oregon*, October, 1991; "A Debt is Paid", *River Oak Review*, Spring 1997; "They Do Not Have to Nest in Your Hair", *360° A Revolution of Black Poets*, 1998; "lessons in lying", *Long Shot Review*, Palanquin Press, September, 1996; "dedicated to the domestics", *Long Shot Review*, Palanquin Press, Winter 1997; "back road", *Birthmarks*, Nightshade Press, 1993; "The Major", "One Million Men Marching II" and "Keep a Good Thought", *Million Men Marching II*, 1996; "HELP", *Colored Women Colored Wor(l)ds*, 1996; "Nuclear Peril", *Louisiana Literature*, 1999; "Port Townsend Poems", *Louisiana Laurels*, Baton Rouge Arts Council, 1991; "In Oklahoma", *360° A Revolution of Black Poets*, 1998; "jesus' song" and "swinging doors of knocking-wood cowards 8 for us", *Obsidian: Black Literature in Review*, 1982, *Confirmation An Anthology of African*

TABLE OF CONTENTS

THE MEMORY OF LANDSCAPES

After the 200th White Person Locks Her Car{....}	Bruce A. Jacobs	3.
Exits from Elmina Castle: Cape Coast, Ghana	Toi Derricotte	4.
Born	Yao (Hoke S. Glover, III)	8.
Trying to Sleep After Studying Color Photos{....}	Monifa A. Love	9.
Invisibles	Joanne M. Braxton	10.
Barrage	Ruth-Miriam Garnett	12.
The Woman Who Jumped	M. Eliza Hamilton	14.
Bound	Odetta D. Norton	15.
Soul Roots	Felicia L. Morgenstern	16.
1619. Virginia	Gale P. Jackson	17.
1691. Tituba of Salem	Gale P. Jackson	18.
From the Spirit of Phillis Wheatley {....}	Karen Williams	19.
Gone	Calvin Forbes	21.
If Harriet Tubman Were Alive Today	Verneda (Rikki) Lights	22.
Circumcising Pandora	Mirlande Jean-Gilles	24.
Praisesong: From Son to Mother	Lenard D. Moore	26.
Harvest	Stephen Caldwe Wright	27.
Dream of Mango	Rohan B. Preston	28.
thermometer	giovanni singleton	29.
defensive driving	giovanni singleton	30.
Locks	Joy Dawson	32.
Port Townsend Poems	Pinkie Gordon Lane	33.
Haiku	C. Yaphet Brinson	36.
Memorial	Charmaine A. Gill	37.
Memory of Wings	Jabari Asim	38.
Returning the Water	Angela Shannon	40.
I Am a Creature of the Obvious	Keith Antar Mason	41.
Refugee	Gideon Ferebee	44.
Moons...tides	André J. Baldwin	45.
Legacy	Sydney March	46.
When Africa Speaks	Jude Chudi Okpala	47.
African Sunrunner	Wanda Winbush-David	48.
Senegal Sestina	Odetta D. Norton	49.
Tattoo, or Henna	Odetta D. Norton	51.
Meditations I	Duriel E. Harris	52.

white	*Ronaldo V. Wilson*	*54.*
Blue	*Carl Phillips*	*56.*
Passing Through This House	*Yao (Hoke S. Glover, III)*	*57.*
Objects of Desire	*Monifa A. Love*	*59.*
Poem for the Purchase of a First Bra	*Allison Joseph*	*62.*
Michele	*Afaa Michael S. Weaver*	*64.*
At Five	*Oktavi*	*65.*
HELP	*Rosamond S. King*	*67.*
another day	*Rosamond S. King*	*69.*
Washboard Wizard	*Marilyn Nelson*	*70.*

LANDMARKS: PEOPLE AND PLACES

The Prayer of Miss Budd	*Marilyn Nelson*	*73.*
Drifter	*Marilyn Nelson*	*75.*
Love Song of a Red Cap	*Sam Cornish*	*76.*
Landmarks	*Claude Wilkinson*	*77.*
for my 27th birthday	*giovanni singleton*	*78.*
A Debt is Paid	*A. Van Jordan*	*80.*
Boy at the Paterson Falls	*Toi Derricotte*	*81.*
Walking On: A Declaration of Wholeness	*Saddi Khali*	*82.*
Something Terrible Something	*Sam Cornish*	*85.*
Pretty White Girls	*James E. Cherry*	*86.*
Gentleman at the Barbershop	*S. Brandi Barnes*	*87.*
Roots	*mawiyah kai el-jamah bomani*	*88.*
Black Drag Queen	*A. Van Jordan*	*89.*
fruitbowl 1	*Imani e. Wilson*	*90.*
I Know I Aint Hip No More	*Peter J. Harris*	*91.*
Revolutionary Thoughts	*Crystal Williams*	*93.*
Christmas Eve: My Mother Dressing	*Toi Derricotte*	*95.*
In Search of Aunt Jemima	*Crystal Williams*	*97.*
Raindrop Women	*Mariahadessa Tallie*	*99.*
What I Am	*Terrance Hayes*	*101.*
To the People of a Small Town in Ohio...	*William Henry Lewis*	*103*
The Tar Baby on the Soapbox	*Carole Boston Weatherford*	*105.*
Beaches	*Zak Robbins*	*106.*
Vivian, Take 57	*Bruce A. Jacobs*	*107.*
Annuals and Perennials	*Janice W. Hodges*	*109.*
Mississippi on the Doorstep	*Sam Cornish*	*111.*
The Love of Travellers	*Angela Jackson*	*112.*
Smile	*reuben jackson*	*113.*
Work to be Done	*Sam Cornish*	*115.*
The Fitting Room	*Angela Jackson*	*116.*
Land of the Lost	*Charles Porter*	*118.*

City in You	Michael Hill	119.
Peace Be Still	Esther Iverem	120.
Untitled	Eli Goodwin	122.
American Sonnet (46)	Wanda Coleman	124.
Black on Black	Bruce A. Jacobs	125.
Memorial Drive	Willie Abraham Howard, Jr.	127.
Sunday	Angela Shannon	129.
Going Home	Toneka N. Bonitto Burwell	130.
Leaving Winston-Salem	Toneka N. Bonitto Burwell	131.
charleston, south carolina	Christopher Nickelson	132.
My Mother	Melvin E. Lewis	133.
We	Janeya K. Hisle	134.
Gullah Women	Melvin E. Lewis	136.
JoNelle	Angela Shannon	138.
Things No One Told Me	Opal Palmer Adisa	139.
Integration	Angela Shannon	141.
Dirt	Stacy Lynn	142.
After an All Day Skirmish with the Clouds	Eli Goodwin	143.
Blackbottom	Toi Derricotte	144.
Baltimore	Afaa Michael S. Weaver	145.
Lost	Bruce A. Jacobs	147.
Child in the New Delhi Sun	Garrett McDowell	148.
Threnody	Kalamu Ya Salaam	149.
Soledad	Yao (Hoke S. Glover, III)	152.
Meridian Hill Terrace	Wendy S. Walters	153.
7-30-96	Erren Geraud Kelly	155.
Brother is a Star	Rachel E. Harding	156.
Call and Response	D. J. Renegade	157.
Snapshot: West Philly	Kimmika L. H. Williams	158.
The Bible Buckle	Rozell Caldwell	159.
Saints	Lana C. Williams	160.
How to Make It	Yvonne A. Jackson	161.
Audre's Son	John Frazier	164.
It's a Dog's Life	Bruce A. Jacobs	165.
dungle sublime	Ronaldo V. Wilson	166.
Yellow is Me, But All the Same Are We	Joan Adams	167.
An Irresistible Light	Dorothy Phaire	168.
April 19, 19—: A Sonnet	George Elliott Clarke	170.
Bruised Children	Janice W. Hodges	171.
Worry All the Time	Alison Morris	172.
Midnight in Mississippi	M. Eliza Hamilton	175.
For the Man I Met on Georgia Ave.	Matthew Watley	176.
My Family	Nyere-Gibran Miller	177.
Mother's Day at McDonald's	Patricia Elam	178.

The Major	*Bernard Keller*	*180.*
Hazing	*Brian Gilmore*	*181.*
Father and Son	*D. J. Renegade*	*183.*
father's shoes	*tyehimba jess*	*184.*
father country	*tyehimba jess*	*185.*
100 Times	*Arnold J. Kemp*	*187.*
those I love are sometimes white	*Imani Tolliver*	*188.*
Paralyzed	*Willie Abraham Howard, Jr.*	*189.*
The Museum Cashier	*Yona Camille Harvey*	*190.*
dedicated to the domestics	*Nzadi Zimele Keita*	*192.*
Astrology?	*Valerie Jean*	*194.*
Moon Daughters	*Artress Bethany White*	*195.*
Passing	*Carl Phillips*	*196.*
Sterling Brown	*Ronald D. Palmer*	*198.*
Matisse, Cut Outs	*Trasi Johnson*	*199.*
Stranger in the Village	*Lorelei Williams*	*200.*
They Do Not Have to Nest in Your Hair	*Carolyn Joyner*	*201.*
Rain Making	*Dana Gilkes*	*202.*
Thoughts From a 747	*Dana Gilkes*	*203.*
Space	*Verneda (Rikki) Lights*	*204.*
High School	*Toi Derricotte*	*207.*
Tattooed Girl	*Monica A. Hand*	*209.*
Cross Burning Black	*Willie Abraham Howard, Jr.*	*210.*
She-Ghosts of Tiresias	*Monica A. Hand*	*211.*
The Science of Forgetting	*Yao (Hoke S. Glover, III)*	*213.*
The Lock and Key	*Vicki-Ann Asservero*	*215.*

DANCING ON THE SHORE WITH SPIRITS, SINGERS AND MUSICIANS

Spirit of the Dancer	*Lisa Elaine Johnson*	*219.*
As Dancers	*Lisa Teasley*	*220.*
Help is a Discotheque	*Eddie Bell*	*221.*
for lester	*Reggie Timpson*	*222.*
Bird	*James E. Cherry*	*223.*
Mom Used to Listen to Erroll Garner	*Everett Goodwin*	*224.*
John Birks Gillespie: an appreciation{....}	*Everett Goodwin*	*225.*
Chittlin's	*Cornelius Eady*	*227.*
Thelonius	*Afaa Michael S. Weaver*	*228.*
Monk	*Gaston Neal*	*230.*
Monk's Misterioso	*Sydney March*	*231.*
The Fourth Supreme	*Allison Joseph*	*232.*
Stevie Wonder	*Lyn'elle Patrice Chapman*	*234.*
The Mighty Blood	*A. Anthony Vessup*	*235.*
Noon Talk at Georgia's Coffee Shop	*Allison Joseph*	*236.*

Burn Rubber on Me	*Derrick X (Goldie Williams)*	*238.*
Photo of Ron Carter, Playing His Bass	*Cornelius Eady*	*239.*
Savannah Brass	*Verneda (Rikki) Lights*	*240.*
Set Piece	*Houston A. Baker, Jr.*	*242.*
A Thousand Marionettes	*Sydney March*	*243.*
verbal gun shots	*Reggie Timpson*	*244.*
Dr. Jack	*Thomas Stanley*	*245.*

BLOOD AND DISAPPOINTMENT IN THE LAND

Vipers, Flies, and Women of the Cloth	*James Coleman*	*249.*
Visiting Hours	*John Frazier*	*250.*
Concerning Violence	*Ruth-Miriam Garnett*	*251.*
Rehearsal	*Baba Lukata*	*252.*
Alley Games 6/the ascension	*Ira B. Jones*	*253.*
Glass Box Puzzle No. 1	*André J. Baldwin*	*254.*
December 12th	*Zak Robbins*	*255.*
Examination	*Stacy Lynn*	*256.*
A White Man and the Judge	*Kevin Simmonds*	*257.*
The Good Ole Days	*Harriet Wilkes Washington*	*258.*
I Love You, Though You're Unemployed	*Dawn L. Hannaham*	*259.*
If there's no sugar	*Dawn L. Hannaham*	*260.*
The Edge	*Paul Jamal*	*261.*
the subtle art of breathing	*asha bandele*	*262.*
Who Sez Thunderbirds Can't Fly	*Gary Lilley*	*266.*
Imperialism-The Dancing Do Not Die	*Thomas Stanley*	*268.*
park mole	*Merilene M. Murphy*	*270.*
The Artifice of War	*Brandon D. Johnson*	*272.*
Generation Gap	*Tammy Lynn Pertillar*	*273.*
Funeral	*Gary Lilley*	*275.*
Say Something: A Change is Gonna Come	*Mbali Umoja*	*277.*
Some Solace, Some Yearning	*William Henry Lewis*	*280.*
In Oklahoma	*Toni Asante Lightfoot*	*281.*
black tax	*Nzadi Zimele Keita*	*282.*
what is left	*Nzadi Zimele Keita*	*283.*
A Guard	*John Frazier*	*285.*
Sorrow Song	*John Frazier*	*286.*
1st Lt. Vernon J. Baker: Hero on the Hill	*Jabari Asim*	*287.*
Staff. Sgt. Edward A. Carter, Jr. {....}	*Jabari Asim*	*290.*
1st Lt. John R. Fox: Rain of Fire	*Jabari Asim*	*293.*
The Names of Summer: A War Memory	*Harold L. Johnson*	*295.*
At the Jackson Pollock Retrospective in L.A.	*Harold L. Johnson*	*298.*
Our Second Night	*Viki Radden*	*300.*

Letter from Kuwait	*Lenard D. Moore*	*303.*
a black soldier	*Lenard D. Moore*	*304.*
Four and Twenty Soldiers	*S. P. Shephard*	*305.*
Come and See My Little Toys	*S. P. Shephard*	*306.*
Homeless Vets	*S. P. Shephard*	*307.*
Suicides and Fools	*S. P. Shephard*	*308.*
Lights of the Bigtop	*Garrett McDowell*	*309.*
this mortal coil	*Robert Fleming*	*311.*

BEYOND THE FRONTIER

The Plea	*Calvin Forbes*	*315.*
Girlfriend	*Lori Tsang*	*316.*
To Keep from Shouting Something	*Honorée F. Jeffers*	*317.*
Our Mothers	*Melanie Hope*	*319.*
she kneels at the wailing wall	*Cherryl Floyd-Miller*	*321.*
Color-Struck	*Afaa Michael S. Weaver*	*322.*
For My Mother	*Duriel E. Harris*	*324.*
For My Mother	*Gideon Ferebee*	*326.*
Fallen Bodies	*Gideon Ferebee*	*327.*
The Long Walk Home	*Robert Fleming*	*328.*
back road	*Nzadi Zimele Keita*	*329.*
Grand Diva	*Thandiwe Shiphrah*	*330.*
to adam	*Thandiwe Shiphrah*	*331.*
Grandma	*Thandiwe Shiphrah*	*332.*
While Communing with a Tree{....}	*M. Eliza Hamilton*	*333.*
Friendly Skies	*Bruce A. Jacobs*	*335.*
And all the sisters said...	*Janeya K. Hisle*	*336.*
angry sisters	*Christopher Nickelson*	*337.*
three men	*Christopher Nickelson*	*338.*
Untitled	*Christopher Nickelson*	*339.*
For Fatma and Her Co-wives	*Janeya K. Hisle*	*340.*
What is There for Us?	*Jacqueline Joan Johnson*	*341.*
Be Careful When You Go Looking{....}	*Pat Russell*	*344.*
Rising	*Nzadi Zimele Keita*	*348.*
Cycles	*Nzadi Zimele Keita*	*349.*
Meet in the Conjure Woman	*Gary Lilley*	*350.*
Wet Oak	*Angela Shannon*	*351.*
Hands	*Angela Shannon*	*352.*
The Beelzebub Chronicles	*Artress Bethany White*	*353.*
Stringbeans	*Kay Lindsey*	*354.*
The Star	*Clyde A. Wray*	*355.*
Private Thoughts	*Clyde A. Wray*	*356.*
Sin, 1969	*Afaa Michael S. Weaver*	*357.*

Lines	Afaa Michael S. Weaver	358.
Midnight	Terrance Hayes	359.
Ashy Gal	Baba Lukata	360.
what does a man do	tyehimba jess	361.
Why I Don't Leave the Apartment {....}	Kalamu Ya Salaam	362.
haiku #135	Kalamu Ya Salaam	364.
Grand Canyon	Estelle E. Farley	365.
Home Cookin	Estelle E. Farley	366.
Daniel's Hands	Niama Leslie Williams	367.
cornbread blues	Vincent Woodward	368.
Licorice	Laini Mataka	369.
Can We Talk?	Laini Mataka	370.
Interpretations	Baba Lukata	371.
kiss her that she don't know how	Carletta Carrington Wilson	372.
fisher king	Imani Tolliver	374.
Fire/Water Blues	Darrell Stover	375.
To a Flasher	Dawn L. Hannaham	376.
Finished Poem	Michelle Calhoun Greene	377.
For My D.C. Girlfriends	Michelle Calhoun Greene	378.
Perspective	Lisa Pegram	379.
The New Sestina	Kevin Simmonds	381.
In This, the Fifth World	Jennifer Lisa Vest	383.
Hearts	Melvin E. Lewis	384.
Why I Won't Wear a Tatoo	Tracie Morris	386.
Lover's Total Recall	Tracie Morris	387.
Just Say No Blues	Tracie Morris	388.
Prelude to a Kiss	Tracie Morris	389.
yet another epiphany	Lisa Pegram	390.
Deposed	John Frazier	392.
Untitled	Lauren Anita Arrington	394.
(1/vacant)	Nadir Lasana Bomani	395.
I watched	Kimmika L.H. Williams	396.
my sleeping husband	Nzadi Zimele Keita	397.
Poem #3	Sybil J. Roberts	398.
Love #49	reuben jackson	399.
soul gestures in spring	michael datcher	400.
Word/Life	Charlie R. Braxton	402.
Sextet	C. Yaphet Brinson	404.
Back to the Blues	S. Brandi Barnes	406.
when you say no	Merilene M. Murphy	408.
Voudou Mama	mawiyah kai el-jamah bomani	409.
roots I: {....}	Cherryl Floyd-Miller	410.
roots II: the conjure woman replies	Cherryl Floyd-Miller	411.
taboo	Cherryl Floyd-Miller	412.

lessons in lying	*Nzadi Zimele Keita*	*413.*
Stranger	*Tisa Bryant*	*415.*
More Than Anything	*Doreen Baingana*	*416.*
One More Once	*reuben jackson*	*417.*
Control	*Janice W. Hodges*	*418.*
Imani's Song	*Alison Morris*	*419.*
Crushin	*Stacy Lynn*	*420.*
Obessions are Important	*Primus St. John*	*421.*
Nice Sister-Scholars Need Loving, Too	*David Earl Jackson*	*424.*
Temple of Your Familiar	*Felicia L. Morgenstern*	*425.*
Ride Me Baby, Ride Me	*Felicia L. Morgenstern*	*426.*
Hues of Electric Blue	*Felicia L. Morgenstern*	*427.*
Black Women with Jewish Names	*James Coleman*	*428.*
Loving	*Angela Jackson*	*429.*
Sex	*Viki Radden*	*430.*
When You Talk That Talk	*Viki Radden*	*432.*
Blood	*Viki Radden*	*434.*
jesus' song	*esther louise*	*436.*
Moment	*Angela Jackson*	*437.*

CULTURAL WEBS AND NETS

Zoning	*Joanne M. Braxton*	*441.*
coming to the net	*Brian Gilmore*	*442.*
Untitled One	Kwan Booth	*444.*
Negroes	*Matthew Watley*	*445.*
The Next Malcolm Poem	*Peter J. Harris*	*446.*
Shame of the Writers' Conference	*Allison Joseph*	*447.*
Gale Sayers	*Ta-Nehisi Coates*	*448.*
Brown Bomber	*Sam Cornish*	*450.*
The Knockout	*Sydney March*	*451.*

THE SONG TO COME

And the Birds Sing of Life	*Stephen Caldwell Wright*	*455.*
Confession	*Eli Goodwin*	*456.*
Just Asking	*Carl Hancock Rux*	*457.*
lookin good	*Stacy Lynn*	*460.*
When I Leave My Body	*Rohan B. Preston*	*462.*
As from a Quiver of Arrows	*Carl Phillips*	*463.*
october death	*Kiamsha Madelyn Leeke*	*465.*
October 7th	*Zak Robbins*	*467.*
Haiku for My Brothers	*Ira B. Jones*	*468.*
One Million Men Marching II.	*Bernard Keller*	*469.*
Keep a Good Thought	*Bernard Keller*	*470.*

What My Mother Taught Me	Shara McCallum	471.
Praise the Daughter	Melanie Hope	472.
Ezili Impending	Rachel E. Harding	473.
i am open	michael datcher	474.
Sea Shells	Lorna Lowe	477.
100 Million	Matthew Watley	478.
Storm	Brandon D. Johnson	481.
Mary, Don't You Weep	Honorée F. Jeffers	483.
A Streetwalker Trying to Speak {....}	Elaine Maria Upton	484.
the black experience.	mwatabu s. Okantah	486.
African Morning	mwatabu s. Okantah	492.
market day	mwatabu s. Okantah	493.
Stranger at Home	James R. Lee	494.
Anacaona	Danielle Legros Georges	495.
Another Ode to Salt	Danielle Legros Georges	498.
Jamaica, October 18, 1972	Shara McCallum	499.
Saudades	Jacqueline Joan Johnson	500.
Mississippi: Bell Zone 1	Jerry W. Ward, Jr.	501.
For Brothas That Like to Holla	Kenneth Carroll	503.
a song for serpents	Kysha N. Brown	505.
Yu no send. Me no come.	Shara McCallum	508.
Nuclear Peril	Pinkie Gordon Lane	510.
history of the quilt {....}	Carletta Carrington Wilson	512.
How to Build a Prayer	S. Pearl Sharp	514.
From the Mouth of the Gxara	Carole Boston Weatherford	520.
The Song to Come	Doreen Baingana	522.
Lunching	Lori Tsang	530.
The Beloved Ones	E. Juaguina Watkins-Cothran	534.
swinging doors of knocking-wood {....}	esther louise	535.
At the Threshold of the Moon	Gigi Maria Ross	536.
Surrender	Amitiyah Elayne Hyman	537.
Morning Buddhism	E. Ethelbert Miller	538.
Index		539.
Contributors		558

{....} *Indicates poem title has been shortened for table of contents. Consult the actual poem for the full title.*

Embracing the Blackness at
the End of the Universe

A major turning point in my life occurred when I accepted a visiting professorship at the University of Nevada, Las Vegas, (UNLV) in 1993. It was a wonderful opportunity to not only teach, but to go west, and live in another part of the country. It also provided me with time to complete work on my anthology *In Search of Color Everywhere* (Stewart, Tabori & Chang, 1994). This book was the first anthology I completed on my own. *Beyond the Frontier* is the second.

I have always been interested in compiling collections of African American poetry. *Synergy: Anthology of Washington D.C. Black Poetry* (1975) was made possible because of my work and friendship with the hoo-doo publisher Ahmos Zu-Bolton II. A few years later, I met Barbara Berman, a feminist poet who lived near Dupont Circle. Together we formed Anemone Press and were able to publish books by Lee Howard and Thulani Davis. In 1977, with Barbara's help, I edited *Women Surviving Massacres And Men*, a slender volume praised by such women writers as Adrienne Rich and June Jordan. Working on the campus of Howard University placed me in the company of scholars and writers like Arthur P. Davis, Sterling A. Brown, and Stephen Henderson. Davis and Brown were responsible for such classic anthologies as *Cavalcade* (1971) and *The Negro Caravan* (1941). Henderson, who was my teacher and a major influence on my development as a writer, edited *Understanding The New Black Poetry* (1969), which captured the poetic explosion that took place in the late sixties. It featured representations of the Black oral tradition (work songs, blues, and spirituals) as well as a long introduction in which Henderson attempted to define the unique characteristics of Black poetry.

For a number of years following the publication of *Understanding The New Black Poetry*, Henderson, whose office at Howard was on the same floor as mine in Founder's Library would mention the need for doing another anthology. He wanted to work on a book that would feature emerging writers. He requested my help with the project. I guess this might have been in the early eighties, almost twenty years ago. Why do another anthology of African American poetry? Well, I guess for the same reason a person decides to suddenly pack, leave, and move. Today our world is heading in an exciting new direction. I dream of a place where the air is cleaner, the land richer, and the horizon never-ending in the distance.

Beyond the Frontier is what one needs to travel well. This anthology is a care package of poetry filled with survival songs, cures, and rhythmic potions. It's the type of advice and medicine that one can't obtain over the counter. The frontier is where the outlaws live; people who defy convention and the rules of law. The Black poet has always been an outlaw, a strange bird who found the strength and courage to sing in a strange land. Bars did not silence the songs; they only made them bluer. The frontier is where the oppressor believes civilization ends. However, the new people say the frontier is the new world. They claim the ground. Every breath they take is an act of resistance. *Beyond the Frontier* is not a collection of poets disguised as buffalo soldiers or sentries and witnesses to racism and genocide. This anthology charts the journey of men and women who are explorers and space travelers, embracing the blackness at the end of the universe, and bending light into new images.

This anthology begins with the memory of landscapes and landmarks, presenting poems in the *For My People* tradition of Margaret Walker. It includes a section entitled "Blood and Disappointment In the Land," which in many ways documents the social struggle found in today's headlines. Poems later in the anthology focus on the love which is essential for survival, rebirth, and dreams. Here we are reminded of the importance of faith in the unseen. In many ways, beyond the frontier is where God resides.

At the dawn of the 21st century, we must discover our true beauty. Poetry is a vehicle to transport us beyond forever. Beyond the frontier, beyond this world (which once enslaved us), lies a new consciousness. Poetry like prayer restores faith to the heart. It contains the healing power of love and forgiveness. Words make us human. A common language will reflect the final transformation of the human spirit. This book represents a new genesis as we turn our backs on a century of history and the old civilization.

E. Ethelbert Miller
Washington, D.C.
March 2002

THE MEMORY OF LANDSCAPES

Bruce A. Jacobs

AFTER THE 200th WHITE PERSON
LOCKS HER CAR DOOR AT ME

Makes me wish
my distant cousin
had told the first of them
on the West shore:

"No. This isn't Africa.
Head due south
until you hit ice.
You can't miss it."

Toi Derricotte

EXITS FROM ELMINA CASTLE:
CAPE COAST, GHANA

> Gotta make a way out of no way.
> —traditional black folk saying

The Journey

There is no perfect
past to go back to. Each time I look
into your eyes, I see the long hesitation
of ten thousand years, our mothers' mothers
sitting under the shade trees on boxes, waiting.
There is some great question in your eye that no
longer needs asking: the ball
glistening, wet; the black iris
intense. We know the same things.
What you wait for, I wait for.

The Tour

The castle, always on an
outcrop of indifference;
human shells,
the discards on the way.
Where our mothers were held, we walk now
as tourists, looking for cokes, film, the bathroom.
A few steps beyond the brutalization, we
stand in the sun:

This area for tourists only.

Our very presence an ironic
point of interest to our guide.

4

Tourists' Lunch
On a rise, overlooking
the past, we eat

jolaf with pepper sauce and chicken,
laugh, drink beer, fold our dresses
up under us and bathe thigh-
deep in the weary Atlantic.

Beneath Elmina

Down the long, stone ramp,
chained together, unchained finally from the dead,
from months of lightlessness and the imprisoned stink
(a foot-square breech,
the cell's only opening for air—air
which had entered sulfurous, having passed over
the stocks of ammunition),
they pressed and fell against each other.
The only other way (besides death) had been for the few

women who were hauled up into the sun
to be scrutinized by the officers,
the chosen pulled up to apartments
through a trap door:

If they got pregnant, they were set free—
their children becoming the bastard
go-betweens who could speak both tongues.

●

At the bottom of the dark stone ramp,
a slit in cement six (?) inches wide,
through which our ancestors were pushed—

the "point of no return,"
so narrow because the Dutch feared
two going together to the anchored ship
might cause rebellion,
and because, starved for so many months,

that opening
was their bodies' fit.

Above Elmina

At the top of the castle,
orderly pews.
We enter under a lintel
carved with news:

This is the house of God.

Slavery

It had struck some of the African Americans
in those dungeons beneath the earth—
though we had come to Africa to heal—there was a huge rip
between us: those were rooms through which *our* ancestors
had passed, the Africans' had not.

"Another way to look at it," a Nigerian poet answered levelly,
"is that perhaps your ancestors escaped."

Power

The palace of an African king:
two courtyards (a public and a private) in a complex
of bone white stucco edged with a crimson stripe;
the king, in a huge carved chair,
gold-painted and lioned, wearing an understated robe
of grays and browns, his face a structured pleasantness—
the bones of one who has become
slightly more than human;
his ministers smile from faded velvet sofas—
old men with remarkably intact teeth.

A few of us standing in the courtyard
are surprised by a thin man, boyish, though middle-aged,
who comes toward us signaling he is begging—
one hand outstretched, the other nearly touching his lips—

his robe of subtle greens, his feet bare, his naked shoulder
well defined as an aging athlete's.
" 'The Imbecile Prince,'" our guide explains.
"The only remaining member of the last king's family.
We take care of him as if the present king were his father."

Market

Those huge platters on their heads on which everything
is placed accurately, each small red pepper,
prawn, each orange—arranged in piles so tall they defy gravity—
avocados, crabs, dried fish of silverish brown,
or one great yam, thirty pounds, dirt brushed,
counterbalanced in a kind of aquarium.

A woman approves me with a fluent grin
and offers her light basket for *my* head;
I walk a yard, tottering awkwardly.
The unremarkable commonness —
a beauty shaped by women's hands.

Yao (Hoke S. Glover, III)

BORN

(For Kamau Sekou)

so in every day there is breathe   presence
an arrival from some other place
more beautiful than here   that you have
come there were people gathered to meet
you   to sing into your face and drum into
you skin   all we have to give
we hold you   with our palms
as though life were not as durable as the hardest
steel gigantic stones   we call mountains
or the lonely space   the deep blue   we call sky
that you came down   to travel with us   we
will always remember   that you are headed
somewhere   full of seasons and signs
we know we are thankful
we wait for you to walk and speak
until then and even after
forever   we will   carry   you

Monifa A. Love

TRYING TO SLEEP AFTER STUDYING
COLOR PHOTOS OF GOMA

From a small boat on a large river
I wave to my mother on the shore.

Hundreds of mothers rise from the river,
Their bodies bloated and still.

My fingers spread a net across the river.
My mouth yanked open calls her name.

The sun turns our bodies into glinting, bloody cranes.
The motor roars and kills her name.

She becomes the crowded water and the silenced name.

The clouds spread a net across the river.
My hands are busy with the hail of blades.

Joanne M. Braxton

INVISIBLES

Windward, never leeward, always windward,
Breathing toward Africa, four by five feet,
Thatched with palm, these exile houses, empty now,
Alone on the stoney beach, except for tourist from America,
Come with our cameras and measuring tapes.
Incredulous in Bonaire, island of coral rock
Where even scrub cannot grow.
Mountains of salt at our backs,
Pink, gray and white as far as the eye can see,
They faced East, a pinnacle of torture between them and the sea.
Some refused to work and raised the cry,
"I am a man," stripped and staked to the thing to dry out,
Wind whipping salt and sand like a knife,
An inhospitable place, a bad place to die.

II.

Just offshore, the brother guide nervously introduces "Invisibles":
No further explanation, no particular hazards,
Nothing particular to see.
"Invisible" is what you don't see.
Clearest water in the world.
Ninety feet, turquoise clear to the bottom.
Dropping over the side like a stone, I equalize,
Weightless in descent and eerie silence.
Down and down and down, seventy feet.
Immense flats of sand loom white as the salt above.
Someone who knew this place never became anyone's ancestor.
Down and down and down, eighty-five feet, ninety feet.
Suddenly, the crazy singing of the Saints.
This lamenation is not nitrogen;
And not a living soul can make a

Sound at ninety feet.
Yet I am not in harm's way.
These, who might have been my ancestors,
Beseech me to "Bear Witness,"
And I ascend, following a trail of bubbles.
Below, a black tipped reef shark glides along a boney drop off,
Feasted on African souls of Yoruba and Fanti.
Back on deck, the guide looks fathoms into my eyes and smiles.
"Invisibles," I respond.
And he, "Invisibles."

Ruth-Miriam Garnett

BARRAGE

(for Dawad Philip)

Where does the ark take us, stoics? The gray weather
we imagine to be the helmeted sky of a desert shorn of film,
mined with hungers and indeterminate strangers.

Friend, we are here, seated. You know, like we sometimes were
when eyeing a breach in the trampled road, a path familiar
as a frown next the mirror's inlay.

So much: cousins, old loves, even the dead
attend this seminar or brooding, of sequestered speech.
My tongue is thick from meat pushed around a plate
and from innumerable, visible sins.

My secret was this screaming, what I hold in my hands. The pearl
whose color I want to deepen. My prayer is for blackness, a pearl,
the world to become this. Til then, my language is in tatters

and borne by the day's bosomy rain. As long as there is sound
the believers can gather up on deck to dance. You see them,
how they are given over to each others' thrusts, vocabularies aimed
at the moon. Minutiae; consonant, infinite speech.

We should talk as though this were Casablanca.
We should pull up to a table too small, where I barely escape
your smoking, where you see the words behind my gutless breaths
for the methodists they are, your catholic spate
running alongside my memory with a belt for our tripling waists,
as we realize beauty goes, but keeps its adornments.

We dance also, from memory. Perhaps you and I
we even can run off together, once the white-haired one has docked.
We are not the leaders of this expedition; too odd, too cut
in several places. Unable to hide the gashes our flesh pillows.

It is funny to me, all your children are you, they speak your languages; a pil-
lar, or a pillory. Ask me Wednesday which. But ask.

Tough a thicket's grown wild over my unctuous refusals.
Where you stand, only the top of my head is visible.
I am near drowned, I am doomed to an idea of mating.
I am lain aside, a gourd forgotten by villagers in their packing.

Think, Friend, how we survive the staunchest vessels,
wrestling our tongues from stillness when the day was calm,
from thrashing when the air obeyed no one.

M. *Eliza Hamilton*

THE WOMAN WHO JUMPED

She wants me to gather Her fallen robe around me,
that midnight blue black mantle
separating us five centuries,
and return the way I left.
Middle Passage this time is no different
except, now, I remember
what I could not before.
That is how I stayed alive.
Everything is stored in my ankles
in my wrists
in my womb
in my eyes.
In my tongue thrown at my feet.
In my feet whipped raw
because I dared run for the ocean.
Everything is stored.
And when I cover mySelf with the sky
She once abandoned for me to take hold of -
I will speak Our name in my grandmothers' language.
On the inside of that robe, it is written.

Odetta D. Norton

BOUND

We always had choices:
sharks
or the belly of a ship.

In dimensions of dark
and closed spaces,
we became master

contortionists.
Are meteorites falling? What comes
from nowhere?

Rock, body, rock.

Noah made the journey in his ark,
Moses in his bulrush boat.

We never counted more
than a sixteenth note

Thus, syncopation, rhythmic
                leaps.

Since we were barely living,
rarely stretching
         in those mornings.

Although we must have
extended an elbow here,
              there a hip.

Felicia L. Morgenstern

SOUL ROOTS

Taken in
by my translucent skin
you mistakenly assume
I am of Mayflower kin

But I was as black as coal
an eclipse of the white man's soul
so very many lifetimes ago

Gale P. Jackson

1619.
VIRGINIA.

This morning I steel my eyes open so horror can not seal them
the moon's face is the sky's womb threaded with seabirds
their sheep voice announcing land though this corpse vessel
eclipse the sun the dead child stares before and behind
and I watch my sister rock her baby in bloody empty arms pink
flesh on the bone her mouth a curse of mucus vomit and sperm
she scream her mind into the wind, the dawn, this land they call
"Virginia" I stare it down at the world's end where the sea
is a liar's calm I will outlive them if I must become stone I
will become stone and call myself Isabella I lick her lips I
whisper I feed her the seeds I have hidden, all this time,
under my tongue.

Note: *The beginning of African enslavement in North America dates back to the arrival of a group of Africans to Virginia's shores in 1619. Among these people was a woman 'named' Isabell who worked and perhaps raised the money to 'buy' herself back. Isabell married and the record of her baby's birth was the first of an African American in this region.*

Gale P. Jackson

1691.
TITUBA OF SALEM.

In my mind's eye fields be burning bloody rags
and sunflowers blooming steel grey water they call ocean
marked with bloated bodies floating.
Blackbird caged in cold I nurse them. If you can serve
then you can poison.
Nimble fingers of a story. So by day they may enslave me
but by night I fly away.
My hens are fat. My house is warm. "Black arts!" they cry
and say I'll burn but I confess and will not hang.
What is a witch if not a woman blind to all except surviving.

Note: Tituba of Salem, celebrated in literature and drama, was also of Barbados where the magical practices and storytelling ritual of Bakongo were still very much alive in the seventeenth century.

Tituba was among the first accused and tried in the infamous witchcraft trials of Salem. The evidence against her: a warm house, a lively housekeeping, and an ability to weave a story so seductively her listeners were 'spellbound'. She confessed and did not hang.

Karen Williams

FROM THE SPIRIT OF PHILLIS WHEATLEY
TO THE SPIRIT OF THOMAS JEFFERSON
(A Note 212 Years Later)

*Jefferson once said Wheatley's poetry was beneath dignity of criticism
because Blacks innately could not write poetry. This is her response.*

Kind sir, do listen,
to the zephyr that blows,
and ruffles the fallible threads
beneath your powdered wig. Do you hear it,
it is my voice, a lodestone ardent and sweet,
sage and resolute, the mysterious interface
of dust and gold, of the immemorial,
the now and hopes of our world.

Look about you, kind sir,
to the hills and mountains,
their shadows of eyes looking, dark and keen
waiting not for sleep, but for freedom's leaves
to sprout, sheath and encourage.
Eyes shining with internal and external blood,
and that of the weeper crusting the driver's lash.

This blood of coin, full of shadow and light,
the stirs and whispers of the Muse, lives,
breathes and hisses, procreates and hopes,
breathes and hisses again, angry yet fueled
you and peers have tried to quench its hunger and fire.
212 years later, did you succeed?

The blood of coin too awaits entry into golden gates,
presses it's face to the iron,
into the stories it lives and weaves and remembers.

So kind sir, do listen to me the Afric,
the silenced, the woman,
America in tawny shades,
the screams and songs in the field.

Yes, kind sir, do listen
for I am the peasant and the peacock,
the anchor and the moon
the force behind the eraser,
but better yet I am the quill,
The dollar the buys and frees.

And I am the slave and the slave-owner
the creator and the creation
the knob on doors to me you've closed,
slowly turning,
slowing turning.

I am the sinner and the saved
Footing, a Blackwomanpoet
the walking, courageous bard,
another image of Christ.

Calvin Forbes

GONE

master send me
I get lost
I free myself
this country full
of people with nothing
better to do
than get other people
to work for them
for nothing
master can get
himself
another slave
or pay me
for my troubles
like he pay for me
if you see him
tell him I long gone
with a smile on my behind
signed: freewill freedom
p.s. tell old master he ain't
no kin of mine

Verneda (Rikki) Lights

IF HARRIET TUBMAN WERE ALIVE TODAY

If Harriet Tubman
were alive today
what would she say?
What would she think,
observing
would be warriors
consumed,
like charred leaves
in a burned forest,
as they huddle behind
a cocaine line.

What would she think
'bout snorting white powder
up your nose,
or sellin' your momma
for just one more blow.

I think
she would scream,
yes
Moses would scream,
"my people walk in
darkness as dead
men.
They have no faith
in a promised land.
They've turned their backs
on God
and curse his name,
saying in chic new
religion speak
that Jesus was

just another guru,
maybe,
and being saved is
a faddist's new game."

Perhaps she would enter
some cool sound studio
and sing like Aretha
demanding respect.

Where would
Moses go now?
Where would she indeed.
She who never
lost one soul.
She who never lost
one single soul
would fall down
in fits
rapturous.

One more blow
to her head.
They couldn't kill her.
One more blow
intended deadly.
They couldn't kill her then.
But today,
just maybe
she
      would rather
      be dead

Mirlande Jean-Gilles

CIRCUMCISING PANDORA

These women live in roots darkness
Can make their scent become river
evade salivating dogs and white men
Women who had voodoo
in the whites of their eyes
Silent warriors who can steady
precious stones in streams
Press their ears into conch to understand the tide
Wrapped their hair in fire
Peeled away pores and flesh
to walk through the earth as a breeze.
These are my mothers of magic
Whose voices are only whispers to me now
Their stories coiling into myth-fiction
Family calls them useless fairy tales
Them black angels with universal wing span
Singing butterflies
that could brush stroke the heavens rose
to redefine sky, it was the first sun set.
Dance on the blades of machetes and
strip the whiteness off of doves and wash themselves
in purity
I am told to forget them
But I won't
I set up altars to them
that my father stares at
worries about
I find my candles extinguished when I come home
Lysol where my incense used to be
"Fires," he says, "They will cause fires."
He now listens drumless
Prays soulless

His congregation
defends circumcising Pandora for opening that box
Hitting Eve for talking with that snake
Burnt witches and drowned wizards
But their own son turned day night and nothing to something
They got my dad loving my mom, but not liking her much
Wants to slap her lips when she talks in church
Veil her face and cover her broad hips in loose fitting tunics
Wants to take the belt to me
Saw his eyes flash when I reminded him that Satan was also God's son
and a good looking one at that
Shakes his head, says the devil speaks the language of drums
Resides in the smoke of sage
Florida water his elixir
And my voudoun grandmother clutches her bones tighter
She knows her stone stories will eventually be rubbed smooth
with a bucket of holy water and a leather bound bible

Lenard D. Moore

PRAISESONG: FROM SON TO MOTHER

Mother, I listen hard to hear you speak
how grandfather plowed
behind the largest mule
in dusty sunlight
as nearby elms gave way to wind.
I think of you: how
you picked purple collards
from the backyard garden,
got hog-meat fresh from great-grandma.
This was routine.
At dusk, with father home from teaching mechanics,
you set the redwood table.
We ate by candles.
Nobody spoke, the only sound
the noise of spoons and forks
scraping tin plates.
You guided me through chores:
cooking for younger brothers and sisters
who played daylong in mill-thinned woods;
keeping the large blue house spotless.
Beyond that, you were an artist,
drawing, painting in private hours.
You never knew I saw.
The truth is, I searched out your art
when you were away.
How your love grows into me,
your oldest manchild
praying long this night
that we could pass this praisesong on
to those who ache
to know.

Stephen Caldwell Wright

HARVEST

We Wear this Flesh
Strong to reach Center
    of Space
    at Times
Worth pursuing
Worth Keeping.

We Blink our eyes
At former Lives,

Gape longingly
For future
Resurrections.

Sometimes reflectively,
Oftentimes willingly,
We Wear this given Flesh.

Cast it from us in our dreams;
Embrace it in our ethereal wanderings—

Lost in electric serenity;
Collected in colorful forgetfulness.

If fortunate,
chosen—

Wear it well,
and timely,
We Do.

Rohan B. Preston

DREAM OF MANGO

Sunshine on some ample lips
mango dripping on the chest,
sweeter at the raisin tips
that look out darkly from the breasts.

Mango in the mouth and teeth
stringy diddling on the tongue,
in the throat and in the heat
of a knee-deep, gurgling song.

Mango down the navel coin
on the face of a navel moon,
mango sauce delayed at the loin
but O, dear, it's burning soon.

Mango slurped up in a tremble
in the rushing hush and thud,
in the rise and quivering rumble
boiling up through breath and blood.

Mango in the breeze-open room,
in the dipped-and-dappled glaze,
mango noon and mango night,
mango fans the morning haze.

giovanni singleton

thermometer

and just what color is blue?

names forgive their meaning
sundays are for what a mind thinks

history of touching
stretches out beneath the surface

the only way to sleep is to
imagine it is raining

and it is
raining

wind blows open and over
a final line of defense

what happens happens
far away

giovanni singleton

defensive driving

1.

at night
high beams scan the
unseeable distance

an untitled landscape

black is not
a shade but rather
an impression

oil on canvas

2.

scratch and sniff lawns
on southern streets where
one sips lemonade or

iced tea before hosing
down weeds in
the way of light.

still life with

3.

jars marked and mislabeled for
proper identification
enjambment is a way of doing it.

standing room only

4.

drums do not go quietly
their chained rhythm treads
water and stretches of road.

ocean as enclosure.

Joy Dawson

LOCKS

Tendrils of Strength
Cables of Life
Lines of Curve
Extensions of Freedom
Manifestations of the Past
Statements of Truth
Coils of Care
Sections of Sensuousness
Eels of Electricity
Brandishments of Blackness
Poems of Perseverance
Locks of Love

PORT TOWNSEND POEMS

(for Bill Stafford)

1. Puget Sound. Early Morning

They tell me that the sun
rises more from the north
than from the east —
Alaska-born.

Bright over the sea
it sucks the waves
swelling to shore. No
human voice, no bathers
break the horizon.

Only the gulls, a boat
in the distance, and waist–
high weeds just within reach.

The sky, gray as the waves, flows
into the northern sunrise
that forms a screaming halo
absorbing lowlands and sea,
mountains, and hills.

Clear and without sound
the lighthouse silhouettes
'The Point'—its vigilant
eye resting now,
waiting, but always

there . . .

2. Outside My Window, Unseeing

Hearing sound I
cannot fathom,
I have visions of fluttering
wings, wet
against wind.

It is the voice of loneliness—
unended, trembling
and dark.

I hear its sad, mindless
music —
waiting . . .

3. Coming Home

"Goodbyes" merge now
like the northern lights.

Was it only yesterday that I
listened to the crows
atop the "Kitchen Shelter"
declaring their presence
to the morning mist
while gulls line
the curving beach?

I am ready now for home,
for Louisiana lowlands
cropped by pine trees singing
in the wind,
for a house that hums
between rafters and beams,
for caladiums spreading their broad
leaves to a dying sun.

In this northwest town
I will not be missed. But
that's O.K. I have felt
the presence of Puget Sound outlining
high bluffs,

       have followed a diagonal sky
       screaming to the sea — curving
       beyond sound and rim,

       have climbed a rugged bank in rain
       and wind — ghosts fading in shade
       and light,

       have listened to poems
       in Bill's workshop — new
       voices, familiar, sculptured
       and fine—

Louisiana, my point of reference
its moisture, its azaleas, filling the
earth with sweetness and warmth.

C.Yaphet Brinson

HAIKU

Haiku 10

black, brother, nigga,
african-american:
what the hell am I?

Haiku 30

    Saturday cuties
crossing georgia avenue,
    my brown eyes jaywalk

Haiku 50

"I love you" is a
phrase most commonly spoken
    by those who do not

Haiku 60

    above and beyond
the call of duty, above
        and beyond the law

Charmaine A.Gill

MEMORIAL

Nailah Folami Umoja

burnt sugar skeletons
wave in the wind
memorials
to those once cut
down
whipped into shape
a gritty brown utility
a smooth fiery path
of liquid gold
the crop that binds
is more
than dead
and fields of life
give way to empires
of burnt sugar cones
that messily melt
in the rain

Jabari Asim

MEMORY OF WINGS

I heard a great humming
herald the holy one's coming,
rhythm rumbling as it rose
above the bent backs of the cotton rows.

Through a fold of molten air
a blue-black man with snow-white hair
landed lightly on the trembling field
to share the secrets he concealed.

Faith lifted my eyes
to see an angel in human guise
with human hands black as mine
walk along the planting line.

He urged us all to remember wings
sacred spells and ancient things,
ancient songs and ancient chants
to power the ancestral dance.

Lift up! He said, the sky is yours!
Ride the wind to your native shores!

Many rose swift as thought
singing out the words he taught,
dropping sacks, seeds and hoes
as they climbed above the cotton rows.

Those of us whose tongues were slow
could only watch and remain below.

Driver man cursed the sky
as the flock went soaring by,
black wings against the sun
beyond the bite of whip and gun.

Memories of magic and holy wings
ease the ache bondage brings.
Still I scan the sky and pray to see
the holy one coming back for me.

Angela Shannon

RETURNING THE WATER

We can cry now. After centuries of holding
streams of tears in our bodies until they ballooned,
until they disfigured arms and legs, until
they ached with too much weight and our hearts
became metal, and blood thickened and thinned,
thinned and thickened and turned
toward fire, and our chest cursed our strength
and felt nothing at all—no kisses or pinches
or nails or hammers. And with desert eyes we said,
we can take anything, we are indestructible
we have been beaten, maimed, bruised, burned,
and not one drop has dripped from our right eye.
But now old spirits, we can let go and return
the water to where it should naturally be.

Keith Antar Mason

I AM A CREATURE OF THE OBVIOUS

I am a creature of the obvious.
    i am black
    i am male
when i am running, i am guilty
  the shaming secret swaying in the trees
  do not work here/ i am the torn page out
   of the family, do you remember the old
folk saying tell the truth
    and shame the devil
i am the devil/ the purse snatcher
     needing the nickel and dime
      from that old black woman earth
      there are no excuses between
      me and my father/he didn't keep
      his, word and i ain't making
       none for myself
i do not want what my father wanted
40 hours being a burger fryer
    i am little icarus
       i only fly at night
       i know not to fly too close
        to the sun
         even in the alpine winter
        of freedom's land
i am making the evening news and some don't know
what to do with me...my uzis are singing field hollers
and gospelshouts don't stop the killing, i am the sacred
wanna be b-boys with the hougan ways/papa sam scratch
 knocking on my brotha's head/ and if king is ashamed
 ..of me/it is because my parents quit their job
    and mtv didn't raise me/ i dominate the world
    with my vision of my self/ and whoever don't

love me/ they don't have to watch
but you have closed you eyes
bought up alphabet street
living large with your
bmw's yo' am/pm
solutions
i believe
in myself
i believe
in capitalism
i believe
in getting paid
i believe
in death
don't 'cha
hear me

I can find the exact place
while i laid in the sand
the heat against
my face

i could hear it call my
name, this part of the desert
feel it burn my feet
it was right here
that i found
my heart
pounding naked
my testicles bouncing
painted in sienna
darker than my flesh
i painted myself with the blues
in the corn, and listened
to the whispers of sand
tufts cactus needles drew
blood and we colored
boys
was not suppose to hide out in crazy horse canyon
in red rocks browner than blood soaked bricks
let our muscles harden/by swimming in the green

river and speak to snakes and lizards
what was my black skin telling me
down trails where bandits died
this was an ocean bed
and we could hear slaves
drowning

Gideon Ferebee

REFUGEE

I am a pilgrim adrift upon ancient waters
Allied with an armada of flesh and blood
In flight from familiar borders
I am a crusader
Propelled by all forms of political oppression
A slave, an immigrant, an exile, a spirit without homeland
Hostage to the hospitalities accorded transients
I am denied the dignity of heritage, language, ancestors
The conventional wisdom
Even denies me definitive moral character
For I am of the displaced, a transition of cultures
A spiritual movement of countries, continents
I am a transition of consciousness
An historic transformation of identities
Of both the host and the traveler
I am a refugee
Searching sanctuary where my soul may find shelter
Desiring domicile where my descendants may rest peacefully
Hunting for a habitat where my hopes may take root
I am a refugee
In search of a new horizon
Where my name, the color of my skin, my religion
Will be like a gift to this adoptive community
In search of a new dawning where my quest for freedom
Will be like a blessing at the end of my journey

André J. Baldwin

moons...tides

...riding high

on the waves
floating on my raft
sail full and free

looked down
in the ocean
to see my reflection

liked what i saw
decided to
take a dive

held my breath
jumped in

ocean did not catch me
it let me fall

it moved out of my way...

Sydney March

LEGACY

I belong here
where the waves
rock the fisherman's boat
from dream to dream.
Successive suns
have betrayed the source of my river,
now it is only a trickle.

I have put away my clarinet
with its clever keys,
and my taut skin
becomes once more
the membrane of drums.

Now the music I make
echo songs from the wombs
of my grandmothers' mothers.
For me each night
the rhythms weave a world.

Jude Chudi Okpala

WHEN AFRICA SPEAKS

O! Africans! Here I sing you
A song long overdue
You bleach; you're bleaching;
You're bleached.
More Western than west
Black no more, waiting
On the quicksand of time,
Blurring the boundaries,
Shifting the channels.
The world which you made,
Is roaring past you.
And you are not bewildered, stunned.
Feeding on tension.
Looking back, in you unconscious desires and dreams.
I am here, I am yours.
Come! We are one.
Shall I die with no one to mourn me?
With no grave and epitaph?
No tomb in a high place?
My bones and flesh feast to the birds?
No traces left?
I am thinking.

Wanda Winbush-David

AFRICAN SUNRUNNER

Run in warm sun
Bring legs up Kilimanjaro high
Down Nile river flow
Like mother's milk
Come running to mouth
Nuture all

Run pass Kymit
    pass Mali
    pass Ghana
    pass Nigeria
    pass colonialism
    pass independence
     pass internal strife
    pass revolution
Back to the sun

Odetta D. Norton

SENEGAL SESTINA

Who sews the split calabash? Who mends
the dried gourd? Who boils the peanuts, plants
them in the field? The *Layene* sing
in praise of their founder this evening. A week
ago, the children painted their faces and ran
through the city, banging on cans, expecting coins.

A youth clings to the back of a bus and taps coins,
asks us where we're going while a tailor mends
my dress. We ran
past bougainvillea plants.
Sand fills my lungs, makes them weak.
It's the weekend. Youssou and Lemzo will sing

in the big stadium. Crowds rush to hear them sing.
Fans press bills to their foreheads. Coins
too heavy, though change obsolete during the week.
At the pastry shop we're told politicians promise to make amends.
For the first time, I hear about the fire in the oil refining plants
in the industrial part of town. They say, flames ran

like electric tubers, skimming the ground. Few stories ran
in the Western presses which may be why the *griot* sings:
people listen but don't always hear the news. Rhythm plants
joy in the ear while words like coins
hold variable currency. I missed y*o*u, we say and hope this mends
the distance between us. Less than a week

into Ramadan and violence breaks out. People, hungry and weak,
find strength in Allah. That Abdou Diouf ran
and won the election again is no surprise. Perhaps a country mends
itself by scratching the head of old wounds. The donkeys do not sing

in Fatick, as they might in a fable; they bray. The devout pray and give coins
to *talibe* in observance of one of the five pillars. The *talibe* supplants

the common beggar in the streets. All this asking plants
a certain fear. More needing than giving. The last day of the week,
men bow on prayer rugs in the big avenues, backs shining like coins
in the sun. Heads, tails, they prostrate. The red dust which ran
with the Harmattan winds on their feet and faces. The muezzin sing
from minarets. Language pours from the sky. Mends

in my *tallie-basse* allow me to zip my dress by myself. Mends
like these confound my tailor: a solo woman plants
suspicion here. But as Nina Simone sings
this, so do I live it. Here, rats and roaches are never weak.
The ants march and negotiate a path through all the rooms. I ran
along the *Corniche* in the dry season. My friend coins

phrases more brilliant than coins. Is it the sea that mends?
Other tongues ran in me, sprouted as from two grafted plants.
A lone voice, luxurious but weak. *Adjaraama.* Is peace still singing?

Odetta D. Norton

TATTOO, OR HENNA

Eh, jankh-bi, kaay fii, a woman calls,
tray of kola nuts on her head.

Buyers and sellers haggle
for plastic kettles, flip flops, incense

and *jelli-jelli*: beads worn to jingle
and scent around a woman's haunches.

I return to my neighborhood and see
taxi drivers asleep.

The sidewalk a bed, rock a pillow.
Sand blocks, cement, tin tenements.

I pass closed courtyards and hear girls
sweeping. Goats and children are tied

with *gris-gris* to protect them
from *djnn* and other nefarious spirits.

Rhythm of wood, mortar and
pestle. Word spreads quickly:

the foreigner has been painted
on the inside of her hand. Amina

and her friends come running.

Duriel E. Harris

MEDITATIONS I

(for Erma Jean Weems)

I.

For the beginning and the end
For promise
For moments everything seems just that
For clarity after
For stillness that approaches peace
For wind that moves me
For breath that carries the long line
the comma, the colon, the semi-colon
lull of soft sounds conducive to sleep
For light moving steadily toward us
For the cushion of the earth
For those who have come before
the dead and the living
For the now, this moment, and this one
For the tenacity of the just-past
For memory and revelation
For the path to the lake
For graciousness of trees: maple, oak, willow and evergreen
For the path to the wood that trails to . . .
the bigness and smallness of things
For the work of seasons and their willingness
For those who have come before and their legacy
of strong bones and teeth and flesh
-all moving in unison to become what is human
For those who are still beginning: our shapes, our possibilities
For the now, this moment, and this one

II.

For eyes that reach from sleep and bring morning
    still warm glazed with strangeness
For the arc of the star and the blackening crusts of night's first offering

For dark passages of ears and their shapes and winding
For waves of sound, the major and minor chords, the trill and scat, beat
        and measure
        metronome
        the brilliance that resonates
(Epiphany, divine order echoed in carbon
the molecules rattling the body cage)
            Wound so tightly I would break
            nothing to spare, rationing breath
            all the while screaming
            take it all, take it all, and leave me
And I do break, I do, I do break

For the heaving sigh
For the diaphragm, lung, larynx, tongue and palate

For the receiving palm
For receiving until filled, receiving until unbroken
For the perpetual present-fluid existence-in infinite dimensions
        paper-thin panes (neither barrier nor shield)
        that simultaneously are
        as I am in this moment and all those before and hereafter
For the yes
For the now, this moment, and this one

Ronaldo V. Wilson

white

1.

to a hamster the property of plastic
is sunk in the bath a running tube
click shut as a gas chamber

your fat hairy body makes me sick

2.

metal thread around your wrists
bound like assassin steel around the neck
of a spy filament rip filament death

gold when spun
one ounce to one mile of rope
but what good
your claws anyway?

3.

the pin teeth of a tiny rat head

4.

to rodent scale a corkscrew spiral
the *wahbash cannonball* or *ghost mountain*
demon plunge
a tunnel then the hush of hands bind the back
to hydraulic halt

5.

hand squeezed your pregnant sister shoots milk
her eyes pop the face
blood shot does she struggle through holes?

when we return from holiday:

eaten out stomachs
blood faces a cage
dizzy in sulfur light

6.

you bite you pay

a wall

you hit dazed
like a human

Carl Phillips

BLUE

As through marble or the lining of
certain fish split open and scooped
clean, this is the blue vein
that rides, where the flesh is even
whiter than the rest of her, the splayed
thighs mother forgets, busy struggling
for command over bones: her own,
those of the chaise lounge, all
equally uncooperative, and there's
the wind, too. This is her hair, gone
from white to blue in the air.

This is the black, shot with blue, of my dark
daddy's knuckles, that do not change, ever.
Which is to say they are no more pale
in anger than at rest, or when, as
I imagine them now, they follow
the same two fingers he has always used
to make the rim of every empty blue
glass in the house sing.
Always, the same
blue-to-black sorrow
no black surface can entirely hide.

Under the night, somewhere
between the white that is nothing so much as
blue, and the black that is, finally, nothing,
I am the man neither of you remembers.
Shielding, in the half-dark,
the blue eyes I sometimes forget
I don't have. Pulling my own stoop-
shouldered kind of blues across paper.
Apparently misinformed about the rumored
stuff of dreams: everywhere I inquired,
I was told look for blue.

Yao (Hoke S. Glover, III)

PASSING THROUGH THIS HOUSE

and when you are screaming
I know to be silent
to carry
the groceries into the house
run the bath water
for the children
check the windows
to make sure the house
is safe and sound
like your better half
the one who
in your last days
of pregnancy
held you hand
until it was as simple
as holding your breath
diving to the bottom
of a pool
what else could I do
to say nothing
was to say something
like when the music stops
in the middle of a song
and the musicians are counting
on the same beat
not thinking about their children
the late phone bill, or that no one
will be awake
when the cab drops them
at the front door, 3 a.m.
when we settle
when we begin again

in the next moment
I will tell myself
living is as precious
as the sunrise
everyday
it comes in bits and pieces
until it is day
and done
and when you
are screaming
I pray
my own throat
is empty
to take your words
and swallow
them whole

OBJECTS OF DESIRE

1.

at ten
before i knew
anyone could smell me
all kinds of men started staring at me
on the bus
and reaching up my skirt
as they sat comfortably
and i stood holding on to the pole
an older woman
smacked one for me once
when she saw that hand slithering
for my panties   a good walloping smack
passengers around him
saw her hand flying for his
face and ducked
she talked loud about his mother
and his private parts
my fairy godmother
looked around at the other men
like it was high noon
don't you let them worry you none
she said
the rear door hissing as she left

at ten
i couldn't eat on the street any more
men hanging out of car windows would ask for some
talk about my tongue and mouth
their tongues and mouths
with shark teeth
at ten

i wasn't one body anymore
i was pieces
i didn't know
i had so many
pieces.

2.

the first cannibals i ever saw were black.   they were in the
   movies and on tv. they had big pots. i liked those pots. i
   thought how did they make those? i wondered why did they
   cook people with their clothes on? it seemed silly to me.
   tarzan seemed silly, too, although i thought he swam well.
   then one day while i was examining that jungle scene my face
   close to the tv steadied on my elbow propped hands, my
   brother said those aren't black people those are white people
   with black make-up on. ohhhhhh.

3.

i think of draining myself
taking out the last hint of sex
before i leave in the mornings
i don't want to be misunderstood
better to have no secret message
than to feel like a hand grenade
between somebody's teeth
emptying myself might help me
know my place
my confinement tempo
the boundaries of appropriate passion
if i'm not careful i start to feel free
with my body i catch myself dancing
in the supermarket my hips
finding something in the aborted
rhythm and blues of the piped in music
or i grab myself enjoying a breeze
under my dress. i may need to nab myself
before i am nabbed. i think
about wearing my insides on the outside
to see what men would call me then.

4.

in college
i read an ad for dancers
in trenton
good money really good money
so i stood in line
with spiked heeled
tasty black leather women
who wet their sparkling lips
stroked strands of wayward hair
with blood sculptured fingertips
checked their breasts with long smooth
good really good caresses
they turned me on
just standing with them
and i watched them
as their names were called
taking their jackets off
like it was foreplay
and i watched
them moving
holding on to the poles
of the dancer's cage
for balance
i didn't answer
to my name
i looked around with the others
for the named no woman
they all knew it was me
next next

Allison Joseph

POEM FOR THE PURCHASE OF A FIRST BRA

Let the older accompany the younger.
Let the older woman's purse be full
of salient things: sticks of gum to chew
to ease anxiety away, pretty postcards

of Swiss Alps to placate, distract,
an elegant pair of earrings, silver,
to anoint the younger woman's lobes.
Let the lighting in the store

be casual, kind, so soft that when
the younger woman disrobes, her body
fairly glows, surrounded by light
that doesn't disperse, will not fade.

Let the fitting room be empty
except for three women—the older,
the younger, the saleswoman who brings
various sizes on a velvet tray,

shutting curtains as she departs,
so older and younger can measure
in peace. Let everything be of silk:
the tape measure that spans

the girl's chest, the bras that will
not push or strafe. Let her choose
beyond black and white, let her
choose red, and purple, and blue.

Let the older adjust straps, seams,
make sure that nothing pinches
or twists, admiring the fit, fabric,
easing shoulders so the girl stands

erect, no slouch in her stance.
Let them choose together what suits.
Let the saleswoman wave goodbye,
ringing up no price tags this first time.

Afaa Michael S. Weaver

MICHELE

My baby sister used to get
her baths on the kitchen sink.
We were in our new house
in a neighborhood where white folk
used to live, but they left fast.
Everybody was colored now,
and we did colored kinds of things,
like bathing babies in the kitchen.
That's the first I remember Michele,
brown and naked up on the counter
in that little, plastic baby tub.
She had her legs up in the air,
feet kicking around, smiling.
I tiptoed on nine year-old feet
and looked all over this baby sister.
I looked between her legs
for a long time, just a studying.
Her pee hole looked like a keyhole.
Mama said all girls was like that
and I knew what boys had because
I was a boy. I had questions.
"Mama, if that is a keyhole,
what is the key? Where is the door?
What house is we in anyway?"

Oktavi

AT FIVE

Aidel wore her nightshirt inside out
making it difficult
to undo snaps and buttons.

Her mother would consume
the best of a six pack,
and when she seemed to pass out
he'd turn her on her good ear.

Aidel knew when the footsteps would come.
The house held its breath,
the air went stale.
He'd become verbally dyslexic
calling her Ledia instead of Aidel.

Her mother never questioned
dolls on the window sill,
their mouths freshly taped shut.

Aidel's ambition was to eclipse the sun
so that her thighs would be too heavy
to pry apart.

At fifteen,
she developed a condition
which left her mute and myopic.

She sterilized herself
with a hot coat hanger.

No child of hers and his
would fear
the sound of footsteps,
or speak of this.

Rosamond S. King

H E L P

H is for High water
E is for Eyes closed
L is for Leap frog
P is for hot Peppers

H
E
L
P

I always wanted to do double dutch
they don't do that where I come from
But I am master of the jump rope

I can jump hot Peppers
till the girls' arms are
too tired to turn
I can Leap frog lower
I can High jump higher
Eyes closed is too easy
for me I can do everything
eyes closed b/c it's the slap!

of that rope onto the black
school ground that's all
that matters and you hear
that slap. It's all in the

H   E   L   P

I am master of the jump in these
corduroy dresses Mom makes me
wear My plaits vibrate as my shoes

67

use the ground as a launching pad
I can do leap frog high water
at the same time but I prefer
eyes closed and hot peppers H E L P H E L P H E L P H-E-L-P

Rosamond S. King

another day

sometimes you just get tired
carrying all the things in your hands
all the people on your back and
you stumble
keep going
you cannot fall you
cannot   cannot
                fall
think of the people
men and women who thought your back was strong
cutting their feet on the earth's stones
babies rolling into the mud

Marilyn Nelson

WASHBOARD WIZARD
HIGHLAND, KANSAS, 1888

All of us take our clothes to Carver.
He's a wizard with a washboard,
a genie of elbow-grease and suds.
We'll take you over there next week;
by that time you'll be needing him.
He's a colored boy, a few years older
than we are, real smart. But he stays
in his place. They say
he was offered a scholarship
to the college. I don't know
what happened, but they say
that's why he's here in town.
Lives alone, in a little shack
filled with books
over in Poverty Row.
They say he reads them.
Dried plants, rocks, jars of colors.
A bubbling cauldron of laundry.
Pictures of flowers and landscapes.
They say he
painted them. They say
he was turned away when he got here,
because he's a nigger. I don't know about
all that. But he's the best
washwoman in town.

LAND MARKS: PEOPLE AND PLACES

Marilyn Nelson

THE PRAYER OF MISS BUDD
SIMPSON COLLEGE, IOWA, 1890

I'd known he was enrolled, but still
the sight of a sepia boy
trembled my foundations,
I must admit. Thanks
for your patience.
They say each teacher
gets one student. Thanks
for giving me mine. Already
I've sent him home three times
with ague: Please watch over him.
When they found out he was living
on prayer and five cents' worth
of beef suet and cornmeal,
so many of our good
Simpson boys gave him
their laundry I'm afraid
for his delicate health.
Keep him warm this winter.
He says he paints to reveal truth,
his colors lucent, almost transparent;
sometimes a square inch of his canvas
is enough to break your heart.
He paints with such lostness
I've had to remind him
that you gave us brushes
because they do some things
better than fingertips.

Father, this semester I've seen
an unequivocal exception
to what has always seemed to me to be
your cockamamie sense of justice.
Now I see the chosen really are
the cornerstones the builders toss aside.
All the battles the Israelites fought
to come home, all that wandering.
The poor women.
And Jesus.

A Negro artist.
Father, give me greater gifts,
so I can teach this master.

Marilyn Nelson

DRIFTER

Something says find out
why rain falls, what makes corn proud
and squash so humble, the questions
call like a train whistle so at fourteen,
fifteen, eighteen, nineteen still on half-fare,
over the receding landscapes the perceiving self
stares back from the darkening window.

Sam Cornish

LOVE SONG OF A RED CAP

a country boy
livin' in the city
workin' the rails

I think o'
you
honey
I's hurtin'
fa' away
from home
(a dream of whippo-
will)
a thought
of you
my dusky
lady

your light
brown eyes

Befo' I's put
my red cap
on

"*Love Song of a Red Cap*" *is based on the writings of Paul Lawrence Dunbar and a scene from Eugene O'Neill's The Emperor Jones, starring Paul Robeson.*

Claude Wilkinson

LANDMARKS

Talk about cringing
when Sonny heard sirens
in the muddy wash
beneath Baptist Lane--
even when he'd skinned

to his BVDs,
crab-walked the steep cliff
to the huge culvert's
very tip, it was still
a good thirty-foot dive.

That summer, I knew
we could never last as friends--
I mean, he should've respected
my fear of heights, that brotherhood
of chickens who always toe the line.

Years later, when I heard his woman
had shot him, it was winter, frozen over.
All I cared to think of was us
hunting birds with air rifles, aiming
into a sunburst of pines,

the flinch of a finger
reducing the highest,
gayest of songs into
lumps of bright feathers
hurling toward the cold, snowy ground.

giovanni singleton

for my 27th birthday
a poem longer than 10 lines in which pronouns appear

i do not trust math.
each year i mark its failures.
numbers are more accurate than precise.
what is 27 really? veinte siete.

instead i imagine myself to be an abstract
expressionist painting whose value increases
dramatically as pairs of blue and green eyes
stare afraid to avert themselves without having
it all "figured out."

geometrically speaking

i also imagine myself to be 40. not the
numerical position but its signification.
a right angle. being without apology
and needing no forgiveness.

there is a time and place for everything

but 27 resembles an obtuse angle.
paranoia is the only noise with
a bass beat.

persistence

it's been five days now but i still
notice the two small insect bites
on my left thumb. an appetizer.

and now that the irritation has subsided,
the mosquitoes return en masse
determined to finish the job.

a matter of being

the part of "the one, the only" is now
more complex but i've finally memorized
the lines

i have recently studied the history of
the pencil and found the eraser to be
most fascinating

yes, lovely weather we're having
wouldn't you agree?

i recall the first time i smelled horse
shit. the amount was stupefying but
even more so was the animal's
indifference

oh yes, i've been to Africa, northern
Africa really. one night in Tunisia,
i gazed out over the Mediterranean
and wondered if there was where the
Europeans had dropped the blasted
pieces of nose belonging to the Sphinx.

rhyme should not be obvious.

oatmeal oatmeal eat your oatmeal or else. . .

i have given up wanting to be taller
i no longer desire bigger breasts
i accept the fact that i cannot sing

i am almost convinced that Jesus was
in fact an African-American woman
i believe in meat, vegetables, and dessert

for economic reasons, i have stopped looking
for my self. i am a turtle inside a shell

i can see the sky when the lights go dim
and i dance rather well

A. Van Jordan

A DEBT IS PAID

We younger kids were playing
when Johnny took the stray
dog in his hands,
took a stick,
stuck it in the dog's butt,
broke it off there.

We were just playing
and too afraid to stop
this staged nightmare;
too afraid he'd do
the same to one of us.

Years later, they say,
Johnny owed people.
The news did not surprise me:

He was found naked
hanging like a raw light bulb
from the ceiling of his garage,
body bloated,
hands bound,
a bouquet of credit cards
and dollar bills planted
in his ass. He swung
like that for days till
someone went to see what
the dogs were barking at.

Toi Derricotte

BOY AT THE PATERSON FALLS

I am thinking of that boy who bragged about the day he threw
    a dog over and watched it struggle to stay upright all
      the way down.
I am thinking of that rotting carcass on the rocks,
and the child with such power he could call to a helpless
    thing as if he were its friend, capture it, and think of
      the cruelest punishment.
It must have answered some need, some silent screaming in a
    closet, a motherless call when night came crashing;
it must have satisfied, for he seemed joyful, proud, as if he
    had once made a great creation out of murder.
That body on the rocks, its sharp angles, slowly took the shape of
    what was underneath, bones pounded, until it lay on the bottom
      like a scraggly rug.
Nothing remains but memory—and the suffering of those who
    would walk into the soft hands of a killer for a crumb of bread.

Saddi Khali

WALKING ON: A DECLARATION OF WHOLENESS

i can still see her
crying in the grass
screaming in the darkness
fighting behind those bushes
another prey taken in the hunt. . .

took her   from me   took us   from me
is what they did
fucking bastard thieves stole her secrets
          trespassed on her privacy. . .

     "they raped me," she cried
as we shared a bench under those campus trees
          (hanging trees
           we used to call them
           mocking our campus'
           plantation decor)
     ". . . me & my roomate were passing that park
     on our way home from the store &. . ."
-each tear liquified her words
painting ugly this scene
& falling onto her blouse

          . . . my response was arms
          wrapping her into me
          hoping to squeeze away the pain

we were only 18   freshmen
almost Black man & woman
chasing adulthood at a school lacking care
& we sat there sharing that bench
her face covered in my safety
   words leaving her mouth   making spaces

82

　　　　　　　　spaces once filled with laughter
...& the sun　could not　shine
　　not w/ pain raping the place of light
　　　　those bastards grounded her
　　　　grabbed the butterfly's wings
　　　　her colors still mark their hands

"i'm going back to Indiana," she sobbed in my ear
& iiii selfishly thought of myself
(as men sometimes do)
　　　　　　　　　　-of how helpless iiii was to her
...Blackman/warrior/soul-jah/protector of Blackwoman
　　had allowed this to happen
iiii had not protected her
& my anger made me see her
　　crying in the grass
fighting the weight & strength
of men without souls
　　-slaves with slave-master dreams
　　hiding behind bushes in the darkness

& feeling partial
& fragmentary (in my own manhood)
i asked her for descriptions
i have boys　we will make them pay
　　　　　　　i screamed
　　　　　　　　　　find those cowards
　　　　　　　　　　& hurt them
　　　　　　　　　　　& hurt　them...
but its not what she wanted
/made me stop
eyes begging me not to bring her back
so i didn't.

& soon after
　　　　she was gone...
　　　　in a cloud of unanswered answers
　　　　no address　no phone number
　　　　...back to where she left her childhood
...left me & our bench & the hanging trees
to wonder
if she would ever trust　again
　　　　　　　love　again

                    laugh   again
...she left here feeling incomplete
                    unwhole.
                    with part of her
                    still in that park
...& whenever i pass it
                    i feel her there
                    & in my own unwholeness
i want to dig up the grass
        cut down the trees
        curse the evening   the darkness
            the bushes concealing
            those Blackfaced devils

but somehow i manage
    to walk on

    although it has taken years
    to write this poem
    to speak aloud of the rape
    of me
    within the brutal rape
    of the women i love

    i walk on
    awaiting the close of my wounds
    /seeking the strength
    to nurse the scars
    evil scalpels will surely reopen

    i walk on
    knowing i did what i should
    /for only those with hearts
    can erase the actions of the heartless

    i walk on
    knowing thru love
    she can be whole again

     i must be   whole   again

        we will   be   whole   again

Sam Cornish

SOMETHING TERRIBLE SOMETHING

judgement
is coming
the Black Maria
and the hearse
sometime after dusk
every Friday between
payday and church
judgement
is coming
is a song I sing
to myself
something terrible
something miserable
something
blue

James E. Cherry

PRETTY WHITE GIRLS

(for emmitt till)

Peeking over the horizon of day,
I see the brilliance of new light
tangled in the blonde sunrise
of your sleeping hair.
Your skin pulsating from the morning
chill, draws you to me like a silk magnet and
I count each pore and follow lines into
curves and curves atop pink-capped mountains,
probing down warm hirsute valleys.

In the corners of your yawning eyes, blue
mirrors reflect faceless men, drinking
bitter waters of muddy rivers, eating
red white and blue flames, vomiting
God on the crucified air.
I turn quickly, thinking
I've heard the call of a 14yr old boy, but
it is only the voice of the wind
as I squeeze my genitals
and feel nothing.

S. Brandi Barnes

GENTLEMAN IN THE BARBER SHOP

At the Barber Shop
men rehash dreams, settle wars, and politics
and talk about mothers or ugly women.
They discuss the fate of the Union,
joint around the corner,
and advise on law & child support.
Gentleman in the Barber Shop
relive the great love affair
they didn't marry,
and always, always, give
instruction to the young.
Some talk about how they make women
scream from pleasure
while others exchange glances that know better.
At times the phone rings-asking for
different ones to bring something home
and he knows,
Mamma was only checking.
At the Barber Shop they brag about
female jealousy & insecurities,
and her checking up.
When I take the little one to get
his haircut: They call him champ,
size me up quickly,
and change the conversation from
men talk to small talk.

mawiyah kai el-jamah bomani

ROOTS

there
is a revolution
brewing
within
my hair
and that's
no lye

A. *Van Jordan*

BLACK DRAG QUEEN

My life is what it chose for me.

Manhood varies.
To hell with it.
And the opinions of gawkers,
like has-beens,
living their lives through me.
Desires become incest,
switched genders, or just sticky lust.

From this deck I play
the hand dealt.
Suburban-white-boy-johns, family, gay brothers—
allies that evaporate like
any other non-solid substance.

This is drag queen life.
It takes more than high heels
to keep this back erect.

Imani e. Wilson

fruitbowl 1

plums used to be black
like we was
was already
we was pretty black
plums peeled petals split skin
bent back black
soul sported
strove nights nether
neighbors bend backward
when plumes peeled petals
split spat black blood back
bled sweet bee swarms
betrayed big bellied barrels contents
contexted black be
plums peeled petals parrot plumes
split dripped lips
full pulled mouths magnetic
bites blew open veins aneurism thrombosis
revealed fine line capillaries
criscrossed cornrows
bleed back sweet
bleed black

and already we was that

Peter J. Harris

I KNOW I AINT HIP NO MORE

I make eye contact with babies on the street
look deep into their eyes
to catch my stares
they twist in their parents' arms
ignore shouts against talking to strangers
messages link babyminds & mine
mold their feelings into words
How can you make winds coo in my ears?
What shape is your smile in my eyes?
What place does love claim in my heart?
today
I beam the babies' priorities into my neighborhood
sprinkle talcum powder between warring adults
breathe heated massage oil into frozen egos
tonight
I sneak along deserted streets in your town
paste clown faces over Dewar's Profiles
spraypaint Benson & Hedges with infant smiles
I know I aint hip no more
I cuddle trends that could answer
Marvin Gaye's cry
(save the babies/save the children)
I might as well be wearing red socks & highwaters
to a late 70s GoGo in Southeast D.C.
or wearing lemon doubleknit Sans A Belts
& clapping despite Sandman's pan at the Apollo
clomping in two-tone platform shoes
& escorting a California Girl to a house party
or shading my eyes with a gangsterlean widebrim
& pumping up the volume on the Muzak Top 10
if microwave cool is the style

if the password is kneejerk ideology

if sweet talking power brokers gets me over
I know I aint hip no more
I know I aint hip no more

REVOLUTIONARY THOUGHTS

(About some folk who really bite my nerves—D.C. 1991)

They got them fades now   listening
to revolutionary tapes
talkin all of the talk, remembering times
when they wasn't even born Hind-sighting
about panthers and guns that didn't blow-
except they ain't wearing dysikis and fros.

Malcolm is in.
Malcolm abstracts
Malcolm blacks.
Malcolm back in style
talkin a revolution
(Revolution is about land- is what Malcolm said)

Sandals and Nike gym shoes saying *Just Do It*.   Thinking
isn't real in, not really.
Protesting schools, war - sometimes   not
even knowing why.
There is too much regurgitation,
the smell gets foul sometimes

Brothers are trying to be men and
can't be blamed for that, too much else
they can be blamed for Sistas,
sistas still giving up that sweet thang
'cause they owe it to the revolution.
Land   body   same   &
folk are just trying to survive.

Carved walking sticks from the homeland are in
but ain't nothing impeding their walking but them

running, trying to get the one up, the low down
on who got who to do what when where
we are still not thinking & it's this generation

who still has to read Fannon
'cause momma and daddy didn't tell us. So,
we go about our bizness: college   is
that place where we cultivate rhythm.   But
some folk just can't get the beat down right
(who said all black folk got rhythm?)

There is too much talking on the grass, running
those ever-present mouths (who said black folk
aren't articulate? Some of the best sounding shit
comes from themusme). Its just that this shit
don't have to be so treacherous.
Can't talk too much because things lose

perspective. & truth can't get no hype right now
& it didn't then, neither. The year two-thousand is coming
it don't seem like the fade-wearing-sista-stop-swearing
bruthas care about the real plan. Books.
Same ol' same ol'. Black folk. Young folk.
I guess our excuse is our youth.

But it'll be the same tomorrow & then & then
& then? Just like our mommas & daddies,
driving wheels that cost more than most folk
make in a year.   JUSTIFYING.
Justifying is what we do best, living the Hype
we put down-in our malcolm gear
(don't even know who or what the man was.)

Makes me wonder how many.
How many folk gonna think they gave up the revolution   when
graduation passes? How many folk gonna think
they gave it away? How many gonna think it'll wait
for their sons & girl-children when they never really had it at all?

Toi Derricotte

CHRISTMAS EVE: MY MOTHER DRESSING

My mother was not impressed with her beauty;
once a year she put it on like a costume,
plaited her black hair, slick as cornsilk, down past her hips,
in one rope-thick braid, turned it, carefully, hand over hand,
and fixed it at the nape of her neck, stiff and elegant as a crown,
with tortoise pins, like huge insects,
some belonging to her dead mother,
some to my living grandmother.
Sitting on the stool at the mirror,
she applied a peachy foundation that seemed to hold her down,
    to trap her,
as if we never would have noticed what flew among us unless
it was weighted and bound in its mask.
Vaseline shined her eyebrows,
mascara blackened her lashes until they swept down like feathers;
her eyes deepened until they shone from far away.

Now I remember her hands, her poor hands, which, even then
    were old from scrubbing,
whiter on the inside than they should have been,
and hard, the first joints of her fingers, little fattened pads,
the nails filed to sharp points like old-fashioned ink pens,
    painted a jolly color.
Her hands stood next to her face and wanted to be put away,
    prayed
for the scrub bucket and brush to make them useful.
And, as I write, I forget the years I watched her
pull hairs like a witch from her chin, magnify
every blotch—as if acid were thrown from the inside.

But once a year my mother
rose in her white silk slip,
not the slave of the house, the woman,

95

took the ironed dress from the hanger—
allowing me to stand on the bed, so that
my face looked directly into her face,
and hold the garment away from her
as she pulled it down.

Crystal Williams

IN SEARCH OF AUNT JEMIMA

I have sailed the south rivers of China and prayed to hillside Buddahs.
I've lived in Salamanca, Cuernavaca, Misawa, and Madrid.   Have
stood upon the anointed sands of Egypt and found my soul   in their
grains.

I've read more fiction, non-fiction, biographies, poetry, magazines,
essays, and bullshit than imaginable, possible, or even practical.   I
am beyond well read, am somewhat of a bibliophile. Still,   I'm
gawked at by white girls on subways who want to know why   and how
I'm reading T.S Eliot.

I've shopped Hong Kong and Bangkok out in heat so hot   the
trees were looking for shade-I was the hottest thing around.   I'm
followed in corner stores, grocery stores, any store.

I can issue you insults in German, Spanish, and a little Japanese.
I'm still greeted by wannabe-hip white boys in half-assed ghettoese.

I've been 250 pounds, 150 pounds and have lived and loved every
pound in between. I am still restricted by Nell Carter images of me.

I've eaten rabbit in Rome, paella in Barcelona, couscous   in
Morocco, and am seated at the worst table   by
mentally challenged Maitre'd's
who think my big ass is there for coffee.

I am still passed up by cabs
passed over for jobs
ignored by politicians
guilty before innocent
Black before human.

And I'm expected to know Snoop Dogg's latest hit
Mike's latest scandal
I'm expected to believe in O.J.'s innocence.

And I am still expected to walk white babies up and down 92nd street
as I nurse them, sing a hymn and dance a jig.

Sorry,
not this sista, sista-girl, miss boo, miss it, miss thang, honey,
honey-child, girl, girlfriend.

See, I am not your militant right-on sista wearing dashiki and 'fros
with my fist in the air spouting Black Power while smoking weed,
burning incense and making love to Shaka-formally known as Tyrone.

I am not your high-yellow saditty college girl flaunting Gucci bags
and Armani suits, driving an alabaster colored Beemer with tinted
windows and A.K.A. symbols rimming my license plate.

I am not your three-babies-by-fifteen, green dragon lady   press
on nails whose rambunctious ass is stuffed   into too
tight lycra with a lollipop hanging out the side of my mouf   and a
piece of hair caught in a rubberband
stuck to the top of my head.

I am not your timberland, tommy hilfiger,
10K hollow-hoop wearin
gansta rappin
crack dealin
blunt smokin
bandanna wearin
Bitch named Poochie.

I am not your conscious clearer.
I am not your convenient Black friend.
Notyourprototypenotyoursellout 'cause
massa and the big house is too good.

I am not your Aunt Jemima.

 In my (8957) days of Black womanhood I've learned this:

Be careful of what you say
of what you think
of what you do
because you never know

who you're talking to.

Mariahadessa Tallie

RAINDROP WOMEN

we are raindrop women
fallen from cloud palms
sliding down lightening bolts
speaking in thunderous tongues
our words are like balms,
like tonic, like dance;

no shade in our shadows:
mirrors reflect the darkness
of our dreams, the warm black light
of brown skin draped in gold
thoughts washed in syntax.

Our words shimmer
like sunshine on brass,
moonlight woven through
    ocean waves.
    Our hair tuned
and tucked away
under folds of cotton and silk
headwraps, ancient helmets
against inevitable crashes
    with hostility.

Me? I roam sable streets
searching for white candles and coconuts
to wash chaos from my skin. Still
I have to write it out, make dyslexic
thoughts rearrange,
put order to the recklessness
that is one spirit on three planes-
woman with many names
I see rush hour and think: Middle Passage

spirit crashes into unborn daughters
who will never know my-
this-collective pain.

We are teardrop women
fallen from heaven's eyes
causing ripples in the status quo-
-women refusing to tip toe

we sing march stomp scream write
kick whatever to sever ties
between oppression and ourselves.
we slide from lightening bolt legs of mothers
with prophetic, aching wails
that plastic toys and currency
won't ever pacify.

we are raindrop women
fallen from cloud palms
sliding down lightening bolts
speaking in tongues.

WHAT I AM

Fred Sanford's on at 12
& I'm standing in the express lane (cash only)
about to buy *Head & Shoulders*
the white people shampoo, no one knows
what I am. My name could be Lamont.
George Clinton wears colors like Touchcan Sam,
the Froot Loop pelican. *Follow your nose,*
he says. But I have no nose, no mouth,
so you tell me what's good, what's God,
what's funky. When I stop
by McDonalds for a cheeseburger, no one
suspects what I am. I am at Ronald's poster,
perpetual grin behind the pissed-off, fly girl cashier
that I love. *Where are my goddam fries?*
Ain't I American? I never say, *Niggas.*
My ancestors didn't emigrate. Why
 would anyone leave their native land?
I'm thinking about shooting
some hoop later on. I'll dunk on everyone
of those Niggas. They have no idea
what I am. I might be the next Jordan-
god. They don't know if Toni Morrison's
a woman or a man. Michael Jackson
is the biggest name in showbiz. *Mamma se*
Mamma sa mamma ku sa, sang the Bushmen
in Africa. I'll buy a dimebag after the game,
me & Jody. He says, *Fuck them white people*
at work, Man. He was an All-American
in high school. He's cool, but he don't know
what I am, & so what. Fred Sanford's on
in a few & I got the dandruff-free head &
shoulders of white people & a cheeseburger

belly & a Thriller CD & Nike high tops
& slavery's dead & the TV's my daddy—
You big Dummy!
Fred tells Lamont.

William Henry Lewis

TO THE PEOPLE OF A SMALL TOWN IN OHIO , WHO AS I APPROACH THEM ON THE STREET, ARE AFRAID THAT THIS BLACK MAN IS GOING TO DO THEM HARM

Today, I want to know how your Fall works,
how it times itself for January's advance
and the steady progress of cold. I want
to learn the reason for your silence
and the rhythm of you retreating steps.
I want to answer this:
>   Doesn't everyone expect change
>   of color this time of year?

I want to learn the science of distance;
how a wind-borne leaf finds its place,
the change of light which warns the day
of advancing dark, or, as I approach,
the way you lock doors and cross streets,
your movements stiff and hurried with a chill
unkind for September. I'm looking
for the secret to the turn towards tough
everyone's skin takes, regardless of shade
or shape, steeling[ed] for the unforgiving cold
of what another year won't offer.

>   Where is *my* season?
How can my steps thrive
along your streets, you who love
the spectrum of leaves in Autumn,
but have yet to know my Name?
>   This is your fall:
winds blowing colors that must fade
towards the blanched haul of winter.

Aren't we all waiting
	for a different season
to weather the blacks and blues? Waiting
until we can all manage the tedium
of trying, when smiles are near impossible,
and even deceit feels fresh again?

When Winter arrives, you
will have run out of streets to cross.
	And here I come.
What will you do when Autumn has not flushed
all color from the town, and you have no name
for that fear which has always haunted,
always been just around the corner,
hulking your way down that dusky street,
fixin' to do you bad? This seems far away,
and you won't worry with that question now.

But I know this: time is the answer to distance.
And I am waiting for the season
where color comes, not because you like it,
but because it is time.

Carole Boston Weatherford

THE TAR BABY ON THE SOAPBOX

So Clean and White
—Sunlight Soap slogan, circa 1900

"Snowy white," the tar baby promised;
her eyelet pinafore immaculate—beaming
on the soapbox, beckoning believers.
When no one was looking, she seemed to wink
at the washerwoman. They knew it never snowed
in July. The washerwoman shoveled detergent
as if a grave digger, buried under soil
of other people's sweat. Squeezing lemon juice
and rubbing salt into a stain, she snarled
beneath her breath, "Rich folk sure is filthy."
Raw knuckles throbbing contempt. The soapbox
topped onto the pile of laundry. Then, she saw them—

Tiny hands reaching, feet jutting from the box.
Startled, she blinked hard and shivered.
The tar baby kicked wildly, arms
flailing, cries shrill, tantrum full-grown.
The tar baby squealed, mocking the lowly laundress.
The woman scowled, then slammed the ornery chile
against the scrubboard, dunking it in the suds
until the indigo blush left its cheeks. The woman
bled a little. The tar baby wheezed, its tiny neck twisted
chaste; shrouded in damp linens, cradled
in a willow basket, mouthing white lies.

Zak Robbins

BEACHES

(Lines composed at Dewey Beach)

things of my younger years
i don't come to them often

sun/sand/solitude
i buy in B. Dalton and
look in religious studies
for proof God exists

i hear the unfamiliar tongues
of the wind while reading
the braille in the whitecaped waves
then find myself shaking
hand after hand after hand

until the tide comes in
grips me to stare
fuzz at the ocean ends
where seagulls seem happy

and happiness is free

out there calls to me
but isn't my calling

so i stand at the bank
knowing
that getting my feet wet is enough

Bruce A. Jacobs

VIVIAN, TAKE 57

Cousin Vivian stayed single
all the 60 years we loved her,
and when she died,
in-laws from Philadelphia claimed her:
costume pearls, a thousand LPs
from Ellington to Coltrane,
velour couch, enameled bedroom set.
Blue shag.
They guarded their booty
right up through the funeral.

But,
What do you want of Vivian's?
hissed my mother
as we balanced Vivian's porcelain
on our laps, piled with turkey and dressing.
While kinfolk jabbed corn, dabbed eyes,
my mother's hands worked crowded rooms,
crammed a large purse with our past.

I remembered Vivian barking, "Base hit!"
at TV, cutting her words like the with-it cats
from Detroit who moved beneath crooked hats.
She knew the nod to walking bass,
spoke saxophone in days of Donna Reed,
was hipper even than my Uncle Wilbur
with his hi-fi and whitewalled T-bird.

Vivian, my secret beatnik, in her dietitian's lipstick,
pecking my round cheek with What's Cookin', Baby?
feeding me Oreos, then Miles Davis.
In the deep groove of her den,
all relatives were squares. But her.

From the days I called Tchaikovsky's 1812
"The Boom Song," we sat together,
our one face to the music.

At her funeral, I was thirty-two, unmarried,
did not cry. Until the bundle opened
in my hand: two little ivory elephants
wrapped in a napkin by my mother,
a woman who would steal
only for love or hunger.

Janice W. Hodges

ANNUALS AND PERENNIALS

As we strolled
the last row of yellow pansies,
mama's wrinkles
settled comfortably, deeper

"They'll be back next year," she said.

These last days
mama's rambling
hadn't made much sense

Today was the day
we'd take our final tour
behind the bedroom door,
she couldn't remember

vacuous frames
and varnished tables
stared back

mangled memories
quivered, violet
in this desperate room

we wandered, aimlessly
down a fading hallway

she's forgotten
she sleeps on the tip
of her mattress

usually doesn't raise her voice
and daddy doesn't like his eggs runny

she gets lost
on her way to the mailbox

can't remember
where she put the pans

Today was the day
I had to put her in
one of those place

gripping white knuckles,
she cuddled close
sensing unfamiliar floorboards,
unmortared ceiling

it was like burying her
knowing she wouldn't sprout back
young and crisp or tender

persistent care nor perfect conditions
could bring her back, now

I visit her everyday,
toss and turn in steel arms
on the side chair

she rambles about parallel rows, woody stems

Sometimes, in her eyes I see my name
surface just above the waves
entangle, then plunge deeper
into the black lagoon

I stand,
everything in me swelling

she leans,
eyes staining

and whispers
"Don't forget to water the mums."

Sam Cornish

MISSISSIPPI ON THE DOORSTEP

came north
cross the line

saw Negroes on the street
walking (everywhere a Negro walking)
I learned to read
and still it seemed

freedom was a matter
of crossing the Mason-Dixon line

but no job   no place
to live Mississippi you sit

on the doorstep   like a long lost
unwelcome cousin

Angela Jackson

THE LOVE OF TRAVELLERS

(Doris, Sandra, and Sheryl)

At the rest stop on the way to Mississippi
we found the butterfly mired in the oil slick:
its wings thick
and blunted. One of us. tender in the finger tips.
smoothed with a tissue the oil
that came off only a little;
the oil-smeared wings like lips colored with lipstick
blotted before a kiss.
So delicate the cleansing of the wings I thought the color soft as watercolors
would wash off under the method of her mercy for something so slight
and graceful, injured, beyond the love of travellers.

It was torn then. even after her kindest work,
the almost-moth exquisite charity could not mend
what weighted the wing. melded with it.
then ruptured it in release.
The body of the thing lifted out of its place
between the washed wings.
Imagine the agony of a self separated by gentlest repair.
"Should we kill it?" One of us said.   And I said yes..
But none of us had the nerve.
We walked away. the last of the oil welding the butterfly
to the wood of the picnic table.
The wings stuck out and quivered when wind went by
Whoever found it must have marveled at this
And loved it for what it was and
had been..
I think, meticulous mercy is the work of travellers..
and leaving things as they are
punishment or reward.

I have died for the smallest things.
Nothing washes off.

smile

our city has scrubbed the sleep
from its eyes,
the mayor proclaims;
we are now new york
with a cleaner subway.

and yet the hostess
        at veronique's of paris

grew eyes large
as a georgia moon

as she scrambled
to find someone

who could cut my kinky hair.

what if jesus had been a walk in?
                i inquired,
as she whispered

to first one then two
then four elegantly named folks,

who shook their heads
as if i were joseph
in need of a room.

then tony punched in,
face dark as my mood,

placed a bag
in his cubicle,

and before guiding me to his
chair by the window

offered a most ancient
and knowing smile

Sam Cornish

WORK TO BE DONE

on the land we made
what city Negroes buy
no use
going to Detroit
the promised land
my father slaughtered
hogs worth more
than   dollar bills
my father worked till
he can't work   no more
this ain't starvation
farm working long days
I hated that man his ornery ways
but there was no time
for southern blues
there was a rising sun
and work to be done

Angela Jackson

THE FITTING ROOM

(for Jack LaZebnik and
The Ghost of Senior Hall.)

A person has to try on many lives
before she finds one that fits.
     You know what I mean?
People will tell her anything.
How the hat sits too big, and the slip
clings.
She has to be a child again
and see herself in the mirror
in her training bra, in order to dream
             Of breasts.
Or like when you shop for shoes
you should do it in the evening
after your feet have swollen
from all your little steps.
The pair you choose then,
sensible and pleasing to foot and eye,
is the pair you will wear
until they wear
out.
I don't know what to make of this.
I don't know what this means,
even though I'm telling it to you.
Like love.
You can choose a man, then choose another,
and all he did was change pants.
But he's the same man in the same life
that didn't fit you, but you tried to squeeze in it
anyway and it was two sizes too small.

People look at you sometimes
and try to have you thinking you'll never find
anything with your measurements.
And you can change those if you want to wear
something bad enough.
Or some body can cut you down to size.
And you can let them out do you. Or
leave you in hot water until you draw up.
Then they'll call you country   talk about your trouble
shake their heads and admire how awful you look.
They'll say you a nice person but you got no style.
How does that suit you? Fine. Just fine.
Or

you have to keep taking off garments
and putting other ones on
until you see your self in the seeing glass
as this one has all the glamour and sense you mean
to say what is on your mind.
It looks like it was made with you in mind.
Tell me. You who've lived so long and so little,
        so many lives.
Do you
Do you like this one?

Charles Porter

LAND OF THE LOST

Sidewalks lined with stone cold faces... mysterious like the
sphinx... chiseled by poverty. Ancient Black faces... possessing
secrets of survival. Great... Grand... Mothers... Fathers...
generations removed.

Ghetto archeologists sift through trash... looking for missed
meals... misplaced meals and goods... still good to some... and some
will sell two left shoes... which don't match what others will
do. The clothes from their backs they will remove for you... if you
give them what they want.

Others take offerings like church ushers. Guardians of sacred
shrines... waiting for corner store doors to open so that they may
commune with their God... who removes worries... troubles...
problems... leaving empty bottles... no dreams.

That elder is my child. He asks for allowance... I give him a
quarter... he smiles as kids walk by and laugh. No respect... no
love... no community... just selfishness... as they sell poison to
their homies' mother... and everyone looses in this land of the lost.
Stray bullets roam the streets looking for a home... while ancient
ebony faces... carved like sphinxes look on with sorrow... and cry.

Michael Hill

CITY IN YOU

take 1 for magic

steadying this moment

    eyefulls of manhattan persist
    within clouds of trumpet solos

I have brought expensive silence
    to pour in genteel portions
        between us

my eyes
    children of ships
        have begun to hush

wading in shallows
your smiles incubate themselves
while onlookers check for scars

teething on remnants, we are new
    waiting to swallow one another
still
    the matter of 18 roses
        hangs like a traffic light
          between us

can we go?

Esther Iverem

PEACE BE STILL

The 5:46 train roars, waking me,
Shaking the house and my bed,
Bringing the white people from Long Island.
It has been so long
Since I rested at night,
Since I felt protected.

Me and the baby roll the New Jersey Turnpike.
The engine timing belt
could snap at any moment.
A crazy man stalks me 100 miles to Philly,
Waving his arms, flashing high beams,
Following me off the road.

The secret of this life is this:
We are all touchable unless we fight.
Like the federal agent
Dead, slumped and bloody in the elevator
And Frank Nitti smiling wicked.
Like a pin prick of AIDS, a driveby shooting,
A wife or child suddenly snatched,
Broken, riddled with blood and sperm.
Like James Cleveland testifying:
No shelter or hope is nigh...

Everything has gotten into the house:
Squirrels, birds, rats, termites, a slut.
A mumbling, mad street woman
with wino-red eyes and swollen ankles
Came, smelled and touched my son.
Neighbors beat a quivering path of alarm to my door.
Oh. Get up, Jesus!

There has been a fire here.
My loves and pleasures are water-damaged.
Tumors in my womb grow on anger and

Chicken injected with hormones.
Food has become sex. Trips to deafening, silent
Strip malls, my entertainment. In Waldbaums,
The day's catch measures me as wife and mother:
Strong on produce, not many sodas, no cakes or cookies.
The baby holds his breath until he passes out.

Only once have I heard him
Call me and the baby "my family"
I have concluded that even with him, I am alone,
Carrying heavy bags, nailing up sheetrock,
Driving the dangerous car, drowning in needles.
I am burned so much so that I always seek water
—the memory of all those uterine liquids
of mommy, of this once black love
Bathing me to a safe and snug sucking sleep.

The other day, at the tiny, tacky marina opposite Pathmark,
I pulled to the side of the road, climbed the rail
And imagined myself beneath the inky, oily water. Only a glance back
At the baby's little tomato-shaped face, his sharp black eyes,
His puffy little hand waving in protest
Called me back behind the wheel where I shook and shook.
The wind and waves shall obey thy will.

Since then, I have had this recurring dream:
I am running with the baby away from the house.
I am being chased by a man who looks like the devil.
In empty rooms, I build neon dollhouses for my hopes.
On the soundtrack, Fred Ho plays sax and a chorus shouts,
"Only the drums and yells of yeah!"
I am awake again. But this time I roar,
Drowning out the train in the space between my ears.

I say, too many ocean bottom bones
Are shaking and shifting for my life.
I say, too high a blood price has been paid
For the water to claim one more black soul,
For the water to claim all of me.
I say, Peace Be Still..

Eli Goodwin

UNTITLED

The number 1 bus jerks to a stop at Mass. Ave.
Uncomplaining riders fight for balance,
sway in unison, anemones in a current undersea.
My mind drifts, in its own time.
The stopped bus rocks as folks file in,
drop change, find seats.
A woman squeezes her broad bottom
between blue moulded plastic and the
pole that vainly separates her space from mine;
against my arm, my side, my thigh the cool,
soft press of flesh. My reverie and I part company.
A thicket of thin black braids rounds out her dark brown face.
She turns to me apologizing, unashamed;
shifts her weight, then smiles, and says, "I'm fat",
and I smile back and pat her on the shoulder.
Between us just her soft blue cotton shift
and this moment without guile, an ancient knowing shared.
"Hey man," a blast from the doorway—
"what you doin' huggin' my wife?"
Neat trimmed beard beneath a broad brimmed hat,
an expensive tailored suit, dark mustard silk.
His tone sounds like mock anger, but it's hard to read.
"Hey, how's it goin', Brother? " I extend my hand, and
palm smacks open palm in greeting,
"You can slap me five all you want,"
he bellows, waving his cigar,
"but what you doin' huggin' my wife!"
The wife looks back to me, I frown. She chuckles,
"There's enough of me," she says, "to go around."
My mouth, all by itself, performs a little smile

that's neutral, hard to read.
"The man is the boss," he shouts,
to no one in particular.
"None of that shit like back in the seventies.
It's the man makes the rules,
from the president on down.
I don't be hittin' you or nothin',
cause you understand who's boss,"
he tells his wife. warming up now, he
he's proclaiming male supremacy,
in a busfull of people, he's alone.
like a kid in the woods shouting at stones.
a man next to him begins, "Sir, this is the nineties"...
he wheels, and even louder
yells, "No, the man is the boss!
What's wrong with you?
"Sir, you're a sexist"
You must be a faggot.
forget it, I was kidding with you.
You a fuckin' faggot," he persists.
the man stares out the window. His jaw twitches.
Passengers fidget, studying the floor.
"Honey," says the woman, "here's our stop."
Moving down the aisle now, he insists,
"Hey, he jumped in our conversation!"
presses the issue until his wife agrees.
she glances back at me,
"have a nice day," says she.

Wanda Coleman

AMERICAN SONNET (46)

—after Joseph Bathanti

blood-splashed leaves cling to a porous moon-soaked walk
suggest failed escape and ebbing consciousness
emotion-gorged, a trail pocked by steel casings, confused
by the scuffle of the inquisitive sneakers and killer shoes—
angel light—and in its beam the winged intruder descends
crimeward, sinking into a night of blades and blackened eyes.
trees genuflect in the wind, witness swift midnight shushings,
the crude wrench of psyche from soma, shelter newborn ghosts.
after a breakfast of headlines, runners jog the neighborhood,
circle the event marked off by yellow tape and moody uniforms.
sightseeing arouses gratitude—some disquiet in
close whispers, prayers from the fearful lucky—deep
in shock-inured souls like blight unsettling the city
once industry fails and a mean prosperity hurries south

Bruce A. Jacobs

BLACK ON BLACK

1.

Night street an onyx eye unblinking, empty
but for him, black man, hood up,
coat too big, one hand deep in pocket.
Walks too fast, crossing toward me
I see now he's shaggy, 50 feet
and closing but still time for him
to look away, pull out a handkerchief,
to soon for me to jump to how
white people run from us.

20 feet, eyes in the hood are on me,
his angle sharper, no mistake,
watch the hand, watch the hand, still in
that big pocket, street is blind,
shuttered, faceless, look for escape,
see small yard with gate,
close my hand on mace.

10 feet and he has not shaved, the parka is blue
with tattered fur, the hand is shoved to hell
down that huge pocket, in five seconds he will
draw forth flame, in five seconds he will
withdraw magnetic steel and make me slave
to gravity, his eyes are pulling for me,
his mouth about to move, make things official.

Five feet and all sidewalk leads to him,
the hand now cranking from the pocket
like a steam shovel as his lips open,
the words will be the final kiss,
no time to mourn for lost brothers,

Move! I take the gate in three steps running,
make the yard, have gained 10 feet in snow
when his hand clears the pocket
to reveal a driver's license,
his ID, panhandling weapon against fear.

Not gonna rob you, sir, he says. Can you spare some change?

2.

Only after the elevator doors pinch off the night
does the attack come. I strike out, shout,
pound enameled walls for escape, but too late,
I am trapped in this bright cell
with a man who wears my clothes, jingles my keys
and spends our evenings
posing threats from doorway shadows,
holding soft lives hostage.
I have felt him follow me to entrances,
crossed streets against him,
scanned for him before parallel parking,
and handed him my wallet.
I have seen others shy from me
as from a disguised shark, shimmy past as if my hands
were hooks for women's purses.

Now here we are, two black men
within one skin, me alone in an elevator.
Me as the man who might have mugged me.
Me shoving myself against the wall,
blowing mirrors through my own brain.

Willie Abraham Howard, Jr.

MEMORIAL DRIVE

People are watching my eyes,
My feet broken, uncertain
on this old faded blue carpet.
She's calling me, pillow beneath
An adorable head, surrounded
By pink enamel.
Lights, so many relatives
Looking out for me.
Moms was 38, I'm 17.
Some tremble, afraid to kiss her
She didn't belong to AIDS, moms
Was mine I'm kissing that beautiful
cheek. She washed the turnips. Hands
in Tide with palms against my football
uniforms.
People whisper, who she got it from?
You know she was a ho. Rage and tears
Burn my eyes. Grandpa takes my shoulder.
And moms smoked Kools, and sat on the
Kitchen cabinet checking my homework.
Nobody to jone my friends or say,
"get your musty behind in the shower!"
Robes of our choir like spreads blowing
on the lines in this Decatur June.
They sing, "Jesus hold DeAnna's hand!"
None of them held her hand at Grady's
Terminal ward. And I love moms,
Going without her feminine napkins
so that I would have lunch money.
AZT and she won't see my prom suit,
diploma and scholarships.
Double shifts surrounded by cans of Glory

greens at Wayfields. Pulling racks of clothes
At South Dekalb Mall. So many forgot her,
Those shoulders like glass. She held those
friends up before.
No one to ride the 21 Memorial Drive bus
With me. A kiss before I went to Crim High School.
My comedian, Bible scriptures and valiums.
Moms would laugh about the cars,
on her heels down Memorial Drive.
She would yell Stop! by Checkers.
And I'm cold like her hands,
never coming back from that pink coffin
that will hide her. For AIDS hid the ones
who she thought held love.

Angela Shannon

SUNDAY

It could have been the way the Southern
man in his navy suit and skin,
rocked along the church wall,
waddling to the tambourine and falling
at the sides, the way old men do to Blues.

Or the way Sister Nettie got the spirit
all in her feet and behind, quick-stepping,
like an ant hill was under her toes,
shaking her head back and forth in disbelief—

Or the way Deacon Murdock raised
both hands like the police was there,
and started pacing the pulpit—
a foreign street—looking for Jesus.

But something quick came over the church
when Walter's voice slid to his navel
and plucked a piece of an umbilical cord,
tugging the notes from generations gone.

And a sister lost in the crowd screamed,
like when children have their first babies,
and it floated over the pews
and took the congregation rocking

back to the first cry we made
in this freedom-stealing country—
the first scream on the auction block—
and we tried to clap our way out of memory,

to stomp out the sound like sparks of fire
but it was already voiced (and the seer had said,
this child would be different).

Toneka Nathene Bonitto-Burwell

GOING HOME

boarded up churches
keeping out the gods of
Nature
moss and mulch abound
around
withered, weathered
tombstones
from a time
no more
yet it is all
timeless

Toneka Nathene Bonitto-Burwell

LEAVING WINSTON-SALEM

There are secrets
that the woods all hold
run down shacks
fallen limbs
and winding little streams
All through this
I doze
and dream
of you

Christopher Nickelson

charleston, south carolina

we never danced
in a public concert hall
or in a coliseum
we never held hands in a cathedral
or exchanged knowing glances
in public

but we colored this room
into a public arena
our stage
we danced the Charleston
in this little town

you turn the radio down
real low
a lover's whisper
in the dark
and a blue light
colored the room

i tie my bandana
around your arm
and you become mine
i become yours
we sway to the music
and into the night

Melvin E. Lewis

MY MOTHER

My Mother is Alabama
She glows near weaping willows
dreams of red clay soil during January snow.

She is Africa
warm, brown, and buoyant.
She is a front yard pecan tree
carrying spirit songs and legacies in her fruit.

My Mother is a southern Pearl,
is Selma
where Aunt's soaked fruit cakes
from November in cheese cloth,
made shiny leg little girls
bright cotton dresses for Sunday school.

She plants roses and morning glories
near my father's tomatoes and collards,
Wednesday evenings she places a
big pot on her apron,
snaps green beans
as her grandchildren listen
to stories of coal burning stoves
that warmed wooden homes.

She makes cornbread in a black skillet
cleans her greens three times
sings church songs as she recalls land and time
where family was more than country.

Janeya K. Hisle

WE

We women,
We sisters
   you and me.

We be rollin' our necks with our hands on our hips.
We be braidin' our hair.
We be paintin' our lips.
We be peekin' our windows 'cause we just *gotta* see.
But whatever We be...We be beautifully.

We women,
We sisters
      you and me.

We pure gold: We make good Mamas.
And we bold: We bring the drama.
We give a lot.
We play a lot.
We pray a lot cause men stray a lot.
We infiltrate: desegregate.
We complicate.
We instigate.
We always runnin' late
      for a date
           but we so great
               we know they'll wait.

We women,
We sisters
   you and me.

We love.
We love our mothers.

We love our brothers.
We love each other.
And We strong: We be copin'
And We slick: We be scopin'
And no one knows shoes like We.
And no one knows blues like We.

'Cause We earth, moon and stars.
We give birth.
We fix cars.
We cook meals.
We close deals.
We wear pants with high heels.

We got life, love and Spirit in all that We do.
We women,
We sisters
            me and you.

Melvin Lewis

GULLAH WOMEN

Watch out for Gullah woman
they have held something in their memories
they have kept secrets in their language
they know the stories of the frog and turtle
they wear red and know how to watch the seasons
how to catch crab, shrimp and you

My woman is a sea marsh
Her eyes capture the sun and make the
moon dance around her brown pearls

My woman is a Sea Island water,
water that traveled from Benin to Beaufort
o the backs of gray and brown porpoises,
they run over you like a midnight wave
cover you naked body, full and complete

Her lips cover your thoughts,
transpose your dreams, sing in your songs, and motion.
Her smile is an evening wind between Hunting and Flipp Islands,
soft, warm, easy with palmettos blowing on the shores,
eagles flying over the river,
her lips are smooth water, tides that porpoises
play in near the Port Royal Sound, gliding between sand reefs
and flat bottom boats,
waters where African fishermen throw their
hand woven nets to catch fish, her waters have caught me,

Her hands have picked tobacco
Her strokes are smooth and tender
like fine Sea Island cotton
Her hair is thick, strong, and black

She braids her African hair and her
face is my inspiration, her face is Sierra Leone.

Our Daughter is named Maisha,
she is the spirit of the sea,
water turning over from a wave,
she's impatient and reserved.

Our baby girl is stubborn and quick.
I look at her round brown face and see you,
see me, and hear a new sea song,
feel a softer, quieter county song.

Watch out for Gullah women
they know the ways of plants and spells
they'll steal you away.

JoNELLE

JoNelle don't believe in nakedness,
body isn't for all eyes, just
for body's own. She look in the mirror

see Sadie standing on wood-slab,
left breast dripping, ghost men gawking, circling
like huffing vultures,

Evil barking demands: Squat. Lift.
Grin. Turn. Bend. Sadie's mind slipping
to sacred place as the paper women

and children glue their eyes
on her nostrils, ears, thigh. She has
no need to understand spit-words,

or why the duppy* take fire-stick
and brand her heart, leaving a white
A. JoNelle imagines pulling up the ashoki*

crumbled around Sadie's chained ankles,
crowning her hair with tie, and them walking
toward the land whence they came.

*duppy, (Southern) oppressor
*ashoki, a formal Nigerian dress for women

Opal Palmer Adisa

THINGS NO ONE TOLD ME

that being a good mother
was too many jobs for one person

that there was no such thing
as true love

that i could hate so deeply
a person i once loved

that praying didn't ensure
my wishes would come true

that i could be so tired
for so long yet continue
to live what's left of my life

that i would lust after men
especially young hard buck men
the older i get

that i would become
sensitive to the approaching greys
that i would need glasses
to read small print up close

that i would tire of partying
and instead opt for a leisurely walk

that i would still be restless at 40 plus
wanting still to explore the world

that i would continue to believe
housework is a waste of time

that i could love three human beings
who sprang from me so fiercely

that i would still marvel at the beauty
that's nature
that i would still cry
for joy

Angela Shannon

INTEGRATION

One childhood day
in my new neighborhood—
while freely circling
bouncing butterflies
and giggling at
the daffodil's story—

a child in white
ruffles interrupted me
and wiped a forefinger
down my outstretched arm,
asking, "How do you know
when you're dirty?"

dirt

each evening
before she touched us
she cleaned her nails
and scrubbed
too hard at times
to remove the white dirt she'd lifted
from their toilets
amid their slurs
that i might study in white schools
to be taught to hate myself
while receiving a *better* education
among the white trash
amidst their jokes

at night i now scrub
my face and head
that i might remove
the stench of white lies
the bruises of glass ceilings
and false hopes
before i touch
the face of my child
with tears
as will they

Eli Goodwin

AFTER AN ALL DAY SKIRMISH WITH THE CLOUDS

After an all day skirmish with the clouds,
the sun prevails, an hour before sunset.
An old woman in a blue velvet bathrobe
and pink fuzzy slippers stands in her driveway.
One hand grips the flaking paint
of a low white picket fence; the other
meanders aimless, about the corners of her mouth.
Pale light snags on the aura of tangled grey
hair that floats above her like a dark cloud.
She has slipped the surly bonds of decorum.
Facing a lawn strewn with seashells,
Where tall weeds have long held sway,
she stares into a world known but to her.
Under her dark front window, by the steps,
a plastic deer with legs splayed, stands
startled, into stillness frozen,
like Lot's wife.

Toi Derricotte

BLACKBOTTOM

When relatives came from out of town,
we would drive down to Blackbottom,
drive slowly down the congested main streets
—Beubian and Hastings—
trapped in the mesh of Saturday night.
Freshly escaped, black middle class,
we snickered, and were proud;
the louder the streets, the prouder.
We laughed at the bright clothes of a prostitute,
a man sitting on a curb with a bottle in his hand.
We smelled barbecue cooking in dented washtubs,
 and our mouths watered.
As much as we wanted it we couldn't take the chance.

Rhythm and blues came from the windows, the throaty voice of
 a woman lost in the bass, in the drums, in the dirty down
 and out, the grind.
"I love to see a funeral, then I know it ain't mine."
We rolled our windows down so that the waves rolled over us
 like blood.
We hoped to pass invisibly, knowing on Monday we would
 return safely to our jobs, the post office and classroom.
We wanted our sufferings to be offered up as tender meat,
and our triumphs to be belted out in raucous song.
We had lost our voice in the suburbs, in Conant Gardens,
 where each brick house delineated a fence of silence;
we had lost the right to sing in the street and damn creation.

We returned to wash our hands of them,
to smell them
whose very existence
tore us down to the human.

Afaa Michael S.Weaver

BALTIMORE

*(For Donald Faulcon(+), Roger Allen Jones (+), Leonard Spicer(+),
Ronnie Morton(+), Phillip "Lardy" Capers(+), Craig Brock(+),
Bobby Price(+), Herman Gates(+), Otha Walker(+), DarnellDudley(+),
Carl"Sleepy" Miles(+), Marvin Miller(+), Glenford H. Cummings(+),
Ernie Raymond(+), Jeff Miller, Harvell Miller, Horace Miller, Roy Jones,
Butch Reavis, Carl Jones, Mark J. Weaver, Earl "Homeboy" Brown, Melvin
E.Brown, Maurice Reavis, Gary E. Miller, Gene F. Thomas,Roscoe Mason,
Norfleet Barnes,Steve Davis, Kevin Maddox, Melvin Scrivens, Marvin
Scrivens, David Maddox, Donald Drumgoole, David Johns, Frank Jeffries,
Jr., Otis R. Weaver, Michael S. Weaver, Jr.(+,), Richard A. Rowe, Gene F.
Thomas, Erastus Johnson, and Kala Oboi Weaver.)*

Chipped and splintered marble dust,
hopscotch patterns and tops patterns,
knarled hands grabbing their dicks
on corners too full of music to sing anymore,
and someone splatters a baby on a wall.
These are not streets shiny enough to be
remembered in films as the coming of age
boulevards. These are streets with names
down under the curses of Confederate
officers buried in Bolton Hill. *Flip*
pineapple wine busting heads from inside,
holding childhoods down and raping
them in dreams. *Thunderbird* wine
painting yellow streaks in eyes that see
and hope, see and hope until the edge
of nothing rises out of the gritty mists
of steel mills. *White cracker, white cracker,
you can't shine. Bet you five dollars
you can't drink wine.* Drink wine and go
down under the needle, drink wine and blow
away with the dust, drink wine and come

to the bowl like a Buddhist monk and come
no more. The living dead need no sex.

In the missing holes of generations, men
rise up in once bright figures, from the dead-
Butch, gunshot wound in the stomach,
Poochie, heroin overdose,
Lil Mac, heroin overdose,
Boo Boy, dirty needles,
Big D in the Big House, and
none of this is historical because history
doesn't bother itself with the blacks.

Where is the love summoned
from contesting hearts? Where
in this crowded killing is the metal
urging the pure heart to sing its name?
Brave and afraid, young men
ride away from the mills to the liquor,
to the drugs, to the open holler
of night waiting at the corner bars.
To die sweetly in the night is to die
so that you are remembered on coffee
tables lined with pictures of souls.
To die sweetly in the night is to die
as men should die when corralled,
when hustled by hate to such peevish
ways of prospering. To die is to die.
Death to the beast, death to the beast...

Bruce A. Jacobs

LOST

help, she is wailing,
help, from the pavement, help,
from her knees, but her purse is gone,
he is all legs and sneakers, over the hedge,
and she is broken heels and torn hose
and scraped skin in a smart checkered suit and it is
gone, the walking free of larger hands,
gone, the swinging of her arms, gone,
the unclutched rhythm of her pendulum, and she flails
breached in birth from cracked concrete
this world a sidewalk in her wet face,
her mouth moving its small help, help,
a grown woman in ripped black stockings
kneeling blind in sunlight while silhouettes
sift past, none bending close to breathe
it's all right
she will learn to live here
it's all right
she bleeds salt on the tarmac
it's all right
she rises, peeling rock from skin
as her eyes search for home.

Garrett McDowell

CHILD IN THE NEW DELHI SUN

He did not hear her words
at first, her lilting voice
through the clamor and dust
of traffic near the Delhi Y
where she usually found
a foreigner touring the streets
seeking the pleasure of sights
and the nudge of any excuse
to smile with new bought rupees
on a cordial hand. He might have
glimpsed her eyes on his
from a shaded space of wall
as he paused at curbside
collecting exotic differences
rattling past as turbaned taxi carts
and pedal trucks, or as her
standing alone in the heat,
maybe a willowy nine with little brother
clinging by, cleaner in rags
than the usual beggars he had seen—
but he'd stepped off the curb
and almost crossed the asphalt
gauntlet after mumbling "No"
to "Maye Ai doo yourr vishes Sirr?"
before hearing her nuisance
was something beyond a plea.

Kalamu Ya Salaam

THRENODY

Twenty is twenty too many
(for our mothers)

What's your story Atlanta/America?
We should never forget what happened there,
what happens here.

I. Fear

"I'm sorry Mrs. Bell,
we've found your son"

who was not lost
but stolen, sacrificially slain
and left in the underbrush
for search party to seek
for stray dog to eat
left like carrion
to rot in the woods

"Mrs. Jones we must ask you
to identify..."

this America eating our
youth, belching
over the remnants of
children of color, identify
which bones belong to your flesh
identify which of the vultures
circling your misery are
the doves they claim to be,
identify the silenced sound
of your son's brothers and
sisters stonily starring at the space
where once his smile stood shinning

"I wish we could tell
you more, Ms. Watson but..."

tell me how long my son's
been gone, how raging the
world attacking my womb's
issue, how bold this death-
a-month plan going for the
world record of two years
running, how the killer
never slips, how the police
are never sure

"Mrs. Jackson we need to
question your other children..."

and no Black child volunteers
for anything, any longer in Atlanta
the children answer adult questions
haltingly, fear filled that one
of the queries will be
"why don't you come home
with me?"

"Mrs. Lewis I'm afraid..."

so now at night
huddled into coiled balls
of shivering terror, tugging
at covers and mothers for protection,
smelling the rancid odor
of death at every sound
outside the bolted window,
tasting the dry ash of asphyxiation,
Black children lay in bed
restlessly sleeping with
both eyes open

II. Pain

they come to trade in exclusive stories
about dead children,
mothers, their brown eyes moist with misery

are asked to suffer again, to stare unblinking
at blobs of strobe lights and klieg lights,
rigid microphones shoved straight
into these women's faces, the noise
of news hawk's callous questions
concerning the lifestyles of murdered
"street children"

did anyone notice the irony of the pictures
of sobbing women and deceased youth filling
the pages of "Time" and "Life," as if
these killing times were what life is about—
bitter, swollen images swathed in black, images
of pain enlivening dull news broadcasts,
is Black tragedy really news

to our mothers today's news feels
old, ancient, decrepit
looking into a lens that has millions of people
behind it, millions of people staring at you,
looking into that lens it stills seems sometimes
that nobody knows sometimes
how it feels to feel like a
childless mother

III. Disbelief

can we believe
Wayne Williams.
a Black man?
can we believe?

no. yes. could be.
one thing for sure
in America
all things are possible
all things are possible

and that is the problem
anything is possible.

Yao (Hoke S. Glover, III)

SOLEDAD

I have tried
to be beautiful
I have sung
when singing
was brother to pain

I ran
with my arms stretched out
and it slowed me down

I have called you
ever and lasting
and done and begin

I held you
In a lullaby
when where was no sunrise
when my beliefs became
dry and brittle like bread
in the sun

I have shed many songs
that the birds came and ate

And this

Is the only one
I remember

Wendy S. Walters

MERIDIAN HILL TERRACE

crack! a man is crooning to the cement
saying *i'm sorry*
for the mistake he made
what was it?

a cold steel barrel makes his breath tingle
it lifts him up by his chin. crack!
he goes down again.
maybe he has split in two,
each half wobbling like fresh cut fruit.
have I busted open?

he fears he will wash
down the gutter too easily, his body
broken, his blood letting
gone without ceremony.

following careful instructions, he frees
his wallet from his twisted hip,
how have i fallen?
he tries to remember, but first he recalls
his bankcard number. *please.*

there's the fading scrape of sneakers on asphalt
as he tries to reference, flip pages in the memory,
find where this story was told—
he hears the thump of his brain,
closing shut.

if he could, he would call the man back and ask,
what was i thinking?
though he tries to taste the words in his mouth
there is no breath.

before he can cough
or catch it back, a word
bangs like a brick thrown
against a steel door.
it rattles him

       nigger

air fills his chest with fury,
a deep knowledge
of how history performs
he says

o god, not me,
don't take me down in this fire
that can not stop this rush of fear
from my heart

Erren Geraud Kelly

7-30-96

The cop
with the gun full of faulkner
saw the black man
sitting in his car
head bobbing up and down
the cop
with a mouthful of the South's anger
for losing the war
walked up to the
 black boy in his car
sucking, enjoying his youth
off the tongue of his honey

the cop
with the eyes full of anger
because he couldn't accept the verdict
pulled out his gun
and the black man ran, but became trapped
in the circumference of his fear
The cop
pulled out his gun upset
that Jesus escaped the lyncher's noose
and walked along the ruins of churches

to reaffirm their sanctity
the cop
pulled out his gun as if to say
your million man march won't save
 you today

and fired
and the black man lay dead
the south wins the war every time
a cop fires a gun

Rachel E. Harding

BROTHER IS A STAR

Brother
      came back with the roses
      he bought for mom the may Sunday
which all red and tall-stemmed
      went faint
and falling over in so short a time
it was
  ominous
     they said subsequent
one of the signs

    so then when the shot
        knocked him
           days later
down in some southside pool room
    mom knew
it wasn't just
      gas in her heart

little sister
  sat up
at the foot of her bed
  there he was
saying goodbye and I love you
         the life just then leaving
       the strongest body of a brother she knew
 for home
    someplace with no shape
            unless diamond

CALL AND RESPONSE

God No
    Date: 21 Aug 93
Jamal, Jamaal
    Time: 10:48 pm
Oh Jesus please
    Location: 3rd and T
Somebody call 911
    Name: Jones, Jamal
Oh God please make him breathe
    Age: 17
Look at me Honey
    Inj: gunshot wounds
Somebody help me
    HT: 5'9"
Oh Jesus Jamal don't leave me
    WT: 160 lbs
Lord help him
    Hair: blk
Where's the ambulance
    Eyes: blk
Baby can you hear me

Kimmika L.H. Williams

SNAPSHOT: WEST PHILLY

KIDS
PLAYING STICK BALL
IN FRONT OF
DRUNKS
ON THE CORNER;
WHILE
JUNKIES
SIT ON STOOPS
ACROSS THE STREET
WATCHING
JUDGING THE PROGRESS
OF A LITTLE GIRL'S GROWTH
BIDDING HIS TIME
'TIL THE DAY
WHEN SHE TOO
MAY BE FOR SALE
AND "HE"
CAN MAKE A DOLLAR
OFF HER BACK.

Rozell Caldwell

THE BIBLE BUCKLE

Make you wonder
If religion is profound
With a church on every corner
In this town.

Lord they've taken you
Out of heaven
And distributed you
Like a Seven Eleven.

Religion here,
Religion there,
Religion everywhere

Out of all the churches
On any given day,
A minister cannot be found
To lead the way.

Beware the day
They wake up and see
That this religion
Ain't what it ought to be.

Lana C. Williams

SAINTS

They demonize the ripples
on Saturday nights

lay them on the alter
sunrise Sunday

blessing each other's heads
with olives under glass

lying prostrate at noon
fanned awake to dance a jig

at sundown
choir robes hang in closets

separated by sworn secrets
aired dry

in-creased
and winded faces

Yvonne Jackson

HOW TO MAKE IT

If you turn out the bathroom lights
and whisper three times,
Mary Weatherbee, I killed your husband
Mary Weatherbee, I killed your husband
Mary Weatherbee, I killed your husband
the old hag will reach out of the mirror
and scratch your face
so never whisper
those words in dark bathroom
or anywhere else.

Count the cars in funeral procession
and your fingers will walk off
in the middle of the night.
If you and another person
say the same thing
at the same time
knock wood first
so you are the sound
not the echo.

See a dead animal
lying in the road
Spit
to get the bad taste
out of your mouth
Be the first to
wish on the first star
and your wish will come true.

Sidewalk cracks
are your mother's back

fine fissures
in a fragile universe.

An empty wagon
keeps a lot of noise
so be quiet
and you will be full.
When you play jacks
the scatter has to be larger
than the largest hand
in the game or it's
Scatter's over
Learn to conjugate
"to be" and "to have"
and you will.

Do not ask
do not whisper
do not wonder
if someone three streets over
or three time zones over
whispered before you,
I wish I may, I wish I might.

You are too small
to predict the future
so if your mother is late getting home
protect her
imagine the unspeakable
and it will not speak—

She will return to you precious
and mostly whole.

Do not ask
How do you count first,
the starting point on a sphere.
Know you must be the first
and be the first
whispering you rosary dreams
into the squeezed night

of shut eyelids.
I wish I may, I wish I might.

And if you call for
Mary Weatherbee
if you count the funeral cars
if you forget the number of cracks
if you fall asleep
waiting on your mother
and wake too late.
If they will not let you be
first,
You can still
sit up and spit child,
spit
look at the jacks shining
across the dirt of heaven
and demand to see
the hand of God.

John Frazier

AUDRE'S SON

there is a boy who sits outside my window
he sits in the patch of daisies that separate
our homes
the daisies, he says, will remain bright
as long as we still believe in their beauty
he sits there each afternoon
their guardian

Bruce A. Jacobs

IT'S A DOG'S LIFE

We all look at corpses
with the same impending knowledge.
We could give up now, say what's the use
when it all comes to nothing
but hands crossed in plumped silk,
pine bonfires,
the solvent of deep water.

And if this is but a vigil before glory,
why waste time? 70 years is too long
to wait for a bus. You could feel silly
learning bird songs,
chipping your skin toward love
only to declare at last,
"Oh. Here comes mine. The 32."

I say it's a dog's life:
We come when called for sustenance,
but moments have no names.

Ronaldo Wilson

dungle sublime

her finger an elephant trunk discoils
to slouch on a milk crate

to rub the crease
of her polyester leg

she vanishes and i appear
in the kennedy fried chicken
window my blue shades faux silk trench coat
a black fire

suck my ass you blue faggot

she screams my head strands
on heat lamps and lumps of fried meat

last night i ate a center
breast one thigh
a roll

i mouth her a kiss
what does she not hear
my boots clopping?

this is the walk i take when i am hungry

i got two dimes in my pocket to buy
a lousy cigarette
and when i return all cobra and cagey
a cherry tongue steams smoke
out my face

Joan Adams

YELLOW IS ME, BUT ALL THE SAME ARE WE

Don't be mad at me because I have
brown eyes you see. My skin is yellow
but my soul is black. You're only
reacting to the old South's distortion
of facts.

Think, I think, I'm something, I am.
And so are all the others who wallow
in this generational fight about light.

Off the path to empowerment.

Oh My, Oh My, please wake up and see
the real light.

Bright, Light, Dim, Night
Beautiful shades of the
mingling of minds.

Dorothy Phaire

AN IRRESISTIBLE LIGHT

She sits in a corner away from the light.
Her body curves deliciously against black, silk pillows.
Ivory skin is aglow, translucent.
Snow white hair falls in abundant waves down her back.
Soft, crimson lips form a sweet, sculptured smile.
Far sweeter than Mona Lisa's
No one sees the black teeth gripping at her gums.

An eager, young man is seated before her.
She invites him forward,
towards the irresistible light
he accepts.

She is everything she claims to be,
and more.
Hours pass and turn into days, weeks.
She smiles and asks for nothing.

He goes about his normal day,
but the memory of her invades his thoughts.
The machinery he operates demands his full attention,
but her sweet image clouds up before him.
He is drawn back to the small, dark room,
where only she is the light.

Day after day he returns.
Cost is no object.
Slowly, she reveals the magnitude of her power.
When she rears back her head in boisterous laughter,
rotted teeth protrude from her mouth.
He is repulsed and shrinks back,
but it is too late.
He cannot resist.

He discovers she is merciless.
She demands all he owns
Money, jewelry, his car, his home
his mind, and his body.
He cries out in agony and begs for mercy
but she is deaf to his plea.

All that was once normal and mundane in his life,
becomes elusive and beyond his reach.
All that was once taken for granted by him,
is now cherished.

She weaves heartache and despair onto others in his life.
They would not know her if it weren't for him.
She devours a different vital organ each day
Until she consumes all of him
Only a rotting corpse remains.

He needs God's full army to defeat her,
an army that is welled deep within him.
God has given him the weapons to fight
but unless he is ready to go to war,
she will eat away at another piece of him,
Everyday.

George Elliott Clarke

APRIL 19, 19—: A SONNET

I trespass by the harsh, welling canal;
Rain and exploded ice swell feverish,
Entrenching despair in the Ottawa
 River. It's April, I'm ferrying gold
Wafers and songs in my leather satchel;
 I'm off to caress C.H., clandestinely,
After five brute years, I'm dreaming, fearful,
And coupled. *Married*, but I've loved only
Her these feverish, grief-exploded years...
This sorrow-stricken canal, pent-up sea,
April-fierce water charging, ferries moaned,
Shrill news: *I'll love her even down to death.*
I home to the dusk'd café, where she'll be—
Snow and crocus now mingling with the rain.

Janice Hodges

BRUISED CHILDREN

Bruised children
capture raindrops
from violent storms.

Alison Morris

WORRY ALL THE TIME

From the moment I realized

I was carrying you in my womb

I began to worry.

Will it be healthy?

Is it too small?

Why isn't it moving?

Am I eating enough?

Just Worrying All The Time

When you were born

as pretty as you were

You seemed as healthy as could be

I couldn't believe you belonged to me

I was so happy to be in your midst.

Joy was never quite like this.

And then I started to worry.

Will he wake when I'm not there?

Will he fall off the chair?

Are there too many people around?

Is he afraid of all the sounds?

As you began to form I thanked

God everyday

Prayed he watch by you and not let you stray.

Asked that you'd grow up safe,

healthy an strong

Knowing that I'd love you forever

whether you were right or wrong.

And Then, you began to walk

run and play

A part of me wanted to stay near you

every second of the day.

As I watched you from afar

Fear loomed within me

Will he fall?

Is he bleeding?

Where did he get that bump?

He's climbing too high!

He's running too fast!

Though one day not so long ago,

I realized that you never really belonged to me,

but you were your own person.

God created you and I know that

your fate is in his hands.

Still

I worry..

Worry all the time.

M. Eliza Hamilton

MIDNIGHT IN MISSISSIPPI

Emmett Till's ghost hangs between us:
Six black women remembering History out loud.
On this midnight passage in a white van
through land that was never white
only the pecan trees hear our laughter
lilting through windows darkened by night.
The road reveals nothing except
what we leave now and what we now enter.

Emmett Till's ghost hangs between us:
His little-boy body dredged bloated and beaten from the water,
Southern-white-punishment
for a black boy too far from home.
We speak gently of the dead knowing they listen
for their names to be called.
In a brief pause we each hold our breath,
not daring to speak the Truth:
When they threw him in the water
his great-grandmother was there waiting for his return.

Which one of us would have dreamed
our native land would meet us and take us back
like this, dark and silent like our mothers' wombs.
Which one of us would have dreamed
one day we would be unafraid of the pecan trees
whose branches tonight hang only their own fruit.

Matthew Watley

FOR THE MAN I MET ON GEORGIA AVE.

His mustache was graying like my father's,
Calling me sir, and I'm just a boy
Asking me politely for change
I said no
Like always
But those kinky gray hairs
That deep rough voice
I knew him,
But I wanted to forget.

Nyere-Gibran Miller

MY FAMILY

My dad is a cook
My sister is very, very cool
Mom, is out of town

Patricia Elam

MOTHER'S DAY AT MCDONALD'S

In McDonalds, a light-skin boy is crying
with his mouth open and his eyes shut tight.
His mother snatches his high chair so hard
it rocks forward and he almost falls out.
"Shut up," she says. "I told you to shut up
and eat your food." The light in this place
always hurts my eyes. Their electric bill must be high
as I don't know what. A young guy with fresh pimples
mops up spilt ketchup from the floor
like he wish he wasn't there.
He goes right across my feet with the mop.
Somebody in there laughs. Not me.
I count how many people in each line but stay where I am.
The woman beside me can't stand still.
One leg is shaking like it belongs to Tina Turner.
"I coulda cut up my own french fries,
heated the damn grease and cooked em faster
than you mutherfuckers up in here." She spits
when she talks. Her mouth twists around to
the other side of her face.
Her daughter's eyes are big and round,
looking, always looking.
I know she wishes her mother wasn't so loud.
They get up to the cash register before me.
A cardboard display about a Mother's Day McChicken Special
tumbles to the floor and the little girl picks it up
The mother glances at it and sneers.
"I know I ain't gettin me nothin for no Mother's Day,"
she says while the brown-skin girl
behind the counter frowns, sucks her teeth,
waiting for their order.
"Ma, how you know what I got planned?"

the little girls's voice is down low,
stretched thin, barely there.
"I know one thing. I don't want
none of that dollar store shit you got me last year."
Then the mother orders without asking the girl what she wants.

Bernard Keller

THE MAJOR

Wrinkled, callow, calloused fingers
sensitive to the touch of green felt
and a smoothly tapered stick,
hold a life's story.
Jagged, broken lines form at the corners of eyes
reddened in smoke-filled rooms
by endless games of chance.
From his mouth flows a stream of days and friends
long since passed,
of things that were,
and were never meant to be.
Like a general carefully perusing his battle plans,
he contemplates his every shot.
Slowly, he nudges the cue ball forward,
barely scratching the paint
on the number two ball.
Stubbornly, the ball makes its way,
slowly ever so slightly
before coming to rest
deep within the corner pocket.
"Just like it had eyes,"
he whispered aloud to the silence,
"just like it had eyes."

hazing
(for tony new and albee)

i once pledged
my father's fraternity.
the day he came
home from work
unexpectedly
and caught me and my
friends getting
high in the basement.

through the thick
smoky haze of the best
panama red i had ever tasted
my father happened to see his
red and white kappa alpha psi
paddle sitting in the corner.
gripping his paddle tightly
dad immediately placed me on line
despite the fact that i never
expressed any desire to join his
or any other fraternity.

the pledge period lasted
all of ten hits
as i ran through the
thick
cosmic clouds of smoke
that i had been enjoying only
a second ago,

out the backdoor

off line

away from one of those
brothers who takes this greek life
thing a little too serious,

never to get high in the house again,

never to cross those burning sands.

D.J. Renegade

FATHER AND SON

We meet only
in the dark alley of memory
broken smiles glittering
like glass littering the ground
although we wear the same name
first and last
identical scars
you can't remember
what day I was born.
Anger spills over
runs down the side
of my round face
this is all you have taught me:
needles are hollower
than lies
leave bigger holes in families than arms.
Now like an overused excuse
you grow thinner every day
until I can count your T-cells
on one hand.
The phone rings
Mama pleads for me to please
buy a dark suit to wear
I tell her
I wear black everyday
all day
anyway.

father's shoes

these are my father's shoes
holding my feet down to
earth
reflecting dark deep brown
the sky   the trees   my face

these are my father's shoes
freetown's shoe shine boy
spit polish shine and sweat in summer sun

survival lesson learned in depression days
coating my feet in leather sole

these are my father's shoes
built to last
walking to be heard
not made for tip toe
or fancy footwork
or footloose fancy nothing   is free

so
when you hear the footstep
the gravity on my legs
the laughter stomped
when you see scuff and soil
on my sole
you should remember
these are my father's shoes
and i am only
filling in.

tyehimba jess

father country

the country of my father
is a sparse place
a place i do not know well
that lies fallow for moments of
uneasy conversation

the country of my father speaks
mystery even to him
brought here
born here
bred on orange clay and starlight,
returning from motor city steel
and factory fantasy lit skies
to
this quieted place with
syrup slow waves and
southern cousin smiles
lain deep from his past.

there is a journey here
between wind and weed
of empty lots
that once held rusty knees
and playgrounds
for skin brown,
dark as hickory bark
made for climbing.

i smelled the green of
my father's country
standing by his father's grave
sifting through memories of
king edward cigars

world war 2
and greasy corner
"where you can get what you wanna"

i visited the country of my father
to sit still in the house of my grandmother's eyes
searching for my story
staring from old photographs.
hearing the years in her hands.

Arnold J. Kemp

100 TIMES

Lost in rivers of Mars Bars and more coffee to spill on the bus,
Like so many other nights, a rose will silence your expression on film
Her impression of him of little consequence.

Oh my nights and eyes, when I think of those I love,
Those so far away, I cry. When I read the grounds
At the bottom of my coffee cup your image drives me mad.

Because the boys of Guadalajara are so beautiful,
See them still — even here in San Francisco—
With their dark brown hair and oddly shaped noses,
Their long nostrils that, looking at them eye to eye,
One can almost peer into, and the stillness like pools.

Still, when I lie down to love you, I am 100 times a street worth of traffic,
As many engines purring, as many fan belts turning.
Turn to me and you are more than you were from behind.

It didn't start this way at all, my spark plug. The two boys
Were exiting the mall by way of the over ground bridge
Attached to the hotel lobby. One asked the other, in a flirtatious way,
"Well, what do you want to do tonight?" and the handsome one replied,
"I don't know. Go home and think about death," or did he say,

"Sex", totally deadpan? Later that evening, they were sitting in the dark,
Deep in thought and fantasy. Then there was this Japanese drag-queen
Unleashing and practicing her English at the bar's end, saying,
"Black, African-American. Let's go Coco. I'm stinky as a bear!
I am a tiny little minuscule dime-sized penny's worth of a Negro-star."

Imani Tolliver

those i love are sometimes white

everyday
it is hard
getting on the train
seeing the eyes stare back at me
with some kind of hated and feared reflexion
i breathe deep and read this book of poetry, french
and forgive
and believe that god
knows i try to forgive

and everynight
find my young knees
looking for the universal love that we supposed to get
to understand
to live
find
this one sister
praying for one brother to love
and babies
and a degree
and publishing
and find the cords of universal love being broken
each time i open the news
to find fucked up, poor white boys
jamming up all the communication i have been taught to cultivate
find diana's baby potential skinhead
and good friends
potential subversive types
warshipping they no good men
on cold nights
in early december
in north carolina mostly black neighborhoods
where our mamas
can't even speak right
through the prayin'

Willie Abraham Howard, Jr.

PARALYZED

Jet black, once pretty
Like the sisters who ride
MARTA daily.
We unloaded metal,
She stood at the door
Eyes saying hit it up,
I'm a long bag of garbage
Brothers joked, most of them had
crack's yellowed fly-eyes too.
Two dollars man, she'll do you!
I wanted to reach out like Levi Stubbs,
But I wasn't an empty soft drink can
Or baking soda.

Yona Camille Harvey

THE MUSEUM CASHIER

the sky is mine to admire
my eyes a planetarium
projecting the light
of the stars

who are they to get nearer?

selling pictures to tourists
without the consent
of the universe?

who said it was alright?

i am the daughter
of a blue planet
third from the sun
the only one
bearing children

they cannot place
galaxies on visa
they cannot accept checks
for the vision i hold

no, they are not next in line
no, i cannot help them with a smile
to get to the moon to live
selling tickets and postcards
then tell me i cannot
afford to go

i do not believe
in martian chronicles

the sky is mine to admire
from the arms of my mother

whose moon was circled
in sixty-eight when nightmares
smothered a dream. . .

the shuttle will always burn
and i will sell
the matches

Nzadi Zimele Keita

dedicated to the domestics

this one goes out
to all the poems
that drowned in dishwater
and to the poets
who let go
thinking they'd been pierced
by some swimming
kitchen tool

this is for the lost poets
without babysitters
straining for cadence and signals
in the backyard breeze

poets emerging
in traffic
who had to
drop off bring back
stop by pick up
enroute to the wine
and cheese

poets who run
the whole race
passing a baton
from voice to voice
within one body

this one's also
for the poems
wrapped in greasy napkins
sucked down in the scraps
from dinner plates

mashed under the lint
container

poems jetting the pipes
and sewer system
like a hail of sperm

poems bloated
like some shipwrecked survivor

poems belching
as they return to air

poems bursting
like hot oil kissing water
seeking the right mouth
once more

Valerie Jean

ASTROLOGY?

My daughter tells me
I am snake, and she
a tiger- why we argue
all the time. I wonder
at the Scorpion moon
we share, intense, how
her billowing air is
the only element missing
from my chart. Her eyes,
so like her father's, once
trusted me to blot out
shadows, and in her face
was sun enough to light
my days, to forgive all
the promises he broke.

Grown now, she leaps
past my warnings, does
not feel the ground shake
as I do. I tremble at her
daring through rough
jungles- fierce, the power
of his raging in her blood.
At night, I circle, kneel,
beg the moon-ghosts to
keep her safe. As I draw
closer, deeper into earth,
I marvel that my writhing
on this land has carved a lair
for paws that now threaten
to disturb my old uncoiling.

Artress Bethany White

MOON DAUGHTERS

A child once wandered the earth
wearing only a nappy crown of chaos
The skin between its sturdy legs seamless,
its mind clear as water.

The earth roiled beneath its toes in confusion
tried to arrange itself around a creation spit out
a million years too soon. Seeing little promise,
earth attempted to digest its error quickly.

The child, of persistent stock, put up a hellish fight
as feet then legs were sucked into a crusty belly.
Hoarse wails split apart the heavens, prompting the sun
to leap from beneath a cloud and thrust
a fiery arm toward a now shamefaced earth.
The sun tugged at the squirming child all day,
and only managed to rip its body vertically asunder
in partial victory.

The moon, in turn, slid up to claim its domain.
In pity, cast an icy face upon the mischievous earth
and the other half of the child popped out.

The sun and moon, eternally estranged lovers,
were quite aware of the other's spoils
but could come to no accord. So each decided
to refinish their half to individual taste
Thus men and women were born.

Mothers, encourage your sons to be watchful
on full moon nights, as they may come upon a woman
relieving herself standing up
and this woman, if properly amused,
might show them the way
to discover the other half of themselves.

PASSING

When the Famous Black Poet speaks,
I understand

that his is the same unnervingly slow
rambling method of getting from A to B
that I hated in my father,
my father who always told me
don't shuffle.

The Famous Black Poet is
speaking of the dark river in the mind
that runs thick with the heroes of color,
Jackie R., Bessie, Billie, Mr. Page, anyone
who knew how to sing or when to run.
I think of my grandmother, said
to have dropped dead from the evil eye,
of my lesbian aunt who saw cancer and
a generally difficult future headed her way
in the still water
of her brother's commode.
I think of voodoo in the bottoms of soup-cans,
and I want to tell the poet that the blues
is *not* my name, that Alabama
is something I cannot use
in my business.

He is so like my father,
I don't ask the Famous Black Poet,
afterwards,
to remove his shoes,
knowing the inexplicable black
and pink I will find there, a cut
gone wrong in five places.

I don't ask him to remove
his pants, since that too
is known, what has never known
a blade, all the spaces between,
where we differ...

I have spent years tugging
between my legs,
and proved nothing, really.
I wake to the sheets I kicked aside,
and examine where they've failed to mend
their own creases, resembling some silken
obstruction, something pulled
from my father's chest, a bad heart,
a lung,

the lung of the Famous Black Poet
saying nothing I want to understand.

Ronald D. Palmer

STERLING BROWN

Back in 1952
Sterling Brown was my neighbor
And lived
Across Kearny Street in Northeast Washington
Not far from Catholic University
I took my first poems to him
He told me I had no gift
Perhaps he was right
I didn't show anything
To anyone
Until thirty years later

Trasi Johnson

MATISSE, CUT OUTS
STUTTGART, GERMANY

An unassuming curve
Clear. Sharp. Surprising.
Each tone an invention
Blue inevitable
I laugh
I fly with Icarus
I dance
I am Ringmaster
Hold a star to my eye
I will not flinch
I swim the neutral sea
more aquatic than a
rippling sunset
I spin
not sure from one
moment to the next
whether I am
photograph or negative.

Lorelei Williams

STRANGER IN THE VILLAGE

Standing in your same skin
Mr. Baldwin I want
to open your buddha eyes
in my skull
and clothe myself
in your spirit

Ride your sorcerous tongue
that thunders
with hallelujahs
and homecomings
until the holy ghost
sets me back down
on my feet

Will you help me
build a shelter
for my soul
with your confessional palms
and testify to blue eyes
that my tears
are not exotic?

Carolyn Joyner

THEY DO NOT HAVE TO NEST IN YOUR HAIR:
A Tribute to Ron Brown

International blossoms shrivel
on a Croatian hillside as their
Harlem roots give way to bluster
churned by kismet.
Grieving voices unable
to sound out their gloom
wrench global silence
from stunned hearts.
In the ebbing light of a moon
he had hung, shiny
wet sorrow shimmers
on the face of the world.
We look toward the sky,
birds of sadness fly overhead,
but they, too, have song—-
arias of life leaping
death, struggle building corridors
to fair chance, worthiness, freedom—-
soothing harmonies that stir
memories of those delivered
by a man slain on a Memphis
motel balcony, this day,
twenty-eight years ago.
We turned our faces
toward the sky, to see
the birds of sadness fly overhead.
But then, just as now, we did
not allow them
to nest in our hair.

Dana Gilkes

RAIN MAKING

The horizon crawls
Closer inland
Folks hunch down
Inside the thickness
Of rich skins
The sky convulses
And the earth is a sea
Of contemplative rivers
Bursting.

Dana Gilkes

THOUGHTS FROM A 747

Out and across the Atlantic ocean
See where earth has stored the deep
The agonizing waters
Of her sons and daughters
Who long between
Two worlds two cultures
And neither fully blown.

Between my heart and head
A string of cowries
In the lap of the man against me
A laptop opens up with ease
Behind me the whimper of a baby
Beside me the afternoon sun
Is a homing pigeon
I pull the angry shade
On this tiny window to the world
Closing up my fingers
Afraid to span the future
Berating nostalgia.

SPACE

The wind,
cold menacing
wretched howling,
screamed
until it seemed
it must snow
forever.
Freezing bitter
loud   evil
we heard it
and feared
it would swallow
us all.

Where was it coming from?
This cold and hungry force,
screaming from a dream
I had of dark clouds
racing.
Where was it coming from?
This cold and hungry force
my friend identified as
"an evil something
out in space."

"I need room," she said,
"I need air.
My chest is so heavy
and my legs won't move
Why is it so hot in here?
Why am I so cold?"

Wiping beads of sweat
from her upper lip,
she pulled her wet nightgown
away from her armpits.
Gesturing to escape
the heat,
her hands brushed a wave
of ice cold air
across my cheek.
Abandoning my stance,
afraid, I took a seat.

"Seven.
What is it about
that number," she asked,
pacing
crying
as confused, as I was tired.
"Don't leave me," she pleaded,
"Please don't leave me,
cause the evil wants
to swollow me
and you have the energy
to make it back off."

Voices in the wind
screamed all night long.
There was no rest,
no sleep,
'til dawn.

When staring out
at the nearly naked lawn
the snow lay down;
a tired blanket of lace.
A pitiful offering
for such screaming,
I thought.
A pitiful offering
from an angry atmosphere.

Later on
rushing
late for work,
racing against the hours,
I could barely look up.
Then the phone rang.
Voices I know
cried,
"Girl, have you heard?
The Challenger
has exploded!"
I saw:
visions of fire,
flames dancing on ice.
Bodies breathless
burning,
vanished, as ashes
settling as salt
in a wound.

Solomon says,
the hungers
of death and hell,
are never silenced.
Never satisfied.

Vanished,
as ashes from an urn.
Silenced.
Sacrificed in space.
Dying without grace,
the wind
cold,
breathless
screams
on.

Toi Derricotte

HIGH SCHOOL

I didn't want to be
bunched with the black girls in the back
of Girls Catholic Central's cafeteria.
They were my kin,
but sitting there I was aware
of that invisible wall, the others
circling us like stars. The others:

Gintare,
the Ukranian with limbs like silk and childbearing hips.
Kathleen, who would be a nun, whose mother saw the Virgin in
   the suburbs.
Pignalls, whose body had grown into a giant's, who towered
   over the gold prom queens, not like a man, but a child who
   had grown into a monster, her broken speech a path out of
   herself she could not follow.
Donna, her hair hanging over her face like a veil—her knees
   made for kneeling, her stomach for fasts, her genitals for
   the loneliness of the cot, but the rest of her unable to hold
   up holiness.
Jo, who let boys penetrate and shrugged off other wisdoms;
   her long eyelashes held grains of sand, as if tiny pieces of
   eternity were working themselves through her.
Lenore, whose square body threatened the narrow pews;
   expelled, who lived in the back of a White Tower with her
   first woman lover.
Marty, whose palate and teeth stuck out, like some hairy
   specimen of our ancestors, alone with her mother, sleeping
   on the pull-out cot.

None of them called me nigger;
but they were ignorant
as God of our suffering.

Monica A. Hand

TATTOOED GIRL

Frida Kahlo paints
her body with sharp razor lines
to praise the spirits of her fetus
all national treasures are so adorned
then sold in the dollar store
to put back what has been amputated
we create many a freak show

here the great white dome
shoots above our heads
two-hundred and eighty-seven feet
its giant body entombs small men
who postulate our worth in trade
then throw us tiny liberties
at fourth of July parades

beneath these streets
are sacred burial grounds
yet, every year we wave to Lady Freedom
as she dances in bursting light
bangled and bedazzled like Frida
hiding under her big hoop dress
a splintered back and crippled leg

Willie Abraham Howard, Jr.

CROSS BURNING BLACK

Don't need bansaw
Faced klansmen to
Feel like a nigger!
Don't have to see whites stroll
through the anthraxed mouths of
Forsyth, Bensonhurst, Bridgeport or Cicero.
You can be a nigger, with skin tones
like yours. Profane sentences, bullet lined curbs
With Torie Popes, John Wesley Davis and Jeremiah.
Women regurgitate ropes as hostile as men.
Bonfires through elementary school, high school.
What gives the Klan and Aryan Nation the rights
To brag? We've outdone you. We tread nigger
heads at Alto and Rice Street Corrections.
How many incarcerated brothers have prayed
For early morning guard counts? All the pulseless
Women asleep in S.E. Atlanta.
Richard Wright would need
fourteen more lives to novel this.
Down with false black
Love poems, read to crowds to elicit cheers
praises of men and women, while your spirit
Wear those invisible knights covering through
The week.

Monica Hand

SHE-GHOST OF TIRESIAS

I am still wandering.
Still blind with my choice,
a choice that will not deliver me.

I love as a woman loves a woman.
I love as a woman loves a man.
I love as a man loves a woman.
I love as a man loves a man.

This is my curse and my blessing.

Since before the birth of Christ
when I walked barefoot on naked rock
and my skin grew brown in the dry sun,
citizens have sung of me
of my tormented prophecies
They knew the gods used me,
to tell what could not be seen.
I, a mad man, who seven by seven
wears the mask of a whore.

Do not envy or condemn my affliction
It has prompted the quarrel of gods
and society's contempt.
Pity me this paradox.
I see in each of us this sense for complexity.
In each of us this same choice.
I have known more pleasure than is sane:
 for this unusual love I am still the same,
neither man nor woman.
Do not ask me which I prefer.
I answered once
and I am now blind to the distinction.

I do not know if God approves of my knowing.

Certainly you understand this appetite.
You who have drunk the sweet wine of a woman's fire.
You who have experienced the ecstasy of death.

Seven times seven I have been reborn,
shapeshifting.
More than *an old man with wrinkled breasts*[1]
or the warrior queen riding as half man/half beast.
What I am fulfills some larger purpose,
to see with the eyes of one.

[1]T.S. Eliot's The Wasteland

Yao (Hoke S. Glover, III)

THE SCIENCE OF FORGETTING

the simple flush of a toilet
a way to send shit to the same place
trains disappear to as they wind around
the tracks, the future or the past, the dirty
secrets women into time, the smell
you remember, that she was cooking,
chicken the way you like it, or spinach
with garlic and ginger, filling the air
with the thick smell, love becomes
in a house past being new, past its past
that it will stand on its stone, creak
with the wind, break into tiny bits and pieces,
the sing or a door knob, and you will have to fix it,
she was throwing the clothes across the floor
into piles to wash them, thinking you were still
her husband, cleaning the house in a day
dress, pine or some fresh air from a bottle
as you broke out, through the door
and found yourself heavy, sandbags
around you ankles, the damp air stuffed
into the season of rain, the basement of
the old house: the way any man feels
when he leaves, quick steps-exit
the house where the children lie awkward
like dolls in their sleep, legs hanging
over the edge of beds, hands over their eyes
to hide their dreams, trapped in their heads
the worst, he would not come home, ever
somewhere in smoke, in wine
miming his other life before
he made one decision that made a hundred
others like dominoes, beans or rice

the one being insignificant
the whole being nourishment:
this is life once you start running it,
you can't get out, clamped to the edge
of a bar, buying drinks and a stare
into the eyes from whoever will listen
whoever is thirsty for the stories
we all carry like the waste in our bowels
or the hair on our heads
uncountable, to answer to no one
not even love, the trickster, the 98 degrees
we all must carry though it is unbearable
bearing down on the body in summer,
even when you're half naked
something cool would do you right
like running water rolling down you face
there is more love to be made
more love to be gotten, the philosophy
of the Boer, the pioneer, there was a buffalo
and we killed it, there was land
and we made it into miles
so when we travel, we register the senseless
wandering and say we have accomplished
something, so simple, flying across the sea
instead of sailing it, what I am saying
is like my father, many men have found
themselves standing on the tip
of their greatest moment and fell, and thinking
they were climbing, they wandered
the earth, for the rest of their lives
finding no rest, running like water

Vicki-Ann Asservero

THE LOCK AND KEY

#3 For Wam

I went down ole Jamaica way,
"Irie, irie" all dem say.

Reggae, Rasta, Rolling Waves
Play de shore; eat sand all day.

Me see bright blossoms and coconut trees;
den floatin' and splashin' in that Caribbean Sea,
me find an old and rusty key.

I dream of olden treasure chest;
Jah lookin' for galleons sunk in grottos nests;

Me search and scour but me no find
neither jewels or bullion of any kind.

Jah sittin pensive on de shore,
Lookin' wistful at de sea

And sudden, key start talk and it say to me
"Measure wit and humor with profundity!"

Me laugh up crinkle cause this talkin' key
start singin' that "No problem" melody!

So now I know down ole Jamaica way
de people dem happy, God's people dem say
"Irie, irie. . . Serendipity's Jah's play!"

DANCING ON THE SHORE WITH SPIRITS, SINGERS AND MUSICIANS

Lisa Elaine Johnson

SPIRIT OF THE DANCER

I am the dancer. . .
Look into my soul.
I dance for you lord.
I reach out to you.
No words need to be spoken.
Watch me closely.
I dance for you Lord.

Lisa Teasley

AS DANCERS

You can find
whatever you want
a tortoise in the left-hand lane
a sleeper on the train
to Austria in winter
if it suits you
a biker in water
or a poet who lives on lies
I can be your dancer
in a wheelchair
for years and more years
or you can leave me
to find the one who
serenaded you
in the traffic of pigeons
at San Marco Square
The one who saw you
hold your arms out wide
for the birds to sit on
to eat on
to shit on
or you can stay here
in this wheelchair
and we can roll on
together forever
as dancers
if you want to

Eddie Bell

HELP IS A DISCOTHEQUE
(Rio De Janeiro 1996)

So young, so pretty-
their eyes so bright when they smile.
They lean on cars waiting,
waiting to be someone's girlfriend
for the night.
Plying and playing, they wait
We watch with inquisitive eyes.

"It's the economy, they must do something!
And they are happy, No?
See they chat and giggle; and
drink rum with powdered sugar and lime."

So young, so pretty,
these whores of Help.
The men play in their tousled hair
and pat their behinds.
Posing like starlets,
they flash their bodies,
they have no pearls.
All colors of chocolate and cream,
a collection of fruits for the appetites of men.
And oh how they dance
when the music starts!

Reggie Timpson

for lester

every fool
thought
you were
an excuse
for Hawk's absence

James E. Cherry

BIRD

Last time I saw Charlie
Parker, he was shouting 4 o'
clock in the morning blues down
at Minton's on the Square.
It was a resurrected Sunday and
I had been in the grave of hope
lessness for three days, keeping time
to the metronome of solitude.

Bird was bending notes, stretching
tones, breaking rhythms, changing times
and resetting them. And along with
a half pack of smokes, the bitter
lukewarm beer and all the despair that
weighed my head upon the table, I breathed
deeply, taking in cool cathartic moods.

I stepped away, looking back
to a standing ovation and Bird bowing,
riffing to take flight again. Outside,
into the briskness of a dream, I carried each
tune of Birds' like a point of light deep
in the recesses of my soul, illuminating
courage, strength, hope as I
pushed and fought my way down 52nd St.

It was Easter morning.

Everett Goodwin

MOM USED TO LISTEN TO ERROLL GARNER

The cymbals, the drummer, the tasteful buzzing brushes,
The bassman rolling time with his gentle rhythmic thud.
All the while Garner, prancing and skating on top
    of Misty or Angel Eyes.
       In smokey clubs where jazz is good
           and on a right night artist and audience
           are one.
      The Workshop, Paul's Mall, the Cellar Door.
This superb singing of our song
An opening to our art opening my heart with its swing
And, yeah, I'll take mine
Straight, no chaser.

Everett Goodwin

JOHN BIRKS GILLESPIE:
an appreciation and reflection

The famous don't have ages like you and me,
but are forever frozen in memory
at the age they were when you discovered them.

When Diz died,
all of the times I had seen him,
over twenty years or more of joyful virtuosity, came flooding back.

The first encounter came in '62 or 3,
one of my few real college dates,
a concert,
a fine brownskin who I really wanted to impress.

Leaning over,
whispering the names of tunes before Diz called them out—
    "That was 'Round Midnight,'
     that was 'Straight No Chaser.'"
And when the next song was 'Night in Tunesia,'
I announced it with particular joy as it has always been a favorite.

Dizzy puts down his horn
and says in the inimitable humorous tone of his,
    "That was 'Night in Chicago.'"
My date touches my arm
    sympathetically.
    "Well, you were close," she says,
as I manage a small smile.

In 1968 at Charlie Byrd's in Silver Spring,
Diz was running for President.
I thought it was a tongue-in-cheek campaign,
but when he mentioned it, he mentioned it seriously.

225

It was then that I first heard him speak of his Bahai faith,
its emphasis on the oneness of all people.
His marvelously succinct comment stays with me.
　　"If you believe it, live it."

At Wolf Trap in '75 or 6,
they're taping for a future PBS TV series.
Diz, always the iconoclast, is in high form, telling the audience,
　　"It's great to be here tonight,
　　　if for no other reason than it means money in my pocket!"

It's '82 and I'm poet-in-residence
at a high school in a wealthy suburb of Boston.
Diz and group are the centerpiece of an arts weekend.
A man in the bathroom tries telling me how progressive this makes
his community.
　　I know better.

Dizzy said that they called him Dizzy
because they couldn't pronounce intelligent.
Intelligent is what Diz was.
Intelligent and funny and gifted.
But the main thing his detractors failed to recognize
　　was the brilliance
　　　of an eternally luminous spirit.

Cornelius Eady

CHITTLIN'S

According to the chef,
At this small restaurant with its hazy view of the Pyrenees
Dizzy ate nine more of these than I will tonight
It must have reminded him of home, I think,
Whenever he passed through to play the summer jazz festival
In a neighboring town,
And assured him that he wasn't.
And when the dish arrives, hot, pungent,
Its workings disguised in mustard,
Cuisine instead of what's left,

I thought of a friend, who might have said,
When my nose reminds my brain of what I swallow,
Now taste where you come from,
And the sight of the man, waving for another plate,
The insulting stuff turned sweet, digestible: jazz.

Afaa Michael S.Weaver

THELONIUS

It's as if you are given the sky to carry,
lift it on your shoulders and take it to lunch,
sit in McDonald's with it weighing you down,
this business of being black, of staying black
until the darkness of some eternity kisses you.
Birth gives you something other folk thank
God for not having, or else they pray for it,
to have its gift of a body inclined to touch,
inclined to sing. Yet they will not give back
to God the paleness of being able to touch
absolute power. They envy only for so long,
as being black is being bound to danger.

Among us there are masters like Monk,
Who understood the left hand stride
On a brick. In his rapturous dance beside
the piano, he was connected to silence.
He danced the disconnected steps to knowing
the scratch and slide of the shoes leaving
the ground, the shoes of the lynched men.
He carried this thing that we are,
as the mystic he was, reveling in its magic,
respectful of its anger, mute and unchanged
at the hate and envy surrounding us.

One day we learn there is no sky above
this trapped air around the earth.
the sky is but a puff of smoke from
this giant head smoking a Lucky Strike,
pretending not to know the truths.
We learn sometimes in this life,
sometimes in what comes after, where
there is really nothing but everything

we never knew. We learn in silence
the dance Monk knew. We find secrets
for pulling the million arrows
from our souls each time we move
to sleep, to forget that we are both
jewel and jetsam, wanted and unforgiven.

Gaston Neal

MONK

This sound I can hear
that somehow found my head
just drop my mind between
the keys
Ruby, My Dear
and move the rhythm in among
the twisting and grabbing feet
it hurts, this sound
oh god, it hurts

MONK'S MISTERIOSO

If you have to choose
choose nothing but the hippest beat
with criss cross riffs of blues
blown beyond Stravinsky's strut.

Saxophones blow hot
against blue cool of brown skins
mocking metal skies
of steeltowns and mills.

If you have to ask...forget it
there are no answers
just Monk digging deep
into his hip pockets
pulling out melodies, rhythms
holy rolling sermons.

Out of his many hats
flatted fifths leap
to play hopscotch in no man's land
between black and white keys
between Mississippi and Harlem.
The same old song, some say
But it's the dance baby,
Monk does it like nobody
this side of the great walls
of China.

Allison Joseph

THE FOURTH SUPREME

It was really me who came up with that
"Stop! In The Name of Love" gesture,

because I was trying to tell Diane
to shut up during rehearsal

so I could concentrate on the music
and the moves our choreographer

was putting down, intricate motions
all the girls at Motown had to master

if they had any hope of making it.
And we so desperately wanted to—

Flo, Diane, Mary and I—
get ourselves out of the projects

and into the clubs, on stage
where we could strut our stuff,

all of it my idea—bouffant wigs
so we'd never be missed, sequinned

evening gowns that made us look
like royalty, pointy-toed high heels

that made our legs look slender, sexy.
We didn't have to dance like the male

groups did—no Temptation walk for us,
no Four Tops same-old-song

back-and-forth in place turns.
We were there to look good,

sound good—to be the prettiest
black girls in America with

the sweetest voices, making
women weep and men swoon

when we sang about love:
its heartaches, tricky ways.

I wanted to be Motown's sweetheart,
but Diane couldn't stand it,

no record company big enough
for two like us, plus Diane convinced Gordy

I couldn't sing, wasn't cute,
that I was the reason the group

hadn't yet made it big. But that girl
who now calls herself Ms. Diana,

knows I'm the real reason it
worked, that I knew one palm,

held up and out, could make audiences
never forget us—crown us queens

of this new sound all America needed
to hear, a new knowledge of the heart.

Lyn'elle Patrice Chapman

STEVIE WONDER

Most people believe you're blind,
But you're not blind to me,
For happiness is what I find,
In you so good, so free.

You have a Special sight,
That no one else can see,
The sight of love that's dynamite,
Far better than people like me.

People may say I'm crazy,
But you're not blind at all,
For in my eyes and mostly in yours,
Love stands a hundred feet tall.

I would really love to see you,
And have you stare at me,
So in your wonderful precious eyes,
I'll be what you see.

A. *Anthony Vessup*

THE MIGHTY BLOOD

when Tina Turner sings
about rivers all I hear is hot steam
hissing from sealed
lips that shout notes changing pain to
victory
when Tina Turner sings
my erotic nerve twitches
and I go looking for satin legs
teasing silks lines on staffs
manageable
when Tina Turner sings
inspite of being weary in a
dreary world only then life is
more than just a
song.

Allison Joseph

NOON TALK AT GEORGIA'S COFFEE SHOP

What am I supposed to do
when my husband leaves me for a blond—
dye my hair, end up like
some Tina Turner reject?

If it's a white woman he wants,
let him have her, deal with all
the threats and names and ugly
talk. I nod while Georgia speaks,

keep my mouth shut up,
scared to let her know
I'd seen her husband on the street—
his new woman wasn't white.

Georgia, I say, *it'll be okay,*
Howard will come to his senses,
stop fooling with a girl half
his age. Someone will let him know

just how wrong it looks
for him to carry on
with someone's teenage daughter.
Georgia wipes the counter with

a rag, her face so pinched, sad,
I want to fake some obvious sign,
show I know what she's going through.
If she wants to believe this girl

is white, that Howard's left for skin
Georgia can't provide, I should let

the story stand, let her think
her husband's chasing some

low-rent Suzanne Somers. After all,
his cheating is what's breaking her,
and she's entitled to believe
what she wants, needs her version

too. Without my asking, Georgia rests
another cup of coffee by my plate,
a slice of pecan pie she's just baked.
Her hands, ragged from too many

dips in scalding water to scrub
those plates, aren't steady anymore,
each fingernail peeled back
from where it used to set.

Georgia, I say, grasp one shaking hand,
*let me do your nails tonight, the way
I used to, remember?* She pulls it loose
and I see she hasn't wiped the sleep

from her eyes. *Don't ever look old,*
she says, *whatever you do.* She won't
come home with me tonight, though I
have her favorite color—

a black-red lacquer in a fancy
bottle, a color she'll leave
to women whose men don't stray
to sample younger flesh.

Derrick X (Goldie Williams)

BURN RUBBER ON ME

Even watching that Tina Turner movie
brings back painful memories
Of how my daddy beat my momma like a man
Why did he hit her in the eye
I just could not understand
Wanting to do something but not big enough
To bust a grape
Wishing I could transform
like Popeye with that spinach I had ate
The first three digits I ever
learned were 9-1-1!!
All I knew
it meant men in blue
that would have my daddy on the run
He left us
He said
"I'm out the door"
I seen him burning rubber
out the driveway in his Riviera 74
I never ever knew that man
Who put the pedal to the metal
And burned rubber on me
Daddy
Why you want to hurt your family.

Cornelius Eady

PHOTO OF RON CARTER, PLAYING HIS BASS

He is all bark and strung gut.
Taut and loose—it shouldn't be my job to confuse things,
But he's walking while he's standing still,
And as the lens proves its temporal art,

He does time one better, gives it a bottom,
Makes the bottom fleet,
Makes you feel it from the soul of the boot
to the bone's tingling marrow.

Sure, it's a heavy dance,
This lean man holding a curved suggestion
Of a woman in his long, beautiful fingers.
It shouldn't be my job to make things up,
But see how they hold each other in orbit,
How they grind the fleshy notes.
Photo of the young Freddy Hubbard

On the appropriate shoulders
The blues can be a pretty thing.
He is a downhearted strut,
The veracity of spent women and cigarettes.

Luxurious as silk—this black voice.
An intersection in Brooklyn—this black voice.
A blast of audacity and impulse—this black voice.

The slur between whiskey Saturday
And cold mattress Sunday.
Pour the funk into a pin-stripe suit,
Hand him a trumpet.

Verneda (Rikki) Lights

SAVANNAH BRASS

(Composed during a concert by David Murray & Hamiet Bluiett,
Philadelphia, 10-12-82. Donald Smith, Fred Hopkins,
and Ronnie Burage, sidemen.)

A chorus of dark angels
rising from
a tumbling sea of brass,
echoaches of Africa
scream their fierce
lullabye blues.

Each note
a seminal sacrifice
of leaping savannah
animals,
symphonies & melodies
pay homage
to eternal
creativity.

Solo sidemen
try their wings,
crashing cymbals
bells & skins.

Sliding samba
of bass, invites
staccato piano.
Snatching
the anthem
of the universe,
they sing
in black & white
wood & metal.

Strutting chorus
of nightingales,
caress the stars,
then dive
deeper than the whale.

Sweet exchange
of breath,
caribbean spice
a mango sun set;
dancing lighter than
a sleeping elephant.

Houston A. Baker, Jr.

SET PIECE

I was inside Coltrane's blue chords
That bright afternoon,
With bleached clouds
Bare maples and oaks as Medusa's head
Flying past my car.

The lake was frozen motion.
There were no birds at all.

My comfort toward evening was only the grace of knowledge:
Precisely where the sun would fall at 4:43...
The exact corner of the house
Where the new moon would rise,
Without you.

A THOUSAND MARIONETTES

(For Bud Powell)

An athletic tarantula
the handful of fingers
tiptoed at light speed
across uncharted ivory streets.
The echo of ice clinking
in half-empty glasses
carves arcs of boppish lines
across drum tight nights.
They brush past my ears
in brisk breezes.
There is never a hint of stumbling
in the flash of those who run
long before others learn to crawl.

I could not contain
all those sounds
in the vast sphere
of my world.
They spilled over
and rolled away
in different directions
like a handful of marbles
falling
from a child's hand.
Then they would return
to those magnetic fingers
that held all sounds on strings
like a thousand marionettes.

Reggie Timpson

verbal gun shots

(for henry dumas)

ghosts
of sweetwater
made fun
of my dreams
when i spoke
so i
peeled back
my shadow
& hid inside
it's skin
to
shield
the
blows

DR. JACK

The editor said:
        that which I published yesterday is cliché
           that which I have not yet read

   is
   obscure
        Faced with this troubling conundrum,
        the writer
made several unsuccessful attempts to kill
                himself

        Daunted by his own

immortality
he decided instead   to kill   the editor

BLOOD
AND
DISAPPOINTMENT IN THE
LAND

James Coleman

VIPERS, FLIES, AND WOMEN OF THE CLOTH

Slink back with me
To those golden days
    Of yesteryear
When hamburgers cost a dime
And boys wondered if an umbrella
Could parachute them safely
    From the porch roof to earth.

I used to kill fifty flies
A day, and kiss the faces
On the covers of True Confessions.
I was afraid of mice.

One day I challenged God
To make it rain if He
    "Was so all powerful"
And it was that minute exactly
My life began to rot.

I thought you might be angels
Come to absolve me from
The sins I'd committed
But one and all you've caused me pain...

I implore you, cure me Magdeline. . .
Immerse me again
In the baptismal fluids
    Of your cup
Give me water, give me grace. . .
Taste like Salvation

John Frazier

VISITING HOURS

Sit separated by wire-meshed glass
and memories
Show him the cap you're knitting
ask can he try it on
Tell her about the guy one cell over
put in solitary confinement
so the others couldn't get him
how when they brought him back
he whimpered for hours
something about the color of night
bleeding into the color of day

Ruth-Miriam Garnett

CONCERNING VIOLENCE

(for Frantz Fanon)

Because of how we are wed, enjoined, huddled;
our herd of faces and eyes to one of ascots and blunt hairs,
we do not recognize this war. We are merely the survivors
who have slept in the crevices of God's palm.

There are reasons for our madness, its explication
notches down the length of a totem; for our fear of iron dogma,
and of the mask that spits and smiles alternately,
transporting us noiselessly to burial. For such offense,
we kill with our bare hands. This war is like no others.

I have stood to face them, talking their language.
I have stood, facing them, with squared repugnant shoulders.
I have been a cough more silent than breath,
awaiting shares of a religion that rants and rages and spits
its fanaticism of debris, of paper weighted greater than rock.

I have said: My People, come with me under these leaves,
this civilization. Burial is all the same, though bereavement
is sent by the wrong gods, and the hand held out to supply us
is emptied of touch. I have rehearsed feeling,
preparing for wars that history deadlocks.

I have in the same skull grown two minds.
One is the other's warden

Baba Lukata

REHEARSAL

i saw
three little black boys
lying in the grave yard
i couldn't tell
if they were playing
or practicing.

Ira B. Jones

ALLEY GAMES 6/THE ASCENSION

these inner city alleyways connect us
like the veins of life filled with the warmth of flowing family blood
as we stand over James Michael "Peanuts" Woods' closed coffin
the cold-blooded alley war game filled with death
sticks on our hands and in our memories
like red blood separating from yellow plasma on a sacred totem
Peanuts is at the crossroads
In this his last sacred solitary moment of darkness
Burned brown like a golden singed sun
Unable to look into his mother's weary eyes
Dreary with pain of prayers hung on a broken cross
To save his soul transcending before our begging eyes emptying
Our frozen tears dropping mocking the rain gods
Like broken ice white cold glass beneath our natural knees kneeling
While prayers melt this manchild back into the mother earth

André J. Baldwin

GLASS BOX PUZZLE NO. 1

Fist through
a plane of glass

making waves
rippling

shards - pieces
swept up

floating
wind chimes

knocking against
one another,

no harmony.

Zak Robbins

DECEMBER 12TH

The man who raped her
said he was different too
and has sat between us
in movies and lain between us
in beds and it was he
who made her cry
when I tried to hold her
before she slept
on the floor last night
and fretted from nightmares
she has lived since that moment
that counseling hasn't helped
that repeats itself each
time I touch her hand
and tell her how much I care

StacyLynn

examination

with my feet braced
and knees skyward
and only the absence of a restraint
to distinguish between
me and an animal
being prepared for insemination,
I feel him enter me
not unlike a new lover
in exploratory fashion
as though this was his first sojourn.
"i'm going to check on the left,
now to the right"
trained for clinical understanding
but having no comprehension
of the discomfort,
the feeling of being violated,
never having had
an invasive procedure
or internal prodding.
while the remaining fingers
press annoyingly on the outside
the doctor asks
"was it still raining?"
as though we were having tea

Kevin Simmonds

A WHITE MAN AND THE JUDGE

Your honor,
I've committed no crime.
it was night

and I thought that my life was in danger.
Three men approached me and...

Men?

Well, your Honor,
it was night

and they looked like men.

But dey wuz really teenagers.
De bigges' onewuz only but five-foot sev'n,
a 'undred 'n fifteen pounds.
Too small to ev'n swing proper from a tree, huh?

Your Honor?

You shot all three of 'em.
Twice.

You real fas'
in the night.

Tell me somethin'.
Ha' cum all dem bullets wuz in dey backs?

Harriet Wilkes Washington

THE GOOD OLE DAYS

When I lost my job,
The earth opened up, and swallowed me whole.
Bill collectors were drowning me with demands for payments,
And every Morsel of a meal
Reminded me of the Last Supper.

When I lost my job,
The holes in my hopes and dreams
Became lined with tears and fears,
And my kitchen became a shrine
Where food was a new, endangered species.

When I lost my job,
My last paycheck was the only thing
Standing between me and the homeless guy
Whom I used to ignore on my way to work
(because back then, I still had a job....
Those were the good, ole days).

Dawn L. Hannaham

I LOVE YOU, THOUGH YOU'RE UNEMPLOYED

I love you, though you're unemployed,
Despite the fact you smell.
If you wore Brut
and had a job,
I'd love you just as well.
For someday soon you'll get a job,
and sooner—take a shower.
What love is true that can't endure
the idle month and funky hour?

Dawn L. Hannaham

IF THERE'S NO SUGAR

If there's no sugar,
And the water is tainted,
Just suck that lemon.

Paul Jamal

THE EDGE

Everybody says
Why do you live on the edge
Do I ever get scared
In my heart is there fear
Why am I the person I am
Why do I act like.........the person I am

Because I can

Why do I live on the edge they ask
I reply, you must think life is slow,
Life is fast
And then they ask again
Why am I, the person, I am
Why do I act like...........the person I am

Because I can, you wouldn't understand

You see this is the edge, you must make and know your own
ledge
So whats it like on the edge
I'll tell you the truth........it's a great view

the subtle art of breathing

in the middle of everything i'm not doing my doorbell rings it's the
landlady's lost son   i point him up the stairs mildly annoyed to have
been interrupted from my intent viewing of a soap opera one life
to live   ironic   now that i think about it

nobody ever suspects women like me poets politically conscious   watch
soap operas but we do   at least i do grateful   to retreat into the
fictitious chaos of somebody else's life

but this is not a poem about soap operas

it's just that i cannot find another way to begin   i mean how   would
you do it?

would you start with a father's scream lancing the air
with the little sister's indelicate weep
or the acidic gurgle of a stomach self-destruction
maybe you would simply begin like a broadcast journalist scanning a
teleprompter:
in anchorage today a 30 year old black woman was found in her
apartment   dead of an overdose. the incident has been ruled a
suicide....

but this is not a poem about how to begin a poem
or a poem about lost sons and landlady's
this is not a poem about soap operas
in islam they say from Allah we come to Allah we return
leaving   the curious among us hungry
for the story in between arrival and
departure   the person in the center   the thin arms desperate
to stop the steady crush of closing walls   her first wall was daughter
her second was wife not much room there to just be a woman
holy or unholy

but this is not a poem about religion

there are people who have accused me of creating the various
& sundry crises in my life
there are people who have accused me of refusing joy & of
blanketing the sun   but then there are people who know as i know
that even as we laugh   we cannot ignore the wincing in our eyes
we are not crazy or invested in sadness
sister was it that you knew there was no space
to be second best or needy in a country swallowing up the earth
from the inside out   they incinerate their own children here
i have seen them   scraping
their own 8 year olds into garbage bags   or compactors
whatever's efficient &

it might be that this is a political poem

forgive me
i feel guilty borrowing your family's pain   you were not my daughter
not my sister   i never even met you   your name & troubles were a
footnote   at the end of a discussion on lovers and where to go for dinner
that night   i know this space of mourning is not mine to occupy but i
cannot leave   your life reads like the details of my life   & i must
know why   you are dead   i am not   yet we both were 30
black female & fighting histories of drugs violence separation loss
start stop   start stop   again
we are a ritual of everyday blackwoman experience
stories repeated on sally & geraldo ricki lake & the news
nothing unusual
suicide?

been there   done that &

maybe this is a poem about deja vu or a poem about phyllis hyman or billie
holiday maybe this is a poem about my grandmother or your best friend from
back in the day maybe this is a poem about you but it is
definately not a poem about invented crises
fictitious lives or retreating pretending
lying turning away or even praying

this is not a poem about soap operas

once i was told that i was more than all of my hurtings added up
together
if i had know you   i would have told you that too   girl there
was more to you than your violent marriage   more than the brown girl
you became couching   beneath dining room table   more to you
than the baby you lost or the last time you or any one of us gave ourselves
up
like unwilling virgins to   cocaine vodka tonics cheap wine newports
colombian gold   & beer when the money got tight   girl there was clear
skin beneath your bruises   muscle behind the split ribs   a raving
beauty beyond *his* broke up sight & screams of *bitch lemme tell you*
something   you ain't shit nasty funky ass stupid ho
& did you ever see her   even
once & if i did   & if i told you we were the same woman sisters maybe
twins   would you have been able to hear me

can i ask you something?

was this the first time you felt powerful? did you feel   finally some
control   did you say to yourself   can't be yanked out from under this
table gotta hiding place that muthafucka won't never find me in   did
you think at last   a truth no one will ignore   that the world will
believe you   now   i just remember feeling very calm

as i slid into pieces of the splintered wood of my dormroom floor all those
years ago you know what would have happened if you had survived been
surprised by somebody coming back in after the 18th pill?   you would
have tried to fight them as they tried to make you walk   they would
have dragged you up & down the floors til the ambulance arrived someone
would have slapped you to keep you awake   whoever found you
might have read your journals   displayed your diaries   said they
just wanted to understand   at the hospital if you arrived conscious
they would have made you eat a black chalk substance   to induce
vomiting   you would have vomited uncontrollably   in front of
you they would have stirred through it picking out the pills for analysis
     there is no other way to say this   besides i told you

this is not a poem about soap operas but

this may be a poem that warns   breathing is a difficult and subtle art

it may be a poem to say simply   i understand sister after 3 attempts
years past the last one   i understand girl
i think this is a poem that wants to assert itself
i'm proud even glad the i'm a survivor &
sometimes when i am quiet & sometimes when i am alone & sometimes
when i am reflective & sometimes when i am scared & sometimes
sometimes when i am watching soap operas   i say oneday i'm
gonna be even more than a survivor i'll be a celebrant inside myself a
party girl in my own soul   i'll take myself out fancy restaurants
bring
me roses then make love to myself & in the heat of passion call out
my
own name (*asha, asha...*) yes i'm gonna marry myself does that sound
crazy?

martin luther king said *we may not get there together*
but we as a people...
  & What if i do girl? get there &find myself dancing wild in a bright silk
dress &
high heeled shoes will you come too ok   not
  now
   but your next time around   be your own sensual dance partner in
high heeled shoes fine as hell girl & so so so fulla
life

Gary Lilley

WHO SEZ THUNDERBIRDS CAN'T FLY

The streetlamps glow
slashed into my room
across the bed and books
newspapers and clothes
piled on top, it cut through
an empty jack bottle
and into my full face,
this shadow killin light
don't even think
thunderbirds can't fly
let me crank it up
and take a little ride

The bar I'm headin to is my domain,
nappy head thick with blues,
I'm the guy you lookin for
if you want to do anything
just come to me

Sheets of the evening paper
blow like frightened birds
along the wide sidewalk
a man bent into the damp night
face open like a basket
wind wrapped like a pair
of cheap shades around him
An iridescence of gasoline
the next rain will never wash away
it's kinda beautiful when you see it
as I do. I see people
hardwalkers all
doin what they need and strivin

I knew a man
who thought he knew the secrets
His name was Nairobi he smoked the streets
blood fury, dark as wine his weary eyes
he'd say stand and bend the night
like a worried note from a banjo string
just do your thing
Nairobi staggered stumblin step
all the time. He was a ghost
sucked up, burned out tryin to survive
he was an obituary postdated
but ain't we all

So don't blame me
that some are dyin
in the small ways
a stone face cracked
will crumble from within
the soul dies first
being hard all the time
if you trust in God you better believe
in Satan takin what he can
the one long day he's free
cause what is it that keeps us here
thunderbird blue still alive
but the music between those two
so you just gotta turn it up,
rude-boy style, and ride

Thomas Stanley

IMPERIALISM – THE DANCING DO NOT DIE

<Small, where I let you see me,
large where you see me not>

The minstrel and his mask had a conversation.
My only role is for permission said the painted smile
to the broken piece of man behind the mask.
Don't you know greasepaint is a combustible material
said the wounded man to his face of carnival glass —
If you throw a burning clown it may be called a bozobomb
but it will still go boom.

He wants to play his r&b and b left alone
Some say the jews are doomed to wander
 but the minstrel has no home

My only role is for permission
Minstrels are the purest form of misery
ever permitted to roam the earth
they dance their jigaboo judgment
between a pitiful death and a scandalous birth.

Behind his filter of burnt cork and the
cremated remains of
children he could not carry in his mouth,
the dancing clown watches and watches
What is he watching

Don't you know watches tell time!
        said the minstrel
That's what I'm doing — I'm telling on time
                boom

He wants to play his r&b and b left alone
Some say the jews are doomed to wander
but the minstrel has no home

Merilene M. Murphy

park mole

uh-uh-uh
i thought i saw lady day in the park today but
billie's long gone & it's not H would have her now
i saw you today
down deal silver crate home
park mole runaway mother on wheels
mud sister mattress clump
tree table lumpen green & matted as
pus underside of
madness peeled away from
the last hit   from the last pull
through dark holes sitting blue
sky denial beneath
cracked up wings
smoked out
noon shy of the next joke flight craving
shatter lips to fryglass craving
fat havoc & slip bye-bye down another no
lather shortroll
    the habit of smashing
two dollar rock
      throwing motherhood down
dark holes bubbling
sizzling
chasing concrete with
zeroed out vulture eyes
late in the disposable
light of day where
kids mother themselves to school
play you by memory
is your favorite song &
rush tired as your dry pipe whistling

empty as your assassin ghost's pistol
i saw you in the park today
absent your double dutch shadow
fool rope of our laughing kids
dragging home alone

uh-uh-uh

Brandon D. Johnson

THE ARTIFICE OF WAR

My dreams of scaling
your fortress
Hacked to ignoble death

Your eyes, artillery
Slaughter my light bri-
gade

Futile war
This love

I
Surrender

Sun Tzu
Shakes his head

Sighs.

Tammy Lynn Pertillar

GENERATION GAP

"Don't worry bout me,"
She said,
taking her tea in long
swallows,

"My ship is comin in!"
She straightened herself in the
old brown chair.

"Yes...I got a lot to be
thankful for..."

She trailed, clasping her calloused hands.

"Don't you want *more* from your life?"
I asked,
Not understanding what she had said.

A cool breeze sifted through the
threadbare curtains.
She pulled a ragged sweater round her
work-weary shoulders.

"God is good to me. I'll soon
have all the things
I ever wished for!"

The lamp glowed softly
upon her smooth features. Half a century
of hard living had broken her body
but had yet to mark its existence
upon her face.

"Aren't you *tired* of being poor?"
I questioned,
Not listening to what she had just said.

A smiled crossed her lips
as she replied, "Well..."

And I, still not understanding,
walked away.

Gary Lilley

FUNERAL

(In memory of Michael Andrew Lilley)

Naked in eastern mournin sun
let me run
wailing in madness
tired mind weedy and littered roadwide
pain houndin down lazy whore highways north
to prophets proven false who have sent me
death in their tight brick towns
on their asphalt beaches

I have danced in quiet dawn streets
breakin bread with whoever hungry
as I starve for love and God
deliver me sweet Christ
my feet of stone stumble
my soul is a sack of sand

Detox me I'm poisoned and shake with fever
demons my hands tremble
ragged rhythms I thirst one glass savior
in this death damned dawn
I'm alone a flame a solitary candle

(Much too vividly I dreamt I was crucified
on the floor of the lowest shack
in a valley of reachin pines
everything ablaze around me
the rough-cut floorboards smoulderin
toward my outstretched hand)

I have slept in a dead house
boarded up and bare inside

I have improvised
a fitful bed along the obscene wall
while the chosen drank my wine
and as I closed my eyes
late night footsteps scratched
like a moon callin cock
on down the gritty sidewalk

Mbali Umoja

SAY SOMETHING: A CHANGE IS GONNA COME

the funeral grief song
the cleansing wails rising like smoke
over villages once called safe
haven in the familiar
that hooping cry cuts through thin walls/skin
it signals the calling home
and women pull their sons into their eyes
they search them out for a brief glimpse at relief
knowing that kind of holler so close to air
knowing how endangered a species her boy
the diminishing chance of him reaching man
or not knowing enough to know that
and still primal instinct
some mother thing
makes them locate in this universe their black sons
and for one fragile moment more find them alive

the lynch mob has turned into itself
the arbitrary crime the same
a black boy in the wrong place/wrong time
on either side of weapons
zombied hunters armed with self hatred and a gun
they eat their own
they murder for fun

children drenched in hopelessness
stuck frustrated rage
furious at their own being
able to stop it in the blink of an eye
easy to kill   easy to die

once chances were taken to love
on battlefields bloodier than these

in watts   in nam   in detroit
at harpers ferry and mississippi bonfires
(bodies used as kindling)
we loved enough to share the hurt
knowing the pain of loss

how many more funerals
how many more bodies piling heaven high
how many more boys snatched from the loose grip of manhood
just taking hold
how many mammas and poppas
sisters and brothers   sons and daughters
of the sorrowful eyes
what is our collective crime

it's time: say something
find a page   a pen   a corner to shout on
light seven candles in the window
play oscar brown and old gil
play marvin gaye and bob marley
play sam cooke loud
"a change is gonna come"
and know the power in survival calls

say something
about the black boys bodies on corners
ghostly chalk outlining the shadows of their last breathes blood
these boys straining so hard to capture elusive manhood
warrior children   crazy in the craziness
mad in the madness
committing fratricide with the mark of cain furrowing brow

say it's mayhem   murder   madness
and we've cracked under the magnitude of it all
we've cracked and are losing whole chunks
of our families   our nation   our future
trying to fill gaping holes
with sharp dangerous slivers
slicing lives to ribbons
until it's kill or be killed
die a five dollar death and not know why

say something about how we are the solution
who move forward stand firm and live
in spite of carpetbaggers getting rich off the misery they supply
gas on the flames flicking us further away
got to say how much love in
in love with the MEN and WOMEN we must be
to save the villages and rescue the tribes
it is a demand for more than
the least we can be
the least we can stand

say something
say it again
stand rooftop high and catch the words
to the wind roar of approaching storm
say: this much love
this much self love
and still enough for you and you and you and you
will heal the schism and make us lust and lunge
for the true freedom in loving the self
we see in each others eyes.

William Henry Lewis

SOME SOLACE, SOME YEARNING

I.

What remains haunting are not the crematory flames
curling around the body, unfurling into air
and open memory. It is not the stilled face,
and sunken skin, bound to know what comes next.
When the dead embark, eyes closed, arms folded,
they don't seem so lost. What's moving
is their calm; sublime in their leaving,
faces annealed in stillness. Your skin
seems lacking in being left behind. Your face
has forgotten its virtue. What remains
is the air of evanescence, hints of sighs
held back, and the scratch of black seldom worn.

II.

In a picture of my grandfather-a place
where there is no one else to run from
or run to –his smile curves without care.
Beyond him there are elms near blight,
and hedges weeks past their regular trim.
His shirt is open at the collar, glowing
against dark, weathered skin and the pale
canary of his sweater. No need for ties
anymore, he is calm, standing without strain
for as long as I look.
There are grasstips at his calves, moving
with wind that stirs everything movable
forever toward the tattered corners.

The grass. The high green of trees. Wind.
That yellow of my grandfather's cardigan, fading
away from me year after year; a lost hue
betraying the smile of its wearer and the frame
I've trusted to hold him.

Toni Asante Lightfoot

IN OKLAHOMA

shards of retribution jut skyward
leaving minds as devastated
as A-Bombs once left two cities

forgetting words of the prophet
who signed his death certificate
speaking of chickens coming home to roost
president turns Islam into the host of blame
the media drinks the wine of his word
"Cowards" they chorus
like America didn't train the "brave"
to invade Grenada
  kill Libyan children
  and leave star-spangled body bags
  soaked with the blood of our truth-sayers

in Oklahoma
  it's recognized that tragedy struck
  by those blind to tragedies aimed, fired and reloaded
  in my neck of this American wilderness every day
where boys terrorize our girls
  at a rate of one Oklahoma per hour
where girls neglect our children to death
  at a rate of one Oklahoma per minute
where guns doped with vengeance murder families
  at a rate of one Oklahoma per second
and life creates junkies
  at a rate of one Oklahoma per now
the truth hurts
chickens coming home kill

Nzadi Zimele Keita

black tax

we still have funerals
at night, you know
for the parts of us
that shriveled
waiting to be born
for those articles of rage
latched onto the organs
of the body
and stink like
cadavers overdue
for those kindly vapors
we've inhaled
in the course of
any day's duties or pleasure

somewhere
taps will play again tonight
for hypersensitivity
and bitterness
even with a two-for-one
burial they just won't
stay dead
they just won't
stay dead

Nzadi Zimele Keita

what is left

after Toni Cade Bambara

death rides a silencer
into your blood
and swims toward
the mind

what you remember
starts with a smile
raw edge
a single snip
from the someone dead

it is bracelets
or trains or
a taxi,
trailing
her deserted path,

it is the swift traveler, landing
as cat or crow

it is black mastery
presiding over collard greens
hot grits and board games

it is the salt and sugar laughter
of sistahs in darkened
movie houses

that makes it clear
her doubtless eyes are on you

now comes the cruelty
that jerks like vomit
as undenying death
rises from its hiding hole

 now comes the seeking
for she who was that strategist
that sentry
who would walk or ride
who would let you in free
who would put a hex on pain

that which
inside you is glass
pierces the organs
as it shrieks apart

that which
inside you is flesh
shudders across
all the miles you travel

and all the words she said
rain down
a red sound
fanning the streets

John Frazier

A GUARD

I stood in the cold
until my body became numb
Buddhist monks in saffron robes
accomplish more
than me in my gray overcoat
still it felt spiritual to forget the touch of
my own body
to free myself
of its odors
the soft places and hard caverns
momentarily forgotten
I imagined this is how he must feel
and I became envious of him
for I could only make this sensation last for a moment

John Frazier

SORROW SONG

a soldier
we fight with stone loaded muskets
Subcomandante Marcus says inferior weaponry does not matter
because we are a strong people
even our most feeble fight in these hills
in this much underpublicized war
for the creation of new political culture
we would fight with sticks to end our suffering

a laborer
let the Zapatistas fight
for me life is still hard
bondage is knowing how to suffer from birth
sleeping on this dirt
watching my girl cry when she is hungry
selling what I can: fruit, my body, hard candy
fearing my life

Jabari Asim

1ST LT. VERNON J. BAKER: HERO ON THE HILL

(Company C, 370th Infantry Regiment, 92nd Division)

We go up twenty-five strong.
I'm fresh from OCS,
lectures, lessons
ringing in my head.
Press on.
Set an example.
Complete the mission.

Textbooks and games fade fast
when the real thing hits.
We're headed up Hill X in Italy.
Castle Aghinolfi is close enough
to spit at.
How many Nazis are between us
and its ancient stones,
scowling at the dark mystery
gathering below?

We charge
and the air around us changes,
grows heavy with horror
and gray shapes shuffling,
dim outlines of dugouts
and telescopes.
Forward through fear, fury
and the nerve-scraping screech
of artillery, we climb.
We keep our eyes
on the castle, our M-1's aimed
at the hatred ahead.

The ground gives way
to Nazis in our hair
wide-eyed and howling,
eager to take us out
all at once or one by one.
I take seven Germans by myself
kicking in their teeth
with my rifle and my rage.
All around me my own men fall,
slashed and screaming,
their hearts bursting into
bloody chunks.

At OCS our chief of staff said,
"Now it's time for the colored boys
to go get killed."
My company commander,
his pale face flickering red,
runs for reinforcements.
I never see him again.

Killing works two ways.
We blink back blood
and fight until a strange stillness
swallows us up.
Twenty-six Germans
lie twisted beneath our boots.
Their machine gun nests,
their lookout posts and dugouts,
all smoke and splinters now.

Seven of us survive,
sliding and stumbling
until the bottom of the hill
swells to meet our feet.
I sense my stomach
turning against me,

bones and ash under my eyelids,
the smell of flesh
ripped and rotting in the dark.

STAFF. SGT. EDWARD A. CARTER, JR.:
THERE AND BACK

1.

Across the field from a warehouse,
unseen eyes have us all to themselves.
Our tank takes fire from bazookas;
small arms swarm, hornets guarding the hive.

I'm heading a patrol across the field.
Under sniper fire, 150 yards is
a series of agonizing inches,
We begin on our bellies,
dark worms wriggling while Death
waits, patient and inevitable.

One man is stung
as soon as we begin.
I order the others
to pull back and cover for me,
but two shots drop them both.
I hug the earth so hard
my fingernails bleed.

2.

Five bullets find me.
Three in the left leg,
another in my arm,
one more for my hand.
Each impact is a burning taunt:
I've got your name on me, schvartze.
How fast can you move?

3.

I am sweat and mangled muscle.
Thick grit sticks to my tongue.
Agonies, ecstacies swim in my memory.

I see my lady, luminous and lovely,
laughter shining in her sweet brown eyes.
I call out to her and gulp grass.

Breathing burns my lungs,
holds hot matches to my throat.
I am swimming in sand.
The grains wear away skin,
find their way to the slick bone beneath.
I must move while staying absolutely flat,
under Aryan bullets edging my ears.

The warehouse at last.
I roll behind a berm. Hours pass.
Gradually, my strength gathers.
Adrenaline surges, electrifies
arms and legs.

When eight Nazis find me,
I'm a miracle in motion,
the black angel of their dreams.
Six soon fall dead,
 their eyes wide open,
  mouths soft circles of surprise.

I use two as shields,
white wings for the flight back.
Pistols in ribs steer their stumbling.

I hear shouts, commands,
men moving.
My platoon appears.
Helping hands catch me as I fall,
handle the holes in me.

"You made it," a soldier says.
"You made it, man. You made it."

"Yeah," I say.
"There and back."

Jabari Asim

1ST LT. JOHN R. FOX: RAIN OF FIRE

Smoke seeps slowly under the door
of my observation post, this cramped room
where we battled time and dueled doom
with telescopes and maps. From the second floor

of a house in Sommocolonia, a small
Italian village in Serchio Valley,
I've kept watch on our enemies, all
bent for blood. Last night I saw them rally

at our perimeter. At dawn they crossed
through our thin line at will.
Now, as they attack our house, eager to kill
and avenge the lives they've lost,

I have seconds to react,
to forget raging fear
and accept the cold solid fact
of Death's arrival here,

helmeted, heartless and sleek.
This room's secrets are best left undiscerned,
therefore everything in it must be burned.
They must not find the documents they seek.

I radio company command and relay my decision.
My request goes up the chain of unbelieving ears:
"Can he really want artillery aimed at his own position?"
Finally one officer understands what he hears

and gives the order I desire.
He sends a team four guns deep

293

on a final fateful sweep
of vengeance, wrath and fire.

They will converge here, just
ahead of the intruders on the stairs,
and reduce to rubble and dust
the house centered in their cross-hairs.

I'm thinking of all I dreamed and planned
together with my wife, Arlene.
What will they tell her of my final scene,
that I died a hero, with her photo in my hand?

Arlene's face smiles while screams and yells
shake the walls. I pray for silence to drown
out the shrill, shrieking shells
and the fire, raining down.

Harold L. Johnson

THE NAMES OF SUMMER: A WAR MEMORY

(for Jerry Conrath & Joann Geddes)

Early in the war they began to show up on Sundays
at the Washington Junior High School diamond—
the first baseball players I'd seen in uniforms,
twenty or so, wearing white uniforms with red
caps and stockings. At first, they all looked alike,
like a handful of toy soldiers, and their uniforms
seemed like a big white lily that tore into particles
as they piled out of the army truck that brought them
to the field. "Japs," a watching neighbor growled.
Their driver relaxed behind the wheel in his khakis
during games, puffing Camels and flipping through
magazines. He counted heads when they reloaded.

I hung out near the benches to drink in the hitting
and catching, and herd their talk, which was just like
mine. I heard the pitchers' fear of Yamaguchi, a great
lefthanded hitter. Often, he slammed balls
over the rightfielder's head clear to Eighth Street
and he could punch it to left when he took a notion.
Fujitani was a black of muscle behind the plate
in his armor that snicked and clunked as he worked.
He could whip off his mask, sping after a bunt
like a grasshopper and fire to first or second
in one motion. Duncan Matsushita threw
heartbreaking curveballs that dropped suddenly
into the strike zone, and he seldom walked batters.
I began to cheer for my favorites. They laughed
that I could pronounce their names, no stranger to me
than the Deuteronomy, Malachi, Ecclesiastes
I'd been hearing all morning at church.

After a couple of Sundays, they drafted me as their batboy.
Manager Saito gave me staccato instructions: how to
retrieve the bats, how to line them up, how to hustle
after foul balls that looped over the backstop and bounced
into weeds across the street.
      For the rest of the summer
on Sundays, I was waiting at the diamond
as the truck arrived and the players hopped out
and started stretching, playing catch and fielding
fungoes. Sometimes a player didn't show up. I would ask,
"Where's Sadaharu?" "Oh, he signed up for the army,"
somebody would say. And that's all they would say
when somebody signed up for the army.

The war. During the week I played ball, trying
to imitate Kitagawa's nifty pickups at short, or Hongo's
fluid throwing motion from left. And I heard news
about the war, about how we had to beat the Japs,
those funny-talking, slant-eyed sneak attackers
of Pearl Harbor (which we were suppose to remember).
I read comic books featuring heroic American
marines in combat against the bucktoothed, craven
enemy in the island of the Pacific. In one story
a group of marines, victorious, found among other
graffiti on an abandoned cave wall, stick figure
of ballplayers and the legend of "Babu Ruso stenks!"
      But Pentecostal Sunday
morning sealed off the rest of the week, and the town,
except for a few gas stations, rested. First came
Sunday school, then church with all the singing
and praying, testifying and the collection plate.
Some weeks people got baptized. Every week I suffered
a parched crawl across the Sahara of the sermon, trapped
between fat saints who fanned themselves and chanted
"Preach, Brother!" It would end but I knew there'd be
waiting while the grownups finished laughing, shaking
hands and hugging. Then we cruised home in the old
Chevy. I tore into the house, changed clothes
and sprinted to the Washington diamond. The players
arrived in their fresh white uniforms with the red

caps and stockings. Balls popped into gloves that smelled
heavenly of linseed oil and leather. A just-used glove
felt damp, warm, pliant and protective to my small
hand inside. Games lasted until the sparkling uniforms
picked up streaks and smudges of green and brown.
The catchers would be covered with dust, and orange
stains from the leather of the masks printed their faces.

One Sunday before the game, Yamashita told me,
"Sadaharu's in Italy." "Fighting in the war?"
"Yeah," he said, "fighting the Germans." I could imagine
Sadaharu doing swift, heroic deeds for our country.
After the warm up, Manager Saito would gather the players
at home plate and read off the two lineups. The suspense
was like waiting to break out of church, to see
who would be on which team. How will Yamaguchi
handle Matsushita's curveball today? Will Kitigawa
be playing short or second—I know
I'd put Tanaka in center more often.
Then one time Manager Saito said, "Well,
this is the last Sunday, Hallie," and school started
and other seasons, other wars, washed over that summer.
But now here come the names...Genesis,
Exodus, Leviticus,
Inaba, Nakasone, Yamaguchi
Watanabe, Morita, Kitagawa,
Shimura, Fugitani, Matsushita...

Harold L. Johnson

AT THE JACKSON POLLOCK RETROSPECTIVE IN L.A.

Blue Poles, a long painting, mute, manic, American,
its tilted blue members looking strong as rebar
in the chaos they dominate, halted me and legions
of others open-mouthed, as if watching a dangerous
and fantastic aerial performance. All afternoon
I jostled back and forth between giant spattered
canvases. Lacy layered violence in the black and green
masterpiece once bartered for psychiatric help tore
at my schoolish fears. I floated back to my aunt's house
electrified, dreaming those brilliant splashes and drippings
from the wounded alcoholic. But crashed against
the drunken ghost of Uncle George, Aunt Martha's husband,
a tense umber ferret who disappeared for years at a a time,
periodically spotted by cousins in St. Louis,
Cleveland, Detroit, or Los Angeles.
　　　I'd seen him once in person, years ago, looking
depressed and blinky. Mother had a picture of him
in uniform, standing at parade rest outside some tar-
papered Negro barracks. Now here he was, popped up on my face
at Aunt Martha's house. She barely got out, "This is Harold,
Lou's boy. He—" before he leapt into his monologue
about the war: That he was alive because the general,
a southerner, had liked the Negro unit's cooking,
and thus he hadn't had to cook under fire at the front
after the hell of amphibious landing. But he hadn't escaped
shock, or alcohol. He sat there rocking to the progress
of whiskey and war through his heart. An ill wind—
I fought to hang on to the lamppost of my painting dream.
He slapped me on the kneecap—"Do ya hear me, boy!"--
with the back of his hand. War blazed before
his bloodshot eyes, and his voice boiled into my ears.
　　　　　　　　　　He created the whistle of incoming

mortars, uprooted orchards in torn black soil, windfall
apples scattered like flung beads of red and yellow
paint under zinc-tasting smoke. Some boys from Alabama
got wasted in a jeep with a colored captain and a boy
from Memphis who could play the saxophone...boxes
with their names stacked on a corner of a chilly hangar.
he showed how he used to prop his teeth open
with his dogtags to test the notch because he was sure
he was going to bite some o' that sombitchin' French dust—
"That's a long way from Yakima, ain't it, boy," he shouted,
backhanding my knee and fuming the air til my eyes watered.
But that cracker general had liked his cookin
and he'd lived. "You don't think that's somethin'?"
He tried to shake his head into comprehension,
shuddered, rocked, and cursed me for not being
a sport like Virgil, my twin brother, who armed him
with a bottle whenever they met. Then he veered back
to the war, staring bug-eyed into France, blue lips worming,
grey hair frozen straight up like one sitting terrified
piloting his gravebox.

Viki Radden

OUR SECOND NIGHT

We love and talk,
talk and love
I open you like a treasure chest
You are a book with gilded pages
I read with wide open eyes

Just as I had hoped, you are an artist,
a thinker, a man who lives in his head

Your father and brothers,
doll makers
artists in Kyoto, the artists' capital
You, college man, civil servant
dressed in Brooks brothers,
checking your profile in the mirror

Legs wrapped around one another,
we tell our childhood stories
After the war, in your ragged clothes
searching for G.I.'s with chocolate bars
*Gaijin-san, candy-o kudasai!

"Did you see black soldiers?"
"Yes, many."
With my fingertips I caress your face,
close my eyes, remembering
stories my father told me.
In his soldier's uniform,
tall, wide-shouldered,
doling out Hershey bars
to children in Kyoto.

Our lives are enmeshed
I soar
beyond recognition
beyond happiness
Tatsuhiro, you and I,
we are close
close
close

We love and talk,
talk and love

When Mr. Kennedy charged
with unseeing eyes into the
maelstrom, you were in high school
I was playing with my dolls
When I was born, you were fifteen
Did you feel your world rocking?
Did you know lightning had struck?
Did you know a black woman
would one day cross the Pacific,
carrying your shrunken heart
in the palm of her hand?

We love and talk,
talk and love,
on this our second night

My eyes, you say, and my skin,
as sumptuous as the island
of Bali, and my inside,
just as warm

Our hideaway in the heights
breathes cinnamon,
hibiscus, and amber

You are my flying carpet
I think I will ride you
to some languid eastern isle

where we will spend our days idly
in rapturous ease

We love and talk,
talk and love,
my resplendent treasure chest
my book with gilded pages

*Honorable foreigner, give me some candy please!"

Lenard D. Moore

LETTER FROM KUWAIT

Where red sun and sand shine
in desert silence,
we walk through dust
because it spreads out everywhere.
There is the bombed truck—
a charred body stilled
behind the steering wheel,
but we never touch it,
knowing it will crumble.

The desert's evening shadow
rises like a bird's wing
swooping over the earth's face.
Last sunlight floats down
into the Gulf.
And behind the bombed truck
there's a dead soldier, swollen on the sand,
head exploded like a too-ripe watermelon.

Lenard D. Moore

a black soldier

a black soldier
breathing into a saxophone
hot desert wind

S.P.Shephard

FOUR AND TWENTY SOLDIERS

sing a song of wargames a pocket full of grass
four and twenty soldiers going about their tasks
when the mission's over with twenty soldiers dead
i cried just like a baby boy for what the VC said

King Oil is in his castle
counting all his money
the CO in Siagon is kissing all the honeys

the soldiers in the field
will slowly go away
if not tomorrow or next year, they smiled and said...someday!

S. P. Shephard

COME AND SEE MY LITTLE TOYS

little children full of joy
come and see my little toys
monkeys made of American dead
combat boots painted bright blood red
bombs and planes
contaminated rains

armless girls
legless boys
come and see
my little toys

S.P. Shephard

HOMELESS VETS

there was an old soldier
with one pair of shoes
no food to eat
and singing the blues

he found a crumb
and caught a sparrow
and from the bones
he fashioned an arrow

S.P. Shephard

SUICIDES AND FOOLS

there must be forgiveness
for suicides and fools

lost sheep who tread upon dangerous grounds
in heavy snow

Garrett McDowell

LIGHTS OF THE BIGTOP

Stretches of the path are darker
than the rest, hidden from the moon,
wooded places missed by the sun
except on brighter days.
I deny myself the walk
on lighted streets through town,
or displays of faces on the metrorail,
wanting a worthy pilgrimage,
a penance, going the long way
through the valley by the creek,
letting my footsteps mark
the earth by the parking lot
where the circus tent had sent
us laughing at its bulging
red like a giant apple
topped with a foolscap, snagged
on the stage-dark sky;
we even heard the circus
music piping the air,
wanting so hard to believe.
But we never crossed the dazzling
facade, and soon we knew
the trumpeting elephants and drumming
applause, were castles of sound
from our desperately craving
a turn inside on the high wire—
and night seeped through
our canvas spectacular, leaving
the circus, all along,
the zoo, lit after hours,

its gate long closed as I pass
on the street edge of the hill
facing your door, and buzz
the tenuous link for a last
exchange: a blessing for a rose.

Robert Fleming

this mortal coil

"The difference between man's soot and nature's grime
is that nature knows how to cleans up after herself."

-A remark by the head of the
Stanford Research Institute

How can we live in harmony with each other
knowing what we know
acting like we act on this small pebble
adrift in deep space
cursed with our body memory
as beasts trapped in custom and taboo.

The machine in us
has led us farther and farther
from our true selves
from our family nests
to gather in poisonous cities and slums
now we don't even know our way home
our bloodlines
our pedigree or our tribes or clan names.

We rebel against all natural things
we see the rebellion
against our Mother Earth
as a flexing of muscle or testosterone overflow
as a strong whiff or maleness
today and tomorrow
shrinks from all mention of yesterday.

The herbal cures fail now
the illness spreads with the lies
that all important decisions can be erased and set right
by the wrong medicine men
listening to voices no one else can hear
that the Old Ways carry no force.

What have they done to the soul
it now cries out for the venom
which makes it swell, fester and fold
in upon itself
there is no way to beat the clock within
that dooms this house of flesh
no matter how well we cuddle it.

What gives the life force
no voice in that eternal space
between sight and sound
that which expands the inner vision
until all is crystal clear.

We all wish to learn the way to Paradise
to the New World
we all wish to be conquistadors
or Soldiers of Heaven among the heathens
the resistance to the sod is the torture
the sound of the ticking soothes the terror somewhat.

It is our heart and falsely we believe
it is made of stainless steel
that is the folly of Humankind.

BEYOND THE FRONTIER

Calvin Forbes

THE PLEA

Take me home
To your living room
Ride me in your limousine

You got
Brains pretty momma
Yea that put mine to shame

If you leave
Me I'm gonna swallow
The ocean and drown my troubles

You got
A good job good looks
And you live in a big fine house

I'm a poor boy
Poorer than your mice
Dumber than your butler's maid

But I can
Sing you the alphabet
Backwards and make you forget it

I'll love you
Like a candle melts
Slow and hot (just like charcoal)

Cause I need
You like I do a medicine
And my soul's too black to swim

Lori Tsang

girlfriend

says i have
no *community*
like she is not
part of it

i say *my community*
knows no borders
but sometimes i can
count it on my fingers

tonight
there is one
less finger

Honorée F. Jeffers

TO KEEP FROM SHOUTING SOMETHING

I.

This is the story told to me:
The black wife, my father's grandmother,
sits to the side of the casket at the grave sight.
Today she is burying the black doctor who has not
been her husband for over ten years now, the black doctor
who left her for a white woman.
My great-grandmother watches the white wife
sitting right in front by the hole in the ground
and she concentrates on dirt making thumping
sounds on top of the doctor's grave.
She thinks of the land now lost to her,
of the man she is sure this white woman killed
before he can be reclaimed, and she knows
she should keep her gloved hands folded in her lap.
She should remember the ceremonies
of the middle-class. Instead, she starts screaming.
She becomes very colored.
She is not ashamed.

II.

Maybe you think this was a simple story
and you assume who told me and why.
My father, of course.
My father who hated what he understood too well.
What would you say if you knew that all my childhood
I had seen pictures of a white woman in our album,
initials M.E.F., holding my smiling two-year-old father,
his legs short and fat and rounded in an "O"?
It was only after my father's death that my mother
showed me the picture of another woman,

a five-foot-two woman who had held a gun on a mob
of Ku Klux Klansmen to protect her black husband.
A nameless woman with kinky hair piled
on top of her head, her thick lips pursed tightly
to keep from shouting something.

My father didn't speak to me
about this black woman, only the white one.
He said this white woman was the kindest woman on earth.
She kept him from freezing to death one winter in Lincoln.
Her neck was fragrant and she sang in an alto voice.
My mother says this white woman was a good nurse,
one who knew all the right poisons that caused a black man
to forget what he was or made him die trying.

Melanie Hope

OUR MOTHERS

(for Catherine)

Our mothers will always be
Big women
I guess
with big breasts
Trying to hide us beneath them
And we will say thank you
As we were taught
And be shy of kissing in front
Of them
Or under their breasts
Until we become mothers
I guess
Or Moses returns to part these waters
Maybe by then I will turn you
To wine
And drink you dry
Maybe we will never part
Spend our days making plans
Then waiting for them to dance
You can drink me too
Evenly through each breast
Until all of me lands
Inside you
I miss the silence
But not the tears
Of our first nights
Scared your love would
Swallow me up
Or mine would explode
Afraid how mother
Would hear the explanation

Of this love
Myself unclear
As a tadpole's sex
Our mothers will always be
Our mothers
I guess
Even after they die
The dry bones and shriveled veins
Will haunt us
From urn or grave
I hope we never haunt
The lovely creatures
Of our dreams
I hope I am never free of you
Or your round breasts
I would miss you
As dawn would miss
Its reflection in the sea
I want our love to grow
Old and toothless
I want your tongue on my armpit
When my hair there is gray
We will worship together
Whether or not the sun comes
Or the moon goes down on us
We will learn to have each other
And need no more

Cherryl Floyd-Miller

she kneels at the wailing wall

i learned harmony in mama's wails...
over skillets and hot roasting pans,
through fevers and achy bones.

at night when the house quieted,
when all that we could hear
between the buzzing of cozy snores
was the house gently popping with silences,
calming from the commotion of the day,

i tiptoed past mama's room
and saw her kneeling
over a warping mattress,
eyes clamped,

one open hand perfectly slapped
against the other,
gathering pieces of herself
to give tomorrow.

she could *really* hum.

Afaa Michael S. Weaver

COLORS–STRUCK

At your funeral
we had yellow mums
around your casket.
I may be color-blind,
but I like yellow with brown.
You believed in your heart
I was color-struck, hooked
on light-skinned women.
You left without finishing
explaining to me secrets
of how to stop following this
path in my heart. I keep
following my heart and its aches
to where they think love is.
I sometimes do sorta lean
toward high-yellow women.
Sometimes I look at white women,
and they always looking at me.
If I could explain something
to you, it would be that
yellow is the color of Oshun.
Mama, she's an orisha.
She is what you were
because Mark & Marlene
is twins and twins run with us.
Oshun always breaks my heart.
She flirts to break a man down.
Mama, all the way down.
We all carry one of these *orishas*
in our souls, our guardian spirits.
Shango of thunderbolts lives in me.
He is The General who loves

sex & hot sauce on fried chicken.
He can make Oshun behave.
You could have told me this
in your way in your brown wisdom
if you had not died so young.
But I know Oshun will not give me
peace until I show her Sango in me.
He mean like I am inside.
Mama, Shango's color is red.
Remember that red shirt I loved?
All along I been looking for me.

Duriel E. Harris

FOR MY MOTHER

I used to dream of your wake.
I would approach the open casket
stand on tip-toe and stare down into the pit of it.

Sometimes your arms were folded across your chest.
Sometimes they were wedged
in the satin creases of the coffin
so I couldn't see your hands.
Sometimes you were smiling, holding a rose
cut from the bush in our yard,
blood red like May carnations
for those whose mothers are living.
Your corsage was always
white and though it was fresh
it reminded me of tissue paper,
dried baby's breath.

In the dream, your face
was the same beautiful face, mother.
The fullness of your lips moistened by a muted blush.
And I would cry in my sleep and sit up and call to you.
You would appear at my bedside to take me
into your body until I fell back, into some other world
deep in the pillow.

But each night
the woman with your face awaited:
through my closet door
in shadows just beyond the wall.
Palpable and terrifyingly sedate.

It began that day.
I had called to you but you did not come

so I went chattering through the house
and stumbled against the sweet, dim air
of the open doorway. Cloaked in silence
you turned your glistening eyes to the light.
I knew, as only four year olds can know,
just as something had taken your mother,
the woman who gazed out from the creamy soft focus
of the photograph on your dresser—
and she was gone forever—
they could take you.

Now, as we both grow older,
I am even more afraid.
I want to have enough of you.
I know that your body
will find its way into the ground.

Sometimes I watch you while you sleep
and I want to touch your face.

Gideon Ferebee

FOR MY MOTHER
MAGNETIC POETRY SERIES

The Moon's driving, waxing light may suit
The sweet and easy, lazy loves of dreamers
But it has not, yet stilled
The chant of mother's watery white whispers
As they run in and out of cool, misty-blue shadows
Winding through my man-like hair

Nor will it shine upon her gorgeous diamond gifts
And the thousands of honey-chocolate days we lived together
It can never put to sleep the hot, delirious madness
Or stop the flood as pictures pound my head
With a powerful vision of a beloved, crushed red rose
Those sad petals always manipulate my weakly, moaning breast
It beats like summer storms

I mean, like who am I when I recall
Her essential goddess life and think about
The delicate music as death rocked her in His arms?
As a spring-like shadowy symphony sings
Of a woman none so near but barely gone away
I am a boiling, Black Boy
Frantically lusting for Winter rains
To shake a scream on caring,
To take me to some fall-like place
With no memories of bitter crying!
I need some timeless moment
Not to ache and rust at all

Gideon Ferebee

FALLEN BODIES (for garth)

Hanging in the balance
My existence, tentative
Straining towards your   hand
Almost within my grasp, I sense
Your fingertips betray my intensity
Fear swelling throughout my weakening
Wavering muscles

I have looked into my dreadful fate
A chasm strewn with fallen bodies
Do I rationalize too wildly?
They, too, reached out, straining
To find your hand. Didn't they?

Didn't they? Were they too weak,
Too anxious , too late? I cannot
Let go this feeling that you
Did not fully exercise your prerogatives
From the safety of your position
To grab hold those panicked hands
They have plunged to their anihilation

You!...There!...at the very highest point
In the world.   Looking beyond your hand
Deep into your eyes
I struggle to improve my footing,
Straining with outstretched hand
Struggling, also, with the fire
In your eyes which I do not decipher
I must not look down!

Robert Fleming

THE LONG WALK HOME

Neither of them were thinking of me then
it is nearing mid-century and the atom bomb waits on a shelf
in everyone's home

My father fresh from fighting the Nazis
walks along a deserted road at twilight
the image of a young brown-skinned girl in the breast pocket
of his army uniform

He will see her again if the Bible does not get in the way
Or her eagle-eyed parents who smell his intentions
and feel his arms already around their daughter's thin waist

My mother combs her long black hair and imagines her soldier boy
this hollow-cheeked Delta man with his funny words
and clumsy looks at her heart

She cannot tell her father what is on her mind
In church there are names for what she feels
and just the touch of it can leave your breath short

I watched them on the porch together
this tenderness and care now fading in the snapshots
in the torn family albums but still alive then

Theirs was a love that would not be denied
an oil lamp overturned on a stack of yellowed newspapers
soon to engulf the entire house and the fields beyond

Later when asked of this golden time
neither would remember much of their lovers' secrets
the stolen moments in one another's embrace or the promises made
now that the grim word of divorce sprouted like a weed
in their small vocabulary

Nzadi Zimele Keita

back road

sickness hangs on a nail
a yellow rag boiled too many times
to catch the life leaking out

I come back to the house
with my head low-down
for fear of seein' the men
standin' together on the porch,
holdin' short answers to grief
in their folded arms
and the women
inside, movin' together
in twos and threes,
slow hands
ridin' dustcloud dresses

My momma went in the yellow
rag room
to watch Grandma dreamin';
Sissy went next, to see
what was keepin' her
Auntie's out back now,
boilin' everything Grandpa touched;
ain't there a good word for this house?

I come back
with my head low-down
'cause I don't want them to see me
hatin' God while I cry

Thandiwe Shiphrah

GRAND DIVA

When I am old
and have taken to wearing hats
there will be no doubt about it.

I'll be sporting a few of those outrageous numbers
designed especially for women of my caliber.
Something complicated and proud
like the kind they sell in the *Essence-by-Mail* catalog.

Except my hats will have entire worlds spinning around them,
which I will sometimes wear cocked to one side,
and always with such attitude
that people won't be able to stand me.

When I start stepping out
in stunning shades of lavender and fuschia,
they'll be forced to roll their eyes and ask themselves
"just where does she *think* she's going in that hat?"

That's when I'll throw my head back and smile,
knowing full well that I have arrived.

Thandiwe Shiphrah

to adam

have you noticed this desire
to return on bended knees begging
forgive me?

or this one: to spend each day together
tilling the garden,and the nights
with my head upon your shoulder
your fingers caressing my face?

isn't it strange, this desire?
and these defiant times?

oh! to be one

to be naked

and unashamed.

Thandiwe Shiphrah

GRANDMA

Distracted daughters, disoriented sons
trample through her golden years
leaving unblossomed flowers in their footprints.

She nurtures the seedlings – gently, gently –
lifting them from the shade of neglect
into the warmth of her sun.

Her love prunes the first buds of sorrow
from their stems. Her wisdom uproots
the weeds of abandonment.

Though old and infirm,
she is a tireless gardener
watering the soil of a new generation.

M. Eliza Hamilton

WHILE COMMUNING WITH A TREE NEAR MY HOME

Hey girl, you like that tree?
Baby, I got something for you
just as strong, just as thick...

Wheels speed over his laughter.

Girl?   I am old enough to be his mother.

In another time,
the very thing he wants to give me
would be cut from him
by men who never heard him say it,
who only thought he said it;
respected, god-fearing men
whose women voiced their disdain out loud.

In his laughter, he has forgotten
the very thing he wants to give me
is still cause enough to hang him,
his ears sliced from his head,
his body flayed -
blood dripping an unintended apology
for what he might have said, or not,
in a moment of bravado.

This is america.
I am a woman.
I am not white.
He does not remember what he knows:
Once, he was king, warrior, healer, father, husband, brother, son:
    he would have demanded retribution

for that insult flung at my family.
He does not remember who he is.
There is no one to tell him.

It is 1994.

This is america.

Bruce A. Jacobs

FRIENDLY SKIES

Her smile durable as chrome,
she moves seamlessly up the aisle,
courting untold closeness with
200 of the nicest people she has ever met.
She could be my great-grandmother at 25,
quick with coffee over banquets
where a black woman could not sip,
tall cotton waiting as her thanks for affability.

I watch for stress lines, metal fatigue,
a cracking at the corners of the lipstick
but she is just the way I want her:
in love with blind acquaintance,
each offering of her hand a moment's wedding,
each gesture gently powdered with romance.
And by the time she gets to me with "Soft drink? Peanuts?"
I am as certain of what she means
as any guest at a plantation.

In a steel tube above the clouds,
a man can believe anything.

Janeya K. Hisle

AND ALL THE SISTERS SAID...

I
roll my eyes because your
love
makes me dizzy; and
you
complain but you always come back for
more
because you'd rather struggle to death with ebony fists
than
glide through
life
on ivory wings; so I'll gladly search your
black
soul forever praying that you heed your heart and read between my lines,
Man.

Christopher Nickelson

angry sisters

we are angry sisters
who have gathered here
on this mountaintop
to talk loud and ugly
about the man who took
all our shit
our land, our money,
and our peace of mind

one sister says she wants
50 acres and a mule,
another sister says she wants
a dog to guard her land
and keep the man out,
the other sister says she just wants
the stank of this shit
to go away

we are sisters who have gathered
on this mountaintop
waiting on men who ain't ever coming back
and we ain't talking anymore rhetoric,
we ain't talking anymore jive or philosophy
take my land, take my money, and my man,
just gimme back my peace of mind

Christopher Nickelson

three men

three men sit on a stoop
but he is the one with a love letter
pressed into his pocket
his wife left him in the middle of the night
taking everything she could fit into the car.

his every conversation
his every story involves a pretty gal from
the carolinas, or louisiana
who captured his smile
but never a mention of the love letter
that burns a hole in his pocket
next to the bottle.

Christopher Nickelson

untitled

i don't get
the gestures
the hidden meaning
or the reference to
the part to the whole
or the whole to the part
but
it sounds real pretty
it sounds real nice

so
gimme your hand
gimme the part to
the whole

Janeya K. Hisle

FOR FATMA AND HER CO-WIVES

Her husband was regally draped in heavenly white.

He left her standing
with the babies
to come and tell me
that he liked my smile.

When she glared at me,
through her black shroud,
I felt naked
because her eyes were heavy
with duty
and eyeliner

But the sound that came out
as much stronger that I
expected

and so much kinder.

She said an "Asalam Alaikum"
that sounded like "wait 'til I get this muthta fucka home"

I smiled; she nodded
and walked away with hand on one hip-
baby on the other

I wanted to call her back and say
"Sister, I know you are strong

and I like the way you veil swings
when you roll your neck."

Jacqueline Joan Johnson

WHAT IS THERE FOR US?

What is there for us
five generations deep,
we daughters of the dark, open
sinew of our people,
search our mothers' truths
for our own things,
calabash of ancient secrets
eludes us.

What dumb luck some
daughters have
like a village bride
on her wedding night,
we surrender everything,
only to wake up and peer into
some narrow mouth calabash,
our mothers, our grandmothers
call our wealth.
Oh, it is the same one
their mothers passed to them.

A palaver of ancient soundings
raining mercy upon our ears.
Mother carried calabash
of her dreams, silvered,
brilliant on her tongue.
Her hands ammonia reddened,
worked sunup to sundown struggling
to fill that widening, bottomless
bowl, never knowing wicked
satiation of dreams fulfilled.

Even now, we daughters know
a great nothing.
What to do with this rage,
centuries old,
stubborn as naps in the nape of my neck.
We circumference the edge
and beginning of a universe only
we have the keys to.

Some of us know well how to meet
those same women on the road,
holding what knives and sticks we can.
We strip ourselves of all obvious wealth,
hoping to protect our womenselves
from their envy,
age long desire to see us broken,
like the milkless,
flabby tits of a grandma.
These women,
bitter and hard veined believe,
believe, the world is as
small as their vision.

I never expected to bury
new shoots of so many unfurled dreams,
to fight for breath, meaning amongst my sisters,
women who wear my own skin.
I gather courage, and walk
the winding path between
girl and woman. I claim, savor
sweet salt of my woman waves.
I speak in mother tongues, languages,
they don't know here. Just the same,
I scratch the earth for my meaning.

What there is for us,
we daughters wrestle from our mothers' tongues
singing our own songs,
carrying faith larger than that empty bowl,
our vision as wide as this earth,

love stronger than death.
We, who are the calabash and
its contents,
we, the reshaped, renewed clay
know, today,
today is our own!

Pat Russell

BE CAREFUL
WHEN YOU GO LOOKING FOR A MADONNA
CUZ YOU JUST MIGHT FIND A WOMAN

I Am

Myself-Eclectic

I am Strong, I am Weak
I am Invincible, I am Vulnerable
I am Epicurean, I Self Deny
I am Impulsive, I am Controlled
I am Self Assured, I am in Self Doubt
I am Hedonistic, I am Self Sacrificing
I am Boastful, I am Humble

I Love, I Hate

I

Am

Do not Romanticize Me. . .
I am Flesh and Blood
Good and Bad
And When I'm Bad
I'm so-o- Good. . .

I am not an Image
To be Worshipped
I am not a Mule to be Burdened

I am Eristic, I am Complacent
I am Erudite, I am Ignorant

I am Fire, I am Ice
I am Sweet, I am Bitter

I Love, I Hate
I Love to Hate, I Hate to Love

I am Gregarious, I am a Loner
I am an Insomniac, I Sleep too Much
I am Anorectic, I Over Eat
I Bitch too Much, I am Stoic

But. . .

I am Not Your Bitch

A Bitch

Anybody's Bitch

I am a Goddess, I am Demon
I am a Fairy, I am Imp
I am Destoyer, I am Life Giver
I am a Virgin, I am Erotic
I Do As I Please, I am Pleased To Do

But. . .

Please
Do Not Ms. Understand Me
Use Me
Do Not Ms. Use Me

I will Take, I will Receive
I am Your Equal, Your Superior, And Your Subordinate
I am Your Teacher, I am Your Pupil
I am Your Sister, Mother, Daughter, Wife, Mate, Lover

And

I Am Mine

I am Whole, I am Holistic
Quit Taking
Quit Seeing

Only My Pieces
It Disturbs My Peace

I can hurt, I can Heal
I feel Pain, I feel Pleasure
I Touch, I Withdraw

I am Up, I am Down
I am Level, I am Erratic
I am Calm, I am Frantic
I am Deep, I am Shallow

I am an African
     Amerikan
     Womb
     Man

I was Born, I will Die
I Sat in a Birthing Chair
I Stood at a Grave

I am Mediator, I am Instigator
I am Rebel, I am Peacemaker
I am an Agitator, I am Advocate

But. . .
Remember; You Can't Get The Wash Done Without An Agitator

I Tear, I Mend
I Receive, I Send
Ascend, Descend

I am Vulgar, I am Decent
I Laugh, I Cry

Therefore

I Am

If You Take Me
Take All of Me

I Am Not One
I Am All

I Am Eclectic

Nzadi Zimele Keita

rising

we will be brought to recognize
a new wind

rising in the mouths of women
wetting our tongues
for a new century
of battle
evil-keeping calls out for balance
and we will flow, released,
into new forms

Nzadi Zimele Keita

cycles

the moon reaches out
tenuous in its dark home
and finds itself whole

Gary Lilley

MEETIN THE CONJURE WOMAN

My bones burned down
when I met her.
they are still
on fire now.

Angela Shannon

WET OAK

He be a home mender and floor fixer,
his laugh come up fluttering from his root
and he tremble so, sprinklings of joy
like Fall's leaves, float over the kitchen.
He no high yellow nor big muscle man,
he the color of wet oak after dry season
then rain come splattering with deep kisses
like tree and ground was a virgin again
and even hidden spots be holding water,
his hands, broad and playful, full with dreams
that unfold and talk through his silence.
He a man without trying too hard,
with eyes that go soft around sadness
and dance when he watching the galaxy.
He ain't afraid to do some crying
and talk about some old wrongs and hurts.
He let his voice go high as mine
and fall to baritone when he's happy.
He walk like the earth's his Mama
and he aim to respect all he come from.

Angela Shannon

HANDS

When they told us we could have each other,
I didn't know what to do, how to hold you.
I hadn't embraced anyone in years.

I had lost my hands to scrubbing,
stirring, and scraping fabric against iron.
I hadn't used them for touching since David
popped out of me thirty five years ago.

These hands aren't hands, they're just tools
used for cleaning what never going to come clean
with dirt being thrown in the wind.

But I'm going to stretch them out anyway
to see how you feel because you've been tucked
in my heart all of this time and I've loved
you longer than I've had wooden hands.

Artress Bethany White

THE BEELZEBUB CHRONICLES

I.

He played the juice harp and me. Don't judge too harshly
unless you have heard the way notes can leak off sweet plum lips
to crouch down beside your ears. I had his songs glued all over
my body like wet November leaves on a rubber boot.
He would cross his legs, sip red wine between sets.
The first time I saw him, he dipped his big toe into my blood.
I have always had a weakness for the woman inside a man.

II.

I dreamed an apparition dressed in gentleman's black inscribed
with ancient rhyme; a voice that hissed instead of speaking.
He taught me that a body could be encased in a lover's split tongue;
his like knotted twins inside my mouth. I awoke
with the weight of a saddle across my back, a strong desire
to hold the devil between my legs.

III.

The side of my thumb fits snugly into the mark I wear
on my forehead from his horned thrust. Beneath it wash
tepid memories of pointless ears cupped in my hands as he proselytized
on the weakness of the flesh. Words that helped me ignore
dank kisses and white candles that refused to stay lit.

Kay Lindsey

STRINGBEANS

Her boyfriend stood guard—cat eyes on the lookout
While she picked stringbeans
from my garden.

She has longed for something to twist gently—from a mothervine
Inhale the scent of origin still rising from its skin.

Startled, when I appear out of nowhere, she dashes away
Flip-flops pitter patter out of hearing
Skirt tail not far behind.

He probably put her up to it—how he snares his heart's desires
"She won't mind," I can hear him say,
"But I'll watch, while you do it."

The pot of plump beans simmering between the two of them
reduced to a handful, much less
than she expected.

Clyde A. Wray

THE STAR

And for all the adulation
each morning
he awoke

with another warm
body, but
alone

Clyde A. Wray

PRIVATE THOUGHTS

Want to see you
naked
across the room

dancing to flames
tingling ablaze
hotter than kindling

silhouetted against
the wall

your shadow
in rhythm

imagine
your golden sheen
searing scented flesh

hear your voice
trumpeting
an idea

the past
is forgotten

opposites
still attract

nothing is so futile
as when love
is held back

Afaa Michael S. Weaver

SIN, 1969

It was better
than anything I had
ever done in
my whole life.
We took our clothes
off in a bedroom
in Aunt Grace's house
when the grownups
was gone. I looked
at your golden brown
skin near yellow,
and your titties full
and the thick bush
of hair on your pussy.
I was charged
like electric had
taken over my blood.
We made love
without even thinking
about making a baby.
We walked outside.
It was a sunny day.
I could feel the heat
in my chest cause
it was sticking out.
I wondered why anybody
would want this
to be a sin.

Afaa Michael S. Weaver

LINES

(for L.A. Schmidt)

I feel your legs touching
the sides of my face,
your thighs pressing my cheeks.
I slide my fingers down
your arms and the slow tingle
eases my back. I taste
the backs of your knees,
take my tongue along the road
from your hips to your
toes. In your cradle,
I lick the pubic hairs
one by one. I enter you,
and the change happens.
In your eyes I see
time is gone.

Terrance Hayes

MIDNIGHT

You call
Minutes before the train

Worms you deeper
Into the gut of San Francisco

To say a new sun
Is tattooed on your shoulder

I imagine it lighting
Down my throat

At the airport I saw a woman
Finger the neck of her man

I don't remember their faces
I have forgotten everything

But the sound of distance
I had not touched

Myself for weeks
Before now

Baba Lukata

ASHY GAL

they say she used to be 'fine'
coal black and curvy
wide smile and 'lawd have mercy' legs.

today she looks ashy
as she leads a young boy to the park
offering to steal the last of his innocence
for a five dollar bill.

tyehimba jess

what does a man do

after the abortion
when her eyes
gaze through space he fills with
askin
you all right
you sure
and silence of
what to say next
an embrace

after wishin they were ready
wishin for another way
wonderin how it feels to have
you womb sucked out
left dry and waiting

after trying to unmemorize the date
        not to count the years as missed birthdays

what do i do
but sit still   stunned
thinking about the word
        father.

Kalamu Ya Salaam

WHY I DONT LEAVE THE APARTMENT UNTIL AFTER TEN SOME MORNINGS

i like to lay
in the curve
of your physique

you breathing
into the black
of my hair

the pressure
of thigh
to thigh

the beige softness
of your inner hand
slow moving

across
the tubular darkness
of my arousal

my
left arm reached
back massaging

the supple
flesh of your
lower back

for long minutes
quarter hours spent
with nothing

but skin
& pleasure
between us

Kalamu Ya Salaam

haiku # 135

my butterfly breaths
flutter caress the female
flesh of your dark door

Estelle E. Farley

GRAND CANYON

Lying next to you
after love
The canyon between us.
I throw rocks off the edge.
Fingers cross over to touch skin.
Pebbles hit water
as you brush my hand away.
The gulf widens.
Turning away from you in the dark,
I hear only the river's rage.

Estelle E. Farley

HOME COOKIN

Slurp me up like biscuits pick up gravy.
Naw at my bones as you would barbecued ribs
that sizzled all day long.
Take me like the last piece of pie
leftover from Thanksgiving.

Come on home, baby
dinner's on the stove
and I'm about to boil over.

Niama Leslie Williams

DANIEL'S HANDS

daniel's hands rub my back
find all those places i haven't cried out yet

daniel's hands have no callouses
but they know the rough spots in my legs
knead the tender spots gently

daniel's hands know when to touch
and when I must find my way alone

i find daniel's hands in the dark
wrap them in my own
breathe easier.

Vincent Woodward

cornbread blues

"patty cake, patty cake
bake me a man
bake me a man.. as fast as you can."

bake me a brown black taffy corn
golden
dripping
everlasting lip inside my ooooh!!!!...
how you just don't know
how my butter burns bubbling brown
baby slice this bread
in half
ease your tongue
or the tender rounded tip
of your long wooden spoon inside my thick pouring batter
breathe my hurt away baby
breathe it all through me baby
sop me in your dripping hot gravy
sop me in your bowl of collards
sop me up like your grandmamma
who taught her favorite boy
to savor my crispy edges
to languish in my melting thighs
to love me even now
as I laugh inside my beauty
to love me baby once again
with that Sunday dinner hunger
in your eyes.

Laini Mataka

LICORICE

as a child, i hated licorice
didnt like the way it got all up in my teeth
w/out really bein sweet.
i never really thought of it as candy
til i licked yr fingers,
tongued the twisted length
of yr sunburnt legs.
i thought licorice was for kids,
til i tasted yr arms bindin me
shockin my taste-buds into expandin
and includin yr navel as a newly found delicacy.
hatin licorice the way i did
how was i to know
that between yr steel-plated thighs
the delectable grew
good & plenty
forcin me to feast w/out gettin fat.
drink, w/out gettin drunk
yr ability to shift-shape into licorice
has been one of erotika's best kept secrets
and now, every time I see u
i feel like i'm in a candy-shop
measurin by the pound
and it's all i can do
to keep my tongue in my mouth.

Laini Mataka

CAN WE TALK?

can we talk

i have syllables that need to be performed
on the inside of yr thigh.
nouns that need the adjectives
of yr groans to push them into
exclamations of great joy.

can we talk

i know u wanna verb me & i wanna adverb u
right back, until all the question-marks
that we've ever harbored conjugate themselves
into an epicurean nectar
that only libertines drink from.

can we talk

consonant on vowel, taut on soft, ear on mouth
can we hyphenate our own sobs & torture the complexity
of our grammatical gasps & screams
shrieking with pure delight.

can we talk

about the crossroads—those points where
our doings meet to commemorate our sexual oppositeness
when embellished to the highest possible demonstrative degree.

can we talk

cuz i dont have any flights scheduled for tonite
& we both know how badly u wanna get into the sky.

INTERPRETATIONS

he said, "i love you."
she smiled.
he lied.
she knew.
he kissed her.
she pretended it was real.
he turned on the charm.
she turned off the light.
he said, "please?"
she knew he couldn't.
he closed his arms around her.
she opened her legs to him.
he entered into her.
she went some place else.
he moved in closer.
she watched from a distance.
he thought "oh my God this is good!"
she thought "my lord this is wrong!"
he shook and moaned as his body collapsed.
she held and groaned as her heart caved in.
his sweat dripped as he looked to cover his nude body.
her tears fell as she found no shelter for the nakedness of her soul.

Carletta Carrington Wilson

kiss her   that she   don't   know   how

    in powdery blue dark
    she is   *dream/dancing*
    night/so/long   *with him*
    breath beneath breath
    they nod   *into the nape*
      of a melodious song

      violet/black blooms
    bloom in their night nest
    kiss that flies   *comes winging*
    countless radiant petals
    crush against her skin
    skin in the skin   of him

    six times   *her hands*
    transfigured by sweet toil
      cry to themselves
    inside their pink hearts
    the hungry aroma of lips
    the thirsty   *t o n g u i n g*   of a kiss

    involutions… .currings….
    a nocturnal pulse   and him
      an intricate incantation
    of gourd   marimba   saxophone
    wrapped in   the rhythm   of hymns

    kiss her   that she   don't   know   how
      slowly…. *.c e r e m o n i a l l y*
      through labyrinths of longing
    to that place   where breath begins
    where heart's prayers   lie dreaming

where by   the tongues of her mouths
she calls

        in intricate relief
    they submit   to the fall
        delicately eager
    red/moist and shimmering
        in the air/glow
        of water lit fog

    he who sips her in
    is the aromatic mouth
    of all her thirsting dreams
    a trembling vortex
    humid/herbivorous
    volcanic with heat
        he awakens her
        encodes her
    passion dizzying as the abyss of a kiss
        paints sunsets in blush
    blows b l u e s   in a velvety crush
        dances   their silvery
        night lighted hair

Imani Tolliver

fisher king

one net made of the sweetest tears
the finest weave to catch an admirer
the one who will stay

a net cast
like the reddest wine
to stick: lips tongue teeth

you in the water
you in the sea

this net of a prayful fisherwoman
woven thin, woven fine
thrown to feed the children of pregnant villages
sent one hundred times

come: birthed from a warm womb
    moving toward me like an easy birth

one promise
one prayer
one night
one thousand seas
and one net of the sweetest tears

Darrell Stover

FIRE/WATER BLUES

for Mary

The smoke still burns between us.
We pass it on between us,
Figments of a shared consciousness,
Just between us.

Rivers and all sands uncrossed.
We are on the left side of the Nile,
Same side of the Mississippi,
On up the Amazon some place
Spiritually one.

Speaking of water,
Wasn't it at a pool party,
Cool party, we splashed
Lovehappiness all night long?

Smiles of many shades shadow
The love struggles we've outlasted.
We taste the sting of life
And move on.

The smoke purifies the atmosphere
Of this room - full and fresh.
The incense still burns between us.
Hot when you ask,
"Does I love yuh?"
Flaming, I answer, "Yes!"

High humidity,
Warm wetness after the storm,
A shot of vodka,
and the night is on.

The incense still burns between us.

Dawn L. Hannaham

TO A FLASHER

So what! A penis.
Now show me what you have, that
No other man's got.

Michelle Calhoun Greene

FINISHED POEM

the man
was
less man
than
his body
was
I mean
a bed
just aint
     the whole world

Michelle Calhoun Greene

FOR MY D.C. GIRLFRIENDS

we are ladies
of the Quiet Storm
who too many times
measure and weigh
the emptiness
of our lives
by how often
we bear
this
love music
alone

PERSPECTIVE

didn't no
tracy chapman song echo in haunting a capella
when she spit in his face in front of
her friends
the kids
and himself
and
after his shoulders went slack
after she'd taken a bite out of his adam's apple
and left it trembling and infected
venom sliding down his cheeks
serpent gaze daring him to continue standing there
naked
full of knowledge
after he just said nothing else all night
never hauled off and beat her ass the way they didn't realize they
thought a man
would
could
or should
        after the silence
everybody was
laughin
like
shit
slappin' palms / raisin' glasses/ askin' for seconds
rejoicin' and hollerin' bout how much of a
Revolutionary Priestess
she must be to make such a BITCH of him
at his own dinner table
        and he had to sleep with her that night
8 hours kicking and bruisingthat left him no choice but to wear

the pants
　　　　　and in the morning
as she left
crowing to the sun that he was a
faggot-muthafucka-that-worked-her-got-damned- nerves-alla-de-time
couldn't-fuck-worth-shit-and-made-less-money-than-
she
in the morning
　　　　　after she left
there was no one to call
not one of his boys who wouldn't posse up to castrate him with disgust
if he rested his wounds on their shoulders
(a brother tryin not to be
too heavy)
after she left
there was no one to call
no one who wouldn't bittersweetly smile behind sympathy finally be-
lieving in
universal karma
after she left
there was no one to call
and no
tracy chapman song echoing in haunting
a capella.

Kevin Simmonds

THE NEW SESTINA

A new peace hangs like moss,
soaking up shine and rain of death.
In paralysis, I watch
though I can never invite my lover
inside of me again.
He is gone.

I know that he is gone.
The tedious glass of my window is swept by moss
and the deep rose shines again.
But I am stilled by death,
by his demands on my lover,
by the music I watch.

I learned to watch
while everyone was gone.
I learned to accept my young lover
giving in under the moss.

The long-note drones of death
will never sound the same again.
Nothing will sound the same again.
My friends and family watch
as I fill the refusal of death.

He is gone
and I sing under a golden canopy of moss.

Brothers, it was on my watch,
when everyone else was gone,
that I understood the need for death.

The need was not for my death,
but for its black mercy on a young lover.
Now that he is gone,
I will sing again,
renewed by a death-watch
making me moss.

Jennifer Lisa Vest

IN THIS, THE FIFTH WORLD

In this, the fifth world
Sweet green moss
Has a way of climbing
Out of rusty pipes
Into concrete cracks
Breaking and braiding through bricks

Weeds insist on coming up
Instead of other crops
In spite of gardeners' chemicals
Ornate and specific stone paths

And trees

They have a tendency
To climb over fences
Airlift asphalt
Obstruct traffic lights
Drop leaves in the wrong place

But you and me
Are much more orderly

We believe in the bone of brick
The stature of steel
The insolence of iron gates

We've fallen victim to fences
Lines on the highway
The density of plaster

We think the boundaries are real.

Melvin E. Lewis

HEARTS

I wish we had broken up five years ago,
there wouldn't be such a big hole in my heart

In the evening, I want to hold you
Sometimes, I like to look in your eyes while you laugh
Sometimes, I like to sit on the bed and watch you undress

In the morning, I want to kiss you good-bye,
feel your cheeks next to mine.
When you press, lay your lips on mine,
they bring the sun from behind the clouds,
they're sweeter than fresh-squeezed orange juice

I wish we had broken up seven years ago,
we wouldn't have a book of memories to divide.
Who gets the impressions our fingers left in the sand?
Who gets the pictures of Cameron sitting on your lap?
Kia riding a bicycle at 4? Do I give you the pictures of
your Mother kissing you good-bye,
you and her crying when you left?

In the winter who will bring you tea and honey,
know the spot where your back hurts,
in the spring jump across boulders in Rock Creek Park and
blow pussy willows into the air, into your hair?

Who will hear your stories of stringing tobacco,
picking low cotton and lifting buckets of cucumbers
onto moving flat-bed trucks,
who knows that you only eat fruit according to southern seasons?
How do you split the narrow green bridges
that only one person could cross at a time?

I wish we had broken up before we held each other's hands,
knew each other's stories, tears and sadness.
The sands we held too long won't make the strong cement-blocks
the water from our tears won't hold,
make the mortar strong, solid,
hold them together for the bridges we need to cross.

How do you hold the moments,
where you can't tell our breathing,
hearts apart?

If ten years ago, we had walked away from each other,
before the paddle-boat rides, birthday cruises,
midnight strolls through Japanese gardens,
looking out at dawn for the edge of Lake Michigan
we would have had two whole hearts
instead of two broken ones.

Tracie Morris

WHY I WONT WEAR A TATOO

Skin color marks me.
Indelible already.
Been paying for it.

Tracie Morris

LOVERS TOTAL RECALL

Came to me like a
vision. Felt so good I thought
I'd imagined it.

Tracie Morris

JUST SAY NO BLUES

I guess Black men fall
off the wagon more 'cause they
gots no place to go.

Tracie Morris

PRELUDE TO A KISS

"Men must love your lips,"
he said. Sure do. Long as I
ain't saying nothing.

Lisa Pegram

yet another epiphany

much to my dismay
i've allowed you to suffocate me with
inconsistency and those
hershey with almonds
dimples of yours
(both sets.)
tracks of salt keloid cheeks
my soul
trademarks of some
hold me at dusk and then again at dawn
junkie
it's all so beautifully
pitifully
tragic
Good Morning Heartache and all that
jazz
maybe tomorrow i'll wear an orchid
behind my ear
and moan in a shower that echoes regret
damn.
last nite i slept with no one but dreams of you
because i was independent
strong
proud
refusing to let you break me
but mostly because
you left.
i'm in some deep shit that i pretend to not understand because
comprehension makes me vomit these days.
and i don't know when i decided some pretty ass niggah was worth
voluntary ignorance.
so i slam the door in your

august midnite with
two stars and
a full-lipped moon
face
for now
and maybe tomorrow i'll gain the strength to
lock
it.

John Frazier

DEPOSED

The lawyer says
let them know
how he hurt
you
I look back
like what
I'm supposed to say
is thank you
for listening to
my story
but I know
they're not doing this
for me
the woman
from the agency
is here too
telling me
the testimony of immigrants
is crucial
all I do
is stare
thinking
even after
I rinsed the mop
and peeled off
the too
thin
rubber gloves
I smelled him
all the next day
stronger than ammonia
stronger than my will

to learn
the language
to be
a voice
demanding
more

Lauren Anita Arrington

UNTITLED

tomorrow night
when I wear black
what will you see
will I sting your eyes
or will you let them close
until I blend in
to what you want me to be
and this black that I will be wearing
will it be tight
because sex and violence sells
or will it be flowing infinitely
because you'd rather not sell me
and if it is too big or too small
in those particular places
will you not let me wear it
or will you say that
here it should not be exactly
completely
black
because we want to reflect who I really am
and if
I am
by accident
what you don't want me to be
because shit just ain't fittin'
could we let if fit

Somehow
naturally

nadir lasana bomani

(1/vacant)

the day you moved out of my life
i became an empty house
with lights on

Kimmika L.H. Williams

I WATCHED

(for Lucille Clifton)

    My mother
feigned living
after my father
(her husband)
died
and left us;
but left her,
she thought,
finally
after forty-eight years
marriage.

    For three years
I watched her
alternate—
taking off
and putting on
Taking off
and putting on
Taking off
and putting on
Between
the shroud
of mourning
and the guise of living
she'd
cloth herself,
till both
became too heavy.

Nzadi Zimele Keita

my sleeping husband

I sit
with my sleeping husband
and breathe his beauty

he is folded
neatly into brown coves
and smooth, narrow ledges

his shepherd's face
glances over the miles
of his universe
without hunger for conquest;
without need for spiraling grandeur
    or profit
    or slaughter

he is the god of peace
he is the refuge
    all children seek out
    in the dark

Sybil J. Roberts

POEM # 3

today, I'm wearing new love
like a comfortable old sweater
in the Fall
and I keep returning
to the mirror
to admire myself
in it

reuben jackson

LOVE # 49

this is how i felt
hearing gato play
"don't cry rochelle"
in '77.

a saxophone playing
lines lovely as your
hair;

the winter nights
dark as vinyl.

i was probably
lonely and high;

years from believing
there was something

to view at dawn besides
the glorious disk

above this room
where you turn

like the score of a song

soul gestures in spring

(for omone)

soul like marcus bookstore and eso won
tangled in coital postion, caressing on queensized bed
of shredded toni morrison opening lines.
browsing, i fondle each book, laying hands on spines
leafing through black girl histories.
i want to know you.
what page we on.

new years eve.
let the sermon begin:
spirit filled hoodoo mack priest
sobered by your innocence, unsettled by your stare.
coltrane in a maroon crushed velvet dress, sitting indian style
charmed snake off belly, up through cage
made him stand up.
turned his blues into torquoise
bade him sing a new song
what page we on.

virgin lamb:
one heartbreak from a sacrificial one.
crafty those wolves
check the clothes, check the clothes.
you cried your first time.
tears philly joein on my conscious.
inside high hat dreams
i see you twisting and braiding mother wit
into our daughter's hair, greasing her scalp
with nigerian folktales, whispering ibo melodies.

you heavy
but on the secret eternal scale, hidden behind a giant dune of jupiter dust:
    1) your heart   2) a grain of sand from ethiopia's original garden.
your heart is purer, lighter than breath god spoke world into being with.
"let there be light" catapulted your cardiac wonder from scale
through galaxy, past mars, into bed beside me:
understands when my black man life falls short of my black man rhetoric.

last night love so good, tight, start thinking fatback ain't greasy.
love so raw, like wild bee honey
on your flat stomach, a performance space.
my tongue slides south into trance, seduced by oya, severs, transforms
now a naked dreadlocked ice skater slashing, curving, jumping into
impossible backspining triple toe loops.
look up, check the scorecards contorted across your face:
6.0 6.0 6.0 6.0 6.0
you my gold medal.
i wear you on my face, down my neck.
you my cowrie shell choker.
after you come
"don't touch me" barely escapes your lips
your body is 17,000,707 specific sensors
all turned on high.
i turn over, turn on nitelite
reach down, snatch up sliver of toni morrison
hear you whisper, " what page we on."

Charlie R. Braxton

WORD/LIFE

and on that holy day

when you word you

came down in/to

the valley of

my life

your wide eyes

sippin' my soul

sista somewhere somehow someway

we have known each other

in another life perhaps

we walked up/on the nile, niger or nyanzaa

naked of blood and flesh and scars and tears

remember

the time when we were stars

and our smiles would

light up a midnight sky

today we be spirits trapped in a

material world ran by a ghostly machine

pressing the very marrow of our bones together

in search of filthy profits

in this life i've spent days

and nights and seasons

looking for my peeps

saw a few who looked like you but

their eyes

their eyes

their eyes. . . .

weren't thirsty

and then i felt you and your eyes

drink/in my soul and i knew

everything's gonna be alright

word life

everything's gonna be alright

C. *Yaphet Brinson*

SEXTET

1.
your eyes are like
a breeze
walking with me,
arm in arm,
on my way
to your home

2.
kissing you
is like
drinking gin
straight,

let's get drunk
before
we go to bed

3.
I wish
I had
your mind your body
& your soul
so I wouldn't miss you
when you're not here

4.
you look best
in clothes sewn
from the calm air
that surrounds you

5.
in our bedroom
each night is autumn
as our clothes copy
the leave

6.
I can think clearly now
with you
on my mind

S. Brandi Barnes

BACK TO THE BLUES

If you have a sickness
  there's a man around
  mending and soothing cracked up bones-
He's a cure-aid unto himself
  carrying laughing gas for tears
  totes tropical medicine
  for ruptured, frost nipped dreams.
He has the pick-you-ups
  for the downs
  (or down in the mouths)
  and miracle drugs
  for old miseries.
He shouldn't be loose with his radar
  just too many broken rags of dolls around.
He knows the right stroke
  has liniments for your sentiments
  and potions for your notions.
He can sew your heart with his heart
  in no time
  has baby talk to
  make you coo.
You can even see yourself
  in his reflector eye.
Honey 'fo you know it
He'll be your new religion,
  keep you full of holy water.
You'll be thankful! Thankful! Thankful,
  that he knows each painin' spot.
He ain't never out of work
  that one always got a job
  hearts of women folk scruffed and scraped.

Baby, 'fo he finished with you

    he'll see somebody new
     needing repair and drawing salve
    on the black and blues.
You'll go into a relapse,
    start radiating heart trouble:
    gone is the fix-it man and his wonder drugs
    the tropical medicine,
    balms and elixirs
    gone is the laughing gas
    here is a new misery.
So watch where you wobbling, woman
    with your mangled heart.
Them some dangerous man-holes
    leaving you broken down
    in ragged pieces.

Merilene M. Murphy

when you say no

cascade of night aches pray we might
could we tonight
maybe   baby please
alligator bayous cricket thick
rear up gnarly green & snarl
wet & dangerous & deep
lilypads between
mad about you
needeeps
bite me

when you say no
betrayed frog princes stay unkissed
turned off rapunzel goes isaac hayes bald

when you say no
arch pop place my neck says yes
to each yes & every yes one of your kisses
denied a good game of alligator remains unbitten

when you say no
my diva toes curl back ordinary to pace & pout
moon resigns flirtations in champs elysee fountains
zithering bees refuse to buzz in fuschia bonnet bursts
the rain forest folds its green wings in
moroccan belly dancers lose their jewels
the muzzein forgets the words to the call to prayer
his assistant brings them to him in yiddish
jimmy drowns in its a wonderful life
& in spite of all this
all i want to know
when you say no
is
when

mawiyah kai el-jamah bomani

VOUDOU MAMA

beware of a black
woman's hair there are ancient
secrets buried there

Cherryl Floyd-Miller

roots I:
big momma speaks to jimmy's wife

don't care what that hoodoo
chile say 'bout jimmy leavin'

take a lock of his hair
won't go nowhere

say his name three times
while poppin' corn
love you right
night to morn

drop from your monthly
right in his food
jimmy never lose
that do-right mood

do as i say
he'll stay

Cherryl Floyd-Miller

roots II:
the conjure woman replies

jimmy ...

said he never tasted
pink rice

told him it was a
new recipe

he sopped it up between
gravy and bread

gave him water to wash
it down

licked his fingers   was good
to the last drop

Cherryl Floyd-Miller

taboo

can't sleep
on our stomachs
in her house
scared of what
our meddling hands might
trail under the covers

but i am determined
to touch what is mine

so i dream of my
pudgy fingers
finding wet flesh
and fuzz

Nzadi Zimele Keita

lessons in lying

Don't touch a man
while you sweat;
the cling of work and body
to your womanness offends

Don't be long on the phone;
conduct miracles in the meanwhile
and heave your voice without laughter
as he counts time

Eat from a small plate
that you may stand sooner,
wait longer,
and give more
to others

Don't go near a man
with notions that stick
to his food, and don't
tell him how, or how much,
or no

Don't trouble a man's mind
with money, mop water and
cryin' changes,
especially when you know
his lids are unsnapping flesh

Let him go
where he wants and
let him back in
You don't want Rage
stirring the lock

Know, always,
less than he
so that your curiosity
gaps open
for his feast

After all
how else you gonna
get yourself a name?

Tisa Bryant

STRANGER

small birds flit under
the cool boardwalk
of your smile
peck at bits
of sweets noise dropping
from your lips,
soft as the bread
in your hands,
Here. Come on.
I lean to the hopping
little heads.
Shreds of trust and blessing
gulped in their tiny throats.
They eat now what I would save
for last.
Come on. I won't hurt you.
Are you only this
solitary kindness?
Beaks like mica glitter
questions, full of you.
I, too, perched on
your brilliance, swoop down
and steal every word
you say.

Doreen Baingana

MORE THAN ANYTHING

God doesn't fit in
to any box— She is.
Like love, like light,
more than anything.

When I sit quiet to meditate
I see a dark woman smiling
warmth at me, waiting,
working me into myself.

(To see —visions, dreams—
is to keep one's eyes open:
to seek deliberately;
an act of creation.)

 She approves of me
with the old wisdom
of all my Mothers before.
She is where I am going.

A tangled fertile forest
not to fear, but explore,
walking deep. A pond
smooth for my reflection.

We sit, and listen to mystery
flowers pouting open;
there is all the time
to pluck them.

reuben jackson

ONE MORE ONCE

(after Frank O'Hara/for Jeanne)

It is 6:25 in Washington
an autumn-like Monday in May,
and I am washing a head of lettuce and wondering
how the editors at *People* could have omitted you
from their "50 Most Beautiful Individuals in the World
1995" issue.

For who in their right mind would not choose you over
Courtney Cox, or Steve Young or Halle Berry. (this year's lone
African Americans can be kind of attractive entry)

It's clear none of their editors have seen
your face in the day's first chorus of sunlight,
witnessed a night of your sighs and laughter—
or eaten pastrami with you in Midtown Manhattan.

What passes for stardom these days
is not the charisma in your touch,
but competent thespians
with amazingly savvy agents.

The disappointment is enough
to make me start my own magazine.

Janice W. Hodges

"CONTROL"

I cannot control the sun's intensity,
only the length of my own shadow.

IMANI'S SONG

There is a yearning in me to touch your face
I smell your skin
and see you
all of you
so very precious you are to me

Your voice I hear in my sleep
It is the song of a thousand angels
we all sing for you
as I want
hope
and dream
for you Imani
This is your song
Imani's Song

At night we ask the creator
to touch you with life
to move you to a place
prepared for you
There in my womb
where you are protected from all harm
and the wonderous works of our majesty
can begin
to form you
and create in you all that is needed for your journey
in this life
here on earth.

This is our quest for you.
Those who await your coming.
As we sing the song of a thousand angels

Imani's Song

StacyLynn

crushin

this thing of palpitations and
butterflies that appears when
I think of you, this thing of hope,
yearning when you call, makes
me wanna stand at the airport
days before you're scheduled
to arrive, call in sick for weeks,
this thing that makes me think
I love you and we've never even kissed
will break me, yet makes me sing
as it wells up inside me and
spills out in waves, this
blessed, blessed thing

OBESSIONS ARE IMPORTANT

I.

I am just the warm water
In your hands
If you were to bring me up
To your face
It would be a blessing.

II.

I watch your feet
Cross the floor as I dangle
Off the bed.
I think of mice
In an old farm house.
When they get close
I think I'm a cat.

III.

I cannot tell
Where the oil begins
And your back ends.
I can only tell
What soft is
And what it does to my heart.

IV.

When I discovered no one had ever
loved your knees before
I wanted to build elaborate staircases
all over the world,
But I couldn't do that.

Then I began leaving small
gleaming things laying
on the floor
And finally I began to discover what
words made you cross and uncross
your legs—
Obsessions are important.

V.

Whenever I suck your breast
I know you are looking at me.
I can feel it in your breathing.
What are you looking at
The pattern of my balding head,
The arroyo down my back
That leads to my butt,
And what are you thinking about,
This large hummingbird at your feeder?

VI.

Your mouth is such a warm bowl
I can bath in it.

VII.

When I finally staggered
Out of your hair
I realized I had been wandering
Around in the woods for hours.

VIII.

There is a reason I have turned into a
comfortable chair.
There is a reason the brass lamp next to me is
on
And the glass table has the right size book,
A slice of bread and a bowl of chowder,
There is a reason it is raining today

And the fire is blazing:
I would do anything to get you into my lap.

IX.

I like to clean out your ears
With my tongue like they are
little jelly jars.
After all, what are tongues for

X.

You ask me, smiling
Why am I this way?
I think it is because
I am a hungry bear
And you are simply honey.

XI.

But in the end
What your vagina has taught me
Is not simple or soft or warm
Or delicate or wet,
It is that the heart and mind
Cannot thrive without trembling.

David Earl Jackson

NICE SISTER-SCHOLARS NEED LOVING, TOO

Let me get
on my knees,
and lick it.

suck on it.
tongue my baby's
    black mystique
    hidden secret
    bootylicious love fire
    flower swollen open
    with pink red desire.

let my hunger need
get inside and spend
the night eating up all of her
tasty juice cream goodness.

Felicia L. Morgenstern

TEMPLE OF YOUR FAMILIAR

Just watch
the click
of my heel
the whip
to my walk
the coil
to my curl
the sauce
to my smile

Baby,

how can you think
I'd reject ANY part of you?

I LOVE to pray
at the temple of YOUR familiar

And baby,
I take no prisoners

But when I take you
I take
ALL
of you. . .

Felicia L. Morgenstern

RIDE ME BABY, RIDE ME

I am the Silver
to your Lone Ranger

Ride me, baby
Ride me

English
Western
or Side saddle

Just ride, baby
Ride me

I am the Cole- to your –trane
The bump to your grind
The funk to your spunk

Just ride me, baby
Ride me

'Cause baby
When YOU ride me
there IS no me
there is no me to be

 So just ride me, baby
Ride me!

Felicia L. Morgenstern

HUES OF ELECTRIC BLUE

The sky
cries out
in shocking hues
of electric blue

And for one
fleeting moment

I forget I am I
and you forget you are you

Just what is it
we are so fearful to lose?

Even God himself
sometimes suffers
the electric blues. . .

James Coleman

BLACK WOMEN WITH JEWISH NAMES

Suppose there is something
Behind this?
Something more than coincidence
That life should
Pull me this way
And twist me that way?

Suppose all our fears
Are contained in a single teardrop
That wells in the eye
And never hits the cheek?

Black women with Jewish names
That I have known also believe they
Were chosen by God to suffer until
They claim some precious
Promised land.

So I am an Arab to them
Surely less devout and wholly capable
Of defiling the temple they say once stood
Where now there is nothing

Angela Jackson

LOVING

(DAVID AND VIVIAN)

It is
like/making a cake.
The butter must yield/
easy to the the spoon, and the
fall of sugar
The eggs/ warm yolks
spread like sunsets
in the bowl/
Salt pinch/flour pound/ baking
powder be sifted/
shaken down/
It is/ like
making a cake
baked
in the right container
at the
right temperature

It all/ has to be
there.

Viki Radden

SEX

1.

You have a good vagina. It makes me crazy.

Perfect, I think. Perfect.
May you be rendered perpetually crazed
by my good vagina.

2.

You wonder, with your head back and your eyes closed,
just how long I can really go on lingering,
my head buried between your legs
You wonder
but then
I distract you and
you sigh, and
wonder again

3.

Let's sit in the garden again,
my delectable one
dazzled by tulips
purple and white irises
hedge of wild rose
Sooner or later, their beauty
and the nearness of each other
will drive away all thought,
all possibilities
except more love
We'll look at each other,

nod our assent,
then slip back inside
drink once more
from our voluptuous fountain

Viki Radden

WHEN YOU TALK THAT TALK

Speak Japanese to me, lover
Tell me I'm like no other on earth

Late, late,
when the night is silent,
rouse from dreamy sleep,
your hand on my trembling breast
arms encircling
gold on brown

When you speak Japanese to me
a veil lifts
I see you transformed
Ancient, ancient you become
swaggering old samurai
noble of the Heian court

In my loving eyes
you are all
all of Japan

history and destiny
enveloped between my thighs
weak for me,
you beg,
hungry for me,
you cry

Speak Japanese to me, lover

Come
Come inside
Stay there

an eternity
and

Speak Japanese to me

Viki Radden

BLOOD

I tell you,
"Sex is good for menstrual cramps."
Even though you are on the telephone,
I know you are smiling
You say
"I'll be right over."

How a civil service job suits a lonely man
with a mistress only a train ride away!

I put a clean towel
between the bed and me
and I wait for you
my man in the navy gabardine
come to perform his civic duty
a cultural ambassador
showing the foreigner
the many tasty assets of Japan

when you arrive
I undress you and
we roll in the red

You luxuriate
pay homage
cradle of all life
sticky redness
beneath us
annointing us

your fingers stained scarlet
taste on your tongue salty sweet
I warn you against the power

"A man who tastes
the blood of a woman
is forever in her power."
your eyes wide, you nod
You accept the risk
you partake again

When you are in me
cramps vanish
disappearing into
next month's menstrual account
Afterwards, we soap our bodies
and remember the rapture
My blood tints the water crimson

Soap,
semen,
blood
and all,
mingling,
disappearing
like my cramps
and my civil servant
who must now

Get back to work

jesus' song

never could bring myself
into the question of him
bending backwards at night
into his own voice, or what
it was he put inside his pants
after i left, wondering why
this river never runs upstream
like they promised in the ads.
last week's voice was my answer
thinking this place was large
enough for me, my toys and
a picture taken before thirty
showed me here, almost grey,
never wanting more than one night
in the promised land,
unlike its last occupants
who took it for granted before
the flood of knowledge drowned
them in their beds.
if, only, i could learn to swim
backwards like a salmon, i would
know how to double under belly,
soar against the tide,
back into the ground,
singing the song jesus taught me.

Angela Jackson

MOMENT

Each moment is infinite and complete

After you get up to go and I can think of no more reasons
for you to stay that I can say without making it all too plain
more plain than what is safe later to look at after we have both
had our way with each other and we don't know yet where to go
with each other or even if we want to, we stand out in front
of the house like proper would-be lovers courting
in an earlier century.
I start staring up at the stars because I want to see a falling star,
and you follow because you have far more experience at star-gazing
than I. You are quick and see two, but I see none,
only the after-effect of stars in the vicinity of the falling who talk
in coded light after the one goes down, "Yonder he goes; yonder she runs."
That is what I know they say, but say this is not so
I only think it is
and I say it is and how do you know
and you say maybe so.
Then you tell me about light, how old it is and how new, how you first
saw time while you sat close by a river that bent; it was then and
it was now is now and it was easier for you to live after that
or was it before
you know it now.
I do too. You have always been standing under this sky with me.
I have always been here somewhere near you.
When you bend down and I arch up, my breasts ending
like starpoints pushing against you,
we make a bow for a moment. You turn your mouth to my cheek and say,
"You are beautiful." Then you kiss me.
I look over my shoulder at all those stars and see you.
You're beautiful."
Now I say the stars that fall are falling in love.
And what do you say then?

CULTURAL WEBS
AND NETS

Joanne M. Braxton

ZONING

(for MMB)

In the wild zone, we wait and watch and pray.
A small, golden voice, delicate as a fairy flower,
Some lady's slipper shaft of rain-forest sunlight
Speaks up to me, "We are African-American people."
"Yes, we are," I answer; "yes, we are."

In a cosmos of double veils, every answer is twain:
We own this space, if nothing else, and fill it
With twinkling stars and cymbals, common buttercups,
Fire from John Henry's hammer, and cascades of bubbles,
Baptized and baptizing, in the spirit.

Who are we who are known and not known?
Who speak in light-stick riddles of river rock
And kiss the kiss of family, finding in each answer
Not two more questions, but three? From what far,
Distant place we come to enter here?

We inhabit this space, we walk the walk together.
We wear the same name; cut, we bleed the same blood.
In this zone, the unconscious is awake as the Red Sea,
Parted. Enter lightly, the physics of this world.
In the wild zone, we wait and watch and pray.

Brian Gilmore

coming to the net (for arthur ashe)

now we must come to the net
with our rackets
our skills
rushing the net
ready for the lob that our
opponent always seems to rely on.
ready to slam the shot into the
open court
that's all we need now is an opening,
a clear chance to take control
of this match
a double fault
an unforced error
a slow high bouncing return we can handle,
send back with violent force
drive our opponent into the fence so
we can come to the net for the shot
that will make history.

now we must prepare our rackets
back behind us and ready
we just need to keep the ball in
play now
it is match point but we must have the heart
of a champion.
we must all be in grand slam form
wimbeldon
the french
the u.s. open
we are down to our last point
but this is how greatness is
born.

now we must be ready to serve
a hard driving
up in your face
roscoe tanner look alike.
pushing our opponent
back against the fence
telling him we will not
be beat.
we can then come to the net
with our rackets prepared
ready for the lob
checking down the line
determined to turn this thing
around
because all we need is an opening,
and i know we will be victorious
if we all come to the net together.

Kwan Booth

UNTITLED ONE

I wrote a poem,
or two
about niggahs.
but now I want to write
about black people.
not negroes, not coloreds, not African Americans
not jiggaboos, oreos, or Uncle Toms
but black people
I want to write about Black people.
Iwant to write about those luscious, licorice, lovely black people
The ones with the full lips and the kinky hair.
The ones with the big asses and wide noses.
Black people that walk through life not giving a damn
Black people that roll their eyes and suck their teeth
Black people that take two and pass (puff puff give)
Black people that pour it out for the black people
                who ain't here
Black people that love to be loved
Black people that can do it all night
Black people that do it cause they have to
Black people that make ends meet
                    by any means necessary
Black people that struggle
Black people that survive
Black people that LIVE
Yeah,
I want to write
about black people.

Matthew Watley

NEGROES

Negroes don bow ties
And corner the market on blackness
But I really don't see the connection.

Negroes will buy a scrap of kente cloth
And think that they are African kings and queens
But to be royalty you can't just add water and mix.

Negroes grow dreads-smoke weed
Wear boots and hoodies
And instruct me to check myself
But since when did this Russian roulette
Called being black in America turn into monopoly

For the last time
I Define My Blackness!
My Christian, middle-class, fair-skinned
Preppy-clad, Greek-lettered, college-educated
Self is no blacker or whiter than any
Of you Brothers and Sisters.

Negroes
Stop being negroes
Stop defining yourselves by any and every thing
And become the greatest thing anyone could ever hope to be
Yourselves!

Peter J. Harris

THE NEXT MALCOLM POEM

the next Malcolm poem
celebrates the last midnight
a father took quiet giant steps
through the moonlit halls of his home
his whispers a bedtime flute
soothing the breath of his sleeping daughters
humming *Mona Lisa* as he tiptoes
back into their mother's arms
places his spectacles on the night stand
nestles into her drowsy eyes
brushes her cheeks as he pulls
the covers up to her open throat
kissing her mouth to pass on secrets
he learned from his dreaming girls

the next Malcolm poem
celebrates the first morning
the hero's wife took healing giant steps
onto the road past memory toward eternity
her whispers a Coltrane soprano
soloing up the spine of her sheltered daughters
humming *Naima* as she weans them from grief
floats out of widowhood dedicated to the ones she loves
steels herself against the fantastic first–name justifications
steels herself in the spicy occasion
she chose life over death
willing another set of fingerprints
to the biographers who come to praise the name
Shabazz

Allison Joseph

SHAME OF THE WRITERS' CONFERENCE

A heathen in free verse,
not counting syllables or accents,

I'm playing, as some accuse,
tennis with the net way down,

my metrical conduct appalling.
One line I write may lapse

into scansion's territory,
the next so discordant that I

hang my head to claim it,
scoot it to my notebook's

back pages, propping it up
with deletions, compromises.

Don't speak to me of rhyme—
it's never been my talent

or habit, so when I see those
who can do so gliding by,

I envy like I envied girls
far prettier than me, ones

with no paucity of dinner dates.
I have eaten alone for so long

I wouldn't know what else
to do, my poor words no feast,

but enough for me when ornate dinners
are served to the graceful, the metrical.

GALE SAYERS

It is these crisp November days
that are your favorite:
The sound of frosted grass
cracking beneath cleats,
clouds rolling from lips,
Soldier Field's uneasy peace,
like a woman recovering virginity
only to lose it every Sunday.

There is a safety
decked out in a dead-man's colors,
who will be taught with inhuman ease.
the sacred dance
of the grid-iron ballerina.

Sayers at the five,
the ten,
the fifteen,

This is war
a mud-montage of zig-zag footprints
and players left grabbing at sky.
Each of your steps brings a blood-rush,
like a deer running through a mine-field,
as the count-down begins.

He's at the fifteen,
the ten,
the five,

Even on Butkus' face there is pride,
Papa Bear Halas finds a smile.
What they cannot know

is how fate will take you
at your finest hour.
She knows how selfish it all is,
how this is too much music
for one mans legs.

Sam Cornish

BROWN BOMBER

fist: Joe Louis The Brown
Bomber in the ring was the Negro
people sweating and fighting
in the corner store   our small
rooms the pulpit resting
on the marble steps Joe Louis
fighting from radio to radio

THE KNOCKOUT

I woke up dreaming
Sugar Ray Robinson
red shoes dancing
on graves
of dreams.
I woke up
my father's voice
screaming names
Archie Moore, Joe Louis
Willie Pep
Battling Siki.
His favorite Kid Gavilan
swinging his bolo
a machete splitting opponents
into two equal halves.
The Kid always swung
to a Mambo beat.

I woke up dreaming
my old man's voice...
too late now
"Stick and move
stay on your toes
don't waste punches
keep you guard up."

I woke up dreaming
wildly punching air,
the savage bells
invading my silence.
The machete was singing
a lullaby
until the voice interrupted
"What did I tell you?"

THE SONG TO COME

Stephen Caldwell Wright

AND THE BIRDS SING OF LIFE

I fear I shall
Have to remember
This lone Dove
That flies near
The branch,
Over and under it,
But will not
Land, Perch, Rest
Its wings
Nor its feet
To still the thunder
Of Earth's subtle cracking,
Its millennium stretching
Beyond its reach,
Beyond others' grasp—

I shall remember
The wonder of forgetting
That will not come...
The melting of holding
That continually unfolds
Upon the structured
Sense of Resolve
That will not
Quite catch
In Place
And stay
The Mirage
Of tragic Demise—
Itself a Visage
Painted with clouds
Of unpredictable,
Indefinite Conclusion,
Surmise,

And Whispers of God.

Eli Goodwin

CONFESSION

Judge not, lest ye be judged.
                    —Jesus Christ

The Devil made me do it the first time. After that, Ah done it on Mah own.

                    —Willie Nelson

I held your sins against you for so long;

As if The Lord had put me here to judge.

But when I saw how often I've done wrong,

I knew I had to let go of my grudge.

A knotted heart can't give a soul release.

I'm letting go, not just for you, but me.

If blaming you could ever bring me peace,

A long, long time ago I had been free.

Carl Hancock Rux

JUST ASKING

To live to die to die to live to be to
what? To know to then to now
with what? Understanding...
To ask to seek to search
to find to not to say
you do to where
to look to
read to
hear
to

trust to pray
to lose to ask to
not be answered? And
if I should or not or if I
must to bleed to bend or if
and then the gush is not for sure
and if or not if the bow is not promised
anointing after the curtain fall then should I
not or must I then be clear, with who for what
and how? That should and could are not for sure
and *if* or not *if* means nothing anymore to any of us not now...

not ever...well then,

The thought is this: if the thought of being well is just a thought of being
other than what you are and if the thought of being well is just a
thought of being what you are not, then how to know it is a
thought that could bring a state of being if you have never
been in that state at all, having *neverbeen* it? Or if you
think, well then, that being well you once have been
and for now are not then why the thought, why not
the state of being simply willed into the now? If

not, then how to know it is a thought that
could bring a state of being? But if the
thought could very well will the state
then the new thought is this: Could the
thought will the *state* and is it
true that those who die all
willed it so because they
did not think of being
well then? Or as far
as that goes, those
who fail and
those who
fall, all
what? willed
it so by not
being well then
or willing the state of
being well? Well then, if they
did- the young, the old, the in
between- would we know what to will
or want right away (that is life) and what not to
will or want (that is death) and if we did, so *willed* it so,
then why the fear and why the fight? And how could we want
what we do or will such so if the state of life and the being of death
are all inevitable... for one comes first and then the next, the opposite
is still
a thought and not a fact, and still the state of being well, must be a
thought of
being what we have never been, what none of us really are. Well then,
how or why,
could the thought ever be the thing that wills the state, and is it true, at
all, that all those
who

live
and those who
die
all willed it so?

(or have I asked this before?),

and those of us who say we
want
we need
we must be
well

is this what we really want?
or do we know what to want ?
That is, what we are not-
some state of being

well then...

StacyLynn

lookin good

I remember conversations
about death and funerals
and how she was so insistent
        you know what bothers me?
she would begin, each time
someone unknowingly unleashed
the focus of her greatest peeve.
        'Don't he look good?
        He sure looks peaceful' - please!..
she would continue
expressing distaste
for those that would forego reality
and characterize the lifeless
as having beauty and peace.
        I mean, really,
        how can you say they look good? - they're dead
I remember the speech well.

but as we entered the parlor
and walked toward the casket
toward the body of her father
I wondered what she'd feel.

I saw a form much different from my memory.
his piercing look was hidden
behind delicately closed lids.
this stiff and powdered shell looked cold, and empty
and as she had always said, dead.

finally,
        doesn't he look good?
she whispered
and in the quiet of the parlor

out of the light of the truth
I placed my hand on hers
    "yes, mom,
    he does"

Rohan B. Preston

WHEN I LEAVE MY BODY

When I leave my body in this world
please leave it too—leave it be—
whether swirling as chamber dust
or swaddled in sackcloth up front in the yard
under the sweetie mango tree.

Do not finger my skull for secrets
do not tap for water with my bones—
they are their own divining—
please, leave my grave alone.

When I leave this skin, this hair,
these teeth, this femur trunk,
leave them here to dry,
please do not dig them up to check for
the marvels of my eye sockets,

or to read the arrangement
or perished foods and duppy guides,
leave the hieroglyphs and ochre prints
paintings Mum's generation's pride.

Yes, people can live in our home,
even live here haunt free,
if my spirit takes them
and if they let my spirit be.

When I leave my body in this world
free and dead for true,
I may be stiff and brittle at last
but duppy bones can take set on you.

Carl Phillips

AS FROM A QUIVER OF ARROWS

What do we do with the body, do we
burn it, do we set it in dirt or in
stone, do we wrap it in balm, honey,
oil, and then gauze and tip it onto
and trust it to a raft and to water?

What will happen to the memory of his
body, if one of us doesn't hurry now
and write it down fast? Will it be
salt or late light that it melts like?
Floss, rubber gloves, a chewed cap

to a pen elsewhere -- how are we to
regard his effects, do we throw them
or use them away, do we say they are
relics and so treat them like relics?
Does his soiled linen count? If so,

would we be wrong then, to wash it?
There are no instructions whether it
should go to where are those with no
linen, or whether by night we should
memorially wear it ourselves, by day

reflect upon it folded, shelved, empty.
Here, on the floor behind his bed is
a bent photo — why? Were the two of
them lovers? Does it mean, where we
found it, that he forgot it or lost it

or intended a safekeeping? Should we
attempt to make contact? What if this
other man too is dead? Or alive, but
doesn't want to remember, is human?
Is it okay to be human, and fall away

from oblation and memory, if we forget,
and can't sometimes help it and sometimes
it is all that we want? How long, in
dawns or new cocks, does that take?
What if it is rest and nothing else that

we want? Is it a findable thing, small?
In what hole is it hidden? Is it, maybe,
a country? Will a guide be required who
will say to us how? Do we fly? Do we
swim? What will I do now, with my hands?

Kiamsha Madelyn Leeke

october death

(for papa on 10/18/96)

death for me is the transformation of the human spirit
a soulful celebration
to get down on the get down
of the passing of a loved one's soul

no time for funerals
just let the good times roll

let's cut a rug
a jig like some folks used to say
let's pretend that we on bourbon street
mardi gras-ing in our creole masquerade
new orleans jazz
hot, live and in color
celebrating nothing but the good times as they roll right on by

let's shed tears of happiness
use pink and purple polka dot hankies
and shine our kodak color smiles like we did
when nelson was set free

let's paint a picture in our minds
much like jacob
and call it the migration of the soul
knowing,
trusting and
understanding that its movement is fluid
set to no specific music
has its own independent flava
moves only when it is ready to roll

let's cook some red beans and rice
with secret spicy combinations that only grandmas know
and then throw on some funky feel good music like my daddy's
dinah
ella
or nina
the divas divine
and watch time pass by

let's burn some incense like we did for bob marley
frankincense and myrrh
don't forget the sandalwood to clean the air
make it fresh
make it ready
make it right
make it new like we would for Jesus

let's pour some chamomile tea
aunt jessie used to say
that it soothes a body's soul
from the tippy top all the way to the very bottom
and let the good times roll

let's turn out all the lights
and look from our windows into mother midnight's eyes
for the coming forth by day
the great awakening
the transformation of our loved one's soul
and when the night is just about over
let's pour the red wine
slice ahmed's bean pie bought last saturday in bed-stuy
and cut a rug
a jig
like some folks used to say
stomping like we was at the savoy
way back in the day
with chick webb playing at our sides
jitterbugging in our zoot suits and twirley skirts
as we let the good times roll right on by.........

Zak Robbins

OCTOBER 7TH

Prayers have deadlines too
when God stops listening
and waits for us
to get off our knees
and take our hands
away from our faces
and decide
to stop begging
and start performing
our own personal miracles

Ira B. Jones

HAIKU FOR MY BROTHERS

Brothers are kneeling
down within themselves. Bow-down
only unto God

Bernard Keller

ONE MILLION MEN MARCHING II

They did not come to be heroes and legends.

They did not come to wreak havoc

or to preach anarchy.

They came to change the world

to end the killing,

the dying,

the hating

and the taking.

They came to make a peace with themselves

and their God.

They came to be men,

and they came looking to become brothers,

again.

Bernard Keller

KEEP A GOOD THOUGHT

If you must lie,

lie to the fear which clouds your thoughts

and say "I am not afraid."

If you must steal,

steal knowledge in order that you may be punished

with wisdom.

If you must cheat,

cheat failure —

it does not deserve to win anyway.

If you must fight,

fight hopelessness —

for a person without hope

is no person at all.

Shara McCallum

WHAT MY MOTHER TAUGHT ME

When God closes a door, there are no windows.
When the Big Bad Wolf knocks, he knows how to get in.
Be afraid of the dark.

Don't scream.
Don't run.
Don't make wishes you can't keep.

If you drag a horse to water enough, she will drink.
If you don't play with fire, it will find you and burn.
Even careful chickens get caught by the hawk.

Melanie Hope

PRAISE THE DAUGHTER

Imagine we worshipped water
In every home divine fountains
Imagine mothers praised every daughter
Imagine we worshipped water
And every child knew laughter
People praying on top of mountains
Imagine we worshipped water
In every home divine fountains

Rachel E. Harding

EZILI IMPENDING

tree, take my girdle
this strip of cloth around my waist
bind yourself
Mama Ezili is rising in the water
take this cloth from my waist
tree, take my girdle
the wind is in the water
salute her
secure the wind passing among your roots
rubbing herself in your leaves
your branches
salute her
Mama Ezili is rising in the water
tree, take my girdle
this white cloth, this blue cloth
bind yourself:

michael datcher

i am open

walking backwards along shore
foraging for woman answers.
surveying where i have been
where i may return.
cross examining scattered cowrie shells
remains of receding waves.
they woman spirit
compressed into sea stone by osun
for whispering sweet water secrets.

gather seven shells to ear
they afraid to speak.
pounce on nosy seagull
try to pry insight from beak
with long wisdom prayers.
she breaks silence
only after i promise to go down.
she comes mystic shaman tongues
pausing finally to moan:
"what comes around goes around
what comes around goes around."
death chant of progressive macks
urbane snakes who wear goatees
heavy hearts on sleeves.
i am open.
come woman
come woman.
woman whose root doctor breasts
will strengthen spines of my warrior sons
whose seraphic light spirit
will show them god.
woman see me weep waterfall tears

when I cannot write.
see me electric stutter, skipping cd
not glance away.
woman whose third eye expose my cowardice
whose assata courage inspire my change.

woman who be truth.

come woman
come woman.
woman who love to fuck on stove top
like crisco smoking, popping, in black skillet
who make love like morning mist caressing african violet.
who know my scorching sunstar heart sincere
even when salt in peanut gallery doubt me.
woman know i'm afraid of my dreams
call me "punk"
when cave to fear.
woman big lip, french kiss my mind
get sticky wet reading fanon
carry secret ankh shaped vibrator
inside bulging metu neter
see beauty in farrakhan.
come woman
come woman.
Woman say "motherfucker"
with gospel conviction seven languages
then conjugate
woman make me smile.
Cowomanme
come woman.
woman know god a black woman
woman sense enough to worship herself.
who keep my nose open
like fifth street dick's on south central, summer solstice nights.
who perry masons my nigga/nationalist contradictions.
woman let me lick her
like never ending roll, jelly roll morton, 32 cent stamps.
woman serious bout her people.
woman with low hanging
speed bump ass, no speed limit.

woman who can suck some dick.
woman know love oxygen of soul, water of spirit.
come woman
come woman.
woman black love her momma monk deep
got down home, home training.
woman fullmoon, barefoot, damballah dance
to crackling vinyl coltrane.

woman know god.

come woman
come woman.

nigrescent sherlock holmes

sandals, egyptian musk
mystery solving along shore.
searching for soul mate clues
praying waves wash up
cowries in hieroglyphic formation
ocean divination
prophesying my love story.

Lorna Lowe

SEA SHELLS

Baraka says
there is a railroad at the bottom of the sea
sea sailing ships sail on and on
and they cross and befall one another
slicing the brine's imbrued surface   yes
they fall like wretched stepchildren
unsettled
their spirits surfacing to signal the doubters with fear of heights
to hum   this silence is sweet
and they love their people from a watery distance
sail on sail on
while the sea ships sailed on and then
stilled
contemplated retracing her waves for the lost
whose bodies christened the ships' bow and stern
and they turned back   home
Baraka says there is a railroad at the bottom of the sea
sail on and on

Matthew Watley

100 MILLION

One hundred million Africans slaughtered
No burial no tombstones, their graves marked only
By the creamy crests of waves set in motion eternally
By the impact of their corpses upon the water.
Those waves, one hundred million ever moving
Unsettled like the souls of our ancestors.
One hundred million Africans killed
Their memory vanishing in the wind
That blows and shifts, it does not yield
But forces one hundred million trees to bend
It sweeps the earth scattering our sorrows like dust.

One hundred million Africans slaughtered
Lost forever are their stories and names
The smoke of their scorched lives, rises
The sun, 100 million degrees still burns cold
One hundred million suns shine dim
Dim like the eyes of our ancestors now closed to the world
Seeing black the space that parts the stars

One hundred million people, black people
Not slaves, but people, your family
The great great great grandmother you would have known
Had her flesh not been ripped from her bones
By whips on the ship where she was raped
And bled and starved and died to be
Thrown to the sharks to devour the body and hands
That never held the child in her stomach

The child who would never know their older brother
Only five years himself, and his mother dead,
And his brother drowned, and alone to face the stench
Of the feces beneath his cramped body.

Chained to a girl not much older, who can not see him
The captains syphilis had taken her sight.

And night times bring moans and the laughs of men
Drunken as they prod the slave, the man, the black man
Your great great great grandfather whose name was forgotten
As he was forced to stand naked while white men fondled his genitals
Before brandishing their knives to carve his manhood into blood and tears.

One hundred million years can not hide beneath their fabric of time
That which refuses to be covered
One hundred million revolutions of the earth
Can not erase
The greatest crime ever committed
One hundred million drops of rain can not dilute
The blood spilled on the ground from the lips of our ancestors
If an Eagle beat its wings one hundred million times
It could not fly as high as the cries of horror and anguish
Released by mothers who saw their children taken away

Still wet in the afterbirth.
One hundred million grains of sand
Slip through our fingers
With our histroy, our culture, our languages, our names
And who stoops to gather them up?

We
Remember the holocaust and morn for the Jews
We
Feel such pity and compassion for those slain native Americans
We
Cry for the suffering of the Vietnamese
But our tears become caught under our eyes
For those who are flesh of our flesh and bone of our bone
Our tears are dry like the bones of our ancestors
Refusing to depart from their ivory white sockets

We have vanquished that which the sea can not submerge
We have forgotten that which the clouds can not cover
We have erased that which the sun can not burn away
And the earth can not decompose.

One hundred million Africans were slaughtered
Bartered like cattle were sons and daughters
But we sit here proper with pinkie raised
While those children lay dead still unknown.

We kill each other
And feed drugs to each other
And hate ourselves
And bleach our skin
And color our eyes and tighten our butts
And tom ourselves to sleep
And ask to be called African-American
And African-American abbreviated is AA
And we hide our identitites
And are drunken on the lies of the ones who have
Tricked and robbed and raped and killed us for
Hundred of years
And one hundred million Africans were slaughtered
And we forget that they ever lived.

Brandon D. Johnson

STORM

The edges of slave ships are narrow and difficult for footing.

She was gone
Swallowed by wet night that filled her lungs
Before I could call her name
Before I could jump.
Time enough for ropes to restrain me.

My eyes,
Now painted with crimson waves I could not join
Never close
My head
Tossed like a ship in storm

She knows I will come to her
Come when moon's at zenith
When I can no longer stand the waves pummeling
My bloodless heart.

On my knees each sunset
On my mind each dawn
I pray that she still loves me
Though I could not follow her
Could not choose graves with my woman
Could not step into paradise together
Into anything not here
Not bound by earth
Bound by sea
By evil

A bag of feather, soft, yielding, forgiving
Me the indecency of living
Is my only paradise now

I dive in bottles of spirits to find her
Surfacing still lost
Finding only her cries and whispers
Calling...
Calling me
To courage,
To her side
To peace

The ship's sails carried symbols honoring their deity.
If I have come to a holy land
God protect me from your followers.

If she were here
I'd have more than my pillow to lie with
In this land where dark people see no light.

The Conquistadors prevented me from joining her
But nightly I twist my soul to understand
If this was just a convenience
A way to avoid an end
For which she could not wait.

One day I will find my courage
Find her
And leave my pillow behind.

Honorée F. Jeffers

MARY, DON'T YOU WEEP

They sing of Mary and Martha,
the sisters of Lazarus.
Oh, Mary, don't you weep.
Oh, Martha don't you moan.
They sing of the slave woman
who birthed thirteen children,
thirteen children by a slave master
who tells her every year,
you can keep this one,
and every year he forces
her to give up a baby
whose small, blind mouth seeks
emptiness and the slave
woman cannot cry aloud
for fear of her master.
They sing of Pharaoh's army
who got drowned in the Red Sea,
Pharaoh's army of slave masters
who chased Moses into the jaws
of the Promised Land,
and they sing of retribution,
of the soldiers in the sea who are sucking
blood like rivers of milk
and Lazarus arises
from the tomb, shakes dust
from his flesh and cries,
"yes, I proclaim."

Elaine Maria Upton

A STREETWALKER TRYING TO SPEAK TO SOJOURNER TRUTH

I don't know whether it's possible
to have a conversation with you,
don't quite know what it is I'm trying
to say, or whether I should stay.
They say you had your children
sold from under you on the auction block.
I never gave birth to one, who
if she had come, might have been
mine for a while. All those who say
they love me -I keep on leaving them.
Never was close to nieces and nephews
either. Can't seem to make a home.

Sojourner, does that mean I am a wanderer,
too? Some may think I'm a murderer. Then,
some see me as a dreamer, but the   truth
—to speak of a truth with you— is
I don't know why I was born   or if
it matters whose child I am.

I don't know whether you would love me,
because you saints love, if at all,
different than the rest. (But then,
excuse my presumption, I could say
the same about myself.) Sojourner,

did your big bones ever grow cold
all those days and nights on the road?
Did you ever fall asleep and dream?
But what is dreaming, tell me,
if you don't even have a bed?

I keep on moving on, and maybe
I'll find a home. Or maybe
I'll just lie right here and listen.
Don't tell nobody, but I can act
like the dew is a pillow and the black
of night curls over me. That much
I know because I see the stars
rising round. And maybe the crickets
will sing me to sleep right here.

And Sojourner, one more thing
before I go: are you an angel yet?
If so, could you give me a sign
—beat your bright dark wings
in my aching heart sometimes?

mwatabu s. okantah

the black experience

whole populations have been shattered
into people who live
    jagged
edged
lives; human
fragments in search
of discarded
memories that once
held all the pieces together—
everything is upside
down:

Europe has never been a continent.
African history
is not the history of Europeans
in Africa.
African time is ancient.
African time begins
before the appearance of people
who would be called white.
Europe did not
exist.
in the beginning
only black people traveled
down north
from the Mountains
of
the Moon ...

ii.

Columbus did not discover
America.
the New World is old.
America is an alien idea forced
into being.
it did not live
in the dream vision of the native
people who were already
here:

the people who discovered Columbus
no longer exist.
what must it be like
to be
the last of one's
tribe?
extinction.
who remembers their name?
what of their memories?
no glory in Long Walks or
Trails
of
Tears.
Columbus was lost.
he came a stranger
whose intentions
were never
good—
bringer of a New World
        Order
holocaust centuries
before the Hitler years ...

iii.

so-called Red people.
"The Blacks."
Indians. reservations. slaves.

descendents of ex-slaves.
disconnected peoples.
inventions.
figments of a sick imagination
fired in the furnace of white supremacy.
"Native Americans" and negroes.
niggers and smiling
red samboes:

manifest destiny
was just another name for extermination.
a bully nation
created itself out of the destruction
of many.
Europe cast her New World
shadow in blood,
in disease, in death—
all
in the name
of their missionary
God ...

     iv.

strange worlds. new peoples.
how did enslaved
African mothers raise
healthy children?
old, remembered traditions
come together in
       new
ways:

Voodoo.

rebel Africans conjuring in Haitian mountains.
Papa Legba
opened the gates
for Toussaint, Dessalines
and Christophe;
for freedom.

Congolese magic
"in the body of Dan"—
Dahomey.
Damballah. Ayida-Oueddo.
Arada. Petro.
protective spirits.

Candomble.

Holy Mother Mary Yemanjah.
Mother of Waters.
Yoruba. Ifa. Awo.
Samba is Brazil.
the Orisha traveled the
distance across the big water.
it is said the Atlantic
ocean bottom is littered
with African ancestral
bones.

Ring Shout.

they tried to take the drums and dance away.
we clapped our hands,
we stomped our feet,
we shuffle stepped in ritual
        circle
to make a way
for the coming of the spirit
of the Lord.

only one people sang
a new song
in spite of this strange land.
they sang,

        Swing low, sweet chariot,
        Coming for to carry me home,
        Swing low, sweet chariot,
        Coming for to carry me home.

they sang,

> Everybody talkin 'bout heaven
> Ain't goin'there,
> Heaven, heaven.

Holiness Sanctified Holy Roller
Wade in the Water
talkin' in tongues
sweet Jesus rides the backs
of the weary
and wounded
opening a center beyond the massa's reach
and white hot despair.

v.

in this still strange,
but familiar
land,
African ancestors wander,
they are disturbed
        in
their eternal
sleep,
they stand knocking
at the door of our silence.
we hold the key
to the door.

fragments.

a people shattered
into pieces
struggle to become
        whole
once again;
just inside the dark door
of our silence,
Afreekan voiced ancestors stand,
whispering,

reconnecting memories—
water words flow
    rushing
over us
black
into one ...

    Afreeka

mwatabu s. okantah

AFRICAN MORNING

the cock i never see
crows each
new day to announce the sun.
a goat bays,
his bell ringing
just below the compound wall.
morning birds
sing solitary music
to clear Benin City air.

children on the way
to school
sounds
rent the stillness of the Sun's rise.
a woman sings as she draws
water.
Whitney Houston
songs startle
on the clock radio.

African city sounds begin ...

    Nigeria

mwatabu s. okantah

market day

the light flashes red.
traffic stops.
the intersection transforms.

they come. they converge
on waiting cars.
people selling all manner of things.
leather goods,
toilet paper, razor blades,
chew sticks, groundnuts,
newspapers, magazines,
handkerchiefs,
baby clothes ...

they come.
beggars on twisted limbs
with probing eyes.
blind men guided by grim faced
sad-eyed children.
children.
refugee women, wandering, babies
carried in their arms, babies
tied to their backs, babies
held up before open
car windows.
they search each car for soft eyes
to look into ...

the light flashes green.
traffic resumes,
the people wait,
they work,
they market day in Port Harcourt.

       Nigeria

James R. Lee

STRANGER AT HOME

They looked at each other
Both smiling
She spoke to him
In Kikuyu
He continued smiling
Speaking to her
In American English
While circling around him
Looking more confused
Her smile disappeared
She shook her head
In disbelief that
This African man
Who looked
So much like her
Could not speak
Her language
Trying once more
To unravel this
Mystery of history
She threw up both hands
With tears now
In both their eyes
She embraced him
Finally accepting
This strangeness
She motioned him
Inside the house

Danielle Legros Georges

ANACAONA

... and my name will be dropped
                        golden leaf
                            flower

voice of gold

                        the gold

of mountains beyond mountains
     I've crossed to behold my own

                            face

despite my body's death
in double cross
(by a Spanish gentleman's deal/
the sword/the crucifix)

despite divisions of time
of tribes
                        Taino

                        Carib
                          . . .

the island's body itself
its zones:

        Marien
                    Magua
            Maguana
                        Higuey

Xaragua

engulfed
transfigured

my own children
                                 scattered
the *sanba*
                             lost
their tongues
                          scattered

my name buried by music
foreign to me

the mountain-sides bursting
in red

my gestures   marooned

               I have seen what will be
          a mirroring gaze through time
                   a sun in eclipse
                     reflection and

                        reflection

an imprint

                        of my face

the study of

                    my aim

and my name shall sow maize
my name shall breed vision
my girls will be black, bronzed,
their eyes shall be storms

and my name dropped
gold leaf
flower

voice of gold

the gold of mountains
beyond mountains
I've crossed to behold
my own face.

Notes:
Anacaona: *poet and ruler of Xaragua, one of the five regions of Ayiti (now Hispaniola) at time of Columbus's arrival in 1492. In seeking to unite the regions against the Spanish she was ambushed and hanged.*

Sanba: *(Haitian Creole) poet, storyteller, or singer.*

Danielle Legros Georges

ANOTHER ODE TO SALT

We navigate snow not ours
but grown used to, one cold foot
over another, adopt accoutrements:
a red scarf, wind-wrapped and tight,
boots, their soles teethed like sharks,
shackling our ebon ankles, the weight
of wool coats borrowed
from *our ancestors, the Gauls.*

Masters at this now,
we circumvent ice
as we do time,
reach home.

The salt you bend to cast
parts the snow around us.
I bend and think
of a primary sea,
harbors of danger and history,
of passing through the middle
in boats a-sail in furious storms
cargo heavy,
of *mystères*, renamed,
submerged and sure,
riding dark waves,
floating long waves
to the other side of the water
and the other side
and the next.

Note: our ancestor Gauls: ("nos ancêtres, les Gaulois") a phrase from a French children's history text, widely used, (until recently) in Francophone Carribbean primary schools.

JAMAICA, OCTOBER 18, 1972

You tell me about the rickety truck:
your ride in back among goats or cows -
some animal I can't name now -

the water coming down your legs,
my father beside you, strumming
a slow melody of darkened skies

and winter trees he only dreamed
on his guitar. The night was cool.
That detail you rely on each time

the story is told: the one story
your memory serves us better
than my own. I doubt even that night

you considered me, as I lay inside you,
preparing to be born. So many nights
after it would be the same.

You do not remember anything,
you say, so clearly as that trip:
animal smells, guitar straining for sound,

the water between us becoming a river.

Jacqueline Joan Johnson

SAUDADES*

Caporiestas dance in la Marqueta Modelo square,
gourded sound of the berimbau,
drums sounding.
Singers spice my ears in Yoruba and Afro-Portuguese.
Coconut milk and palm oil in all my food.
The smell and taste of Angola,
salted wind on my lips my thighs.
This anago man
gives me his eye,
Bahia nightblack eye.
I samba in his trembling,
he pulls me across time.
Eats the poetry of my mouth whole.
We fly past language and gather
like tendrils of spirit.
Aboriginal reddened locks,
warm my back.
Under narrowed waist, lean and muscular
I reveal all the dances I've ever known.
We lay clean and free
as the yellow fruit of his terriro.
This Anago man
gives me his eye,
Bahia nightblack
spirit eye.

*Longings

Jerry W. Ward, Jr.

MISSISSIPPI: BELL ZONE 1

You need to know, son,
so as not to cut your mouth
the wrong way on sugarcane
or hardtack biscuits — there are
things square
as your haircut
in this world,
but what you got to believe, son,
will damn sure be round in the next.

Sometime it look to be
like that field over yonder,
a closed society of plots,
row after row after row
of grave hope, grave dreams, grave love
laid in the sun and delta dust.

Those things, son, you can't see
till the holy spirit hit you
upside the head like a baseball.
Those things, son, are our lives.

You need to know, son,
your grandfather — at any rate,
your momma and me will
something better for you;
truth be told, I don't care
if kudzu cures cancer
or the blues makes crackers
fall upon their knees in prayer
or the catfish announce themselves to be cuisine —

you need to know, son,
we won't watch you lynch
your life in hushpuppy misery.

Kenneth Carroll

FOR BROTHAS THAT LIKE TO HOLLA

have we come this far,
    bodies clung together in suffocating space
    the roaring ocean just beneath us
    our eyes fixed to stars & dreams
    & voices, calling us to eternal freedom

did we come this far
    to be desolate men, weak & samboish
    like the cracked image in a mirror of gangsta tomishness

did we survive the passage
    through fire & racist storm
    to be impotent men who steal the
    hopes of their women with
    cheap fantasies of being king pimps
    & pharaoh mack daddies

did we struggle to hold
    the rhythms of our drums in our hearts
    only to now dance to tunes sung by backward voices
    to become buck dancing niggas in republican minstrels

did we come this far
    after moonlit escapes & moonless returns
    to reclaim family, only now to surrender them
    for the momentary rush of orgasms
    & the barren caress of funky dollar bills

HOLLA AT ME
brothers, tell me the resounding truth
can we stand comfortably in our father's shadows
can we look confidently into the eyes of our mother's concern

HOLLA AT ME
if we can be men of legacy
if we can be men of boundless tomorrows
if we can be the strong men that haunt our father's poems

HOLLA AT ME
tell me if we can love our women
so faithfullly that we can truly be dangerous
can we struggle to become the men our fathers dreamed about
that our mother's tears & prayers now demand

HOLLA AT ME
brothers, like i'm standing across the street from yesterday.

Kysha N. Brown

a song for serpents

you can't help who you are born with,
but if your brother is a snake,
you should have the courage to say,
"my brother is a snake."
>   —Keorapetse Kgositsile

I.

I see you my brother
in your slimy, snakish ways
hissing unity and revolution
while your tail is wrapped
around your mother's neck
>   having forgotten the days
>   her heart was your attic

I hear even your closet talk
gang bang gossip of secret seductions
sleeping with sisters you don't respect

I must remind you
that lucifer is your slave name

relive the day
of your beautifully black
birth sacred serpent
gliding from
earth   mother womb
into a world wondering
what to do
with your serpentine smooth

shed
your shady ways
and be the new
rejuvenation
of your self

Haiti called you Damballah
crawling out of worn ways
and away from shackles
of oppression
biting your tail
and becoming
circle of life

II.

Join me brother
let us be we
a caduceus of our colony
in this oppressive land
as even the healers knew
it takes two intertwined
in body and mind
head to head
and tail to tail

we will make mistakes
being snakes trying to awaken
a revolution in our people
but we must keep trying

must glide out of and beyond
our indiscretions
and keep on pushing
must make earth
mama so proud
that she will smile rivers

and cry tributaries
inspiring our every undulation

as we
contract
as we
expand
as we
move
as we
change

Shara McCallum

YU NO SEND. ME NO COME.

The first night back and rain falls,
tinging on the aluminum roof.
Trees my tongue had forgotten
return one by one:
        breadfruit, soursop, ackee.

Bougainvillea weigh
with water, fuchsia petals drip
      in disarray.
Love, when you see me next,
      tell me I've changed.

                If we name in order to know:

                  say *apple*
                      it will taste red.

                  say *bird*
                      it will fly
                      from your mouth.

                  say *home*
                      see what stays.

In Negril, a bartender asks where I'm from.
      For the hundredth time today I answer:
          Kingston originally.

For the hundredth time I hear:
      Fi true? But yu so light.
      Yu nuh talk Jamaican.

My sister laughs, offering warning:
  Yu betta not call har no yankee gal, papa.
   She will get well vex wid yu.

Living here again,
  she has the right to say:
   Is fi she country too.

   Long time ago I learned how to mek deketch arredi grow:
   de key is to bruk off a piece fram de parent
   an plant it inna de groun.

    It will sprout up quick.
    De flower dem will come fas
    and grow same way
    as de original tree.

      Dats why it call *ketch arredi* .
      Dats why it call *never die*.

From my sister's porch, the airport stretches below me.
Beside it, sea comes in to land,
touching borders of vegetation and sand.

I search for the lizard on the nearby branch,
nearly call Renée to show her it is both there
and not there: so green, you might almost miss it.

All around me, hibiscus and banana trees
fringe the planes taking off. I wonder when they leave,
what assures them they will come down?

NUCLEAR PERIL

The lights went out
like a thrust of iron
or bone sinking in sand

The hours melt in body
This time I count them
and watch the rain drop
its pellets,   heavy as the leafless
limbs swaying downward --
orphaned waifs

      Landscape stretches
      for miles into a gray
      sky   One figure
      silhouettes the dream

Holocaust is no longer real
no longer imagined
no longer one moment
of dread   Consciousness
hangs on the sharp edge
of night   I wait
for a lingering note,
the song, the music
layered somewhere in a burial
of hills

Lost in the solitude of waiting, I dream
of color, of azaleas
of perfumed gardenias- -
Louisiana now a palmetto
uprooted in a dream
of song

             Who ravishes
this world, the future an
absence of time?   A
spiraling ball takes dominion
writing its brilliant epitaph
in a chain of fire - -

             I reach for you - -
your touch only a memory,
a space - - a center of space,
an absence of space
a song, a dance, a canvass
remembered. . . .

Carletta Carrington Wilson

history of the quilt that heaved life into stars patched, circled, stitched and square

i put my hand to the cloth
and cut and tear and pull
heat rises from the seams
fogs the kitchen table
clouds this room
till each and every window and chair
wears its veil of tears

thrust after thrust i pierce each skin
red flowers blue bruises
sleepless yellow falls across my lap
like ruth in her favorite dress
will in the garden hoeing
john allen chasing after rainbows and cats

these clothes have done their duty
covered our nakedness
pocketed our sorrows
buttoned our joys
strode with us as days opened
then closed across our hearts
like morning glories

i put my hand to their living breath
and sew, sew our lives together
sew till i can't tell where ruth ends
or john allen begins
all the while will fiddlin'
that old black dog beside him growin' meaner
than what i done chewed and spat

when this mornin's light is done
make us whole
make us one cloth
one quilt whose heaviness is no burden to bear
shelter us in the sanctuary of night
bed us in the comfort of days
let us sleep without a sorrowing cold
stealin' into our soul

S. *Pearl Sharp*

HOW TO BUILD A PRAYER

(Notes from a dialog with sculptor and philosopher John Outterbridge, 1995)

1.
With a metal paring knife
I flick the sable seeds from the
ruby meat of sun warmed watermelon
As each falls to its place on the
graveled earth
some distant cousin in Zanzibar
cracks the ruby
eats the seed
and blesses himself.

Swinging the red rind through water
He writes in the river
    the river running through us
    the river
      ancient dog tag
      indentifying us to each other
And his words push through the pavement
to lick my toes like
a tongue come to deliver urgency
On the bottom of my foot I read
"To get inside the watermelon
you have to eat the seed.
Go inside
and look at what we
ask of ourselves."
    And his voice
the river running through us
    river running through us
    river running through us
becomes thought

We harmonize in cerebration,
compelled to create a prayer.

To inherit its blueprint
We beg favor with
supplication as heady as palm wine
        and Georgia clay
invocation as gorgeous as
        thunder and dew
petitions made of cowrie shells
        and my mother's tears
and when the Spirits turn an ear to us
we implore,
Help us build a prayer?

The Spirits
taunt us with stares
tickle our toenails
and mock our absurdity.
        Every moment is a prayer,
        Take what you need
        and build it yourself
        Take what you need
        and build it yourself.

Their leaving is fire
fire red like the ruby that wet my lips
fire orange like the orb that bronzes my skin
fire blue like
                the river that connects me and you
                the river that brands me and you
                the river that sings me and you
The petition falls back on us as
ash and ash
the ash is pure
the ash is white
I bathe my face in it
set out to
gather what I need.

2.

A young woman who knows no rest
because she has no bed
dangles grief on her ankle
like a charm bracelet of broken wings.
I cross her crown with ash
take her pain to make glue
Angry for her absent pain
she begs me leave it
So I take her anger
and it chills me.
An old child
with eyes of mortar
asks questions
without words   I give
answers without solutions
the eyes scatch me
for my inadequacy
I close them and
drop them in my pocket.

A man who knows no peace
because he can find no war
flings laughter against bricks
It flies back to him as
a heartbeat
I unwrap it and find water
and bathe his voice.

In the midnight hour
my sister Olokun carries my feet to
the foot of an olive tree
Yemonja brings sweat
which rolls through me and
softens the earth
Jan raps the rhythm of the work
and I kneed them
        the eyes like mortar
        the laughter like water

the anger like broken wings
knead them with my hands and dreams
until the earth opens to them
    the earth
    foundation of all praise songs
    the earth
    womb of all supplication
    the moist soil
transforms them into song
and some distant cousin in Paramaribo
hears the song and sings it.
I follow the voice the
    river running through us
    river running through us
    river running through us
to the ocean bed
the bed where
there has been no sleep
    since Goreé,
been no sleep
    since Elmina Castle
no sleep
    since Angola
and beg for the singer.

        3.

She comes
comes on feet ancient as sand and sorrow
she is
the daughter of the child with old eyes
she is
the mother of the man without laughter
she is
the son of the woman with no bed
she extends holy ghost arms to me, and we
    dance
    dance
    we
mambo to the swish of falling sugar cane
    dance

waltz to the clank of coffle chains
    dance
boogie to the slap of blood-tipped whips
    dance
line dance on the beat of burning coals
    dance
    dance
she calls for Lamba
and ancestors rise
lift arms
rise,
rise and stomp cries
that become
filaments for the
bricks of a prayer
This is no amazing grace
be clear about this:
never grace that
littered this bed
where there has been no sleep
    since Goreé,
been no sleep
    since Angola
no sleep
    since Dahomey
    since Somaliland
    since Mauritius
and the dance is ritual
and the ritual is revelation
    of why we need a prayer at all

Every ritual is a prayer
every prayer is a moment
every moment is a ritual
understand how important moments are.

    4.

They are drawn to the prayer
like magnets to metal
boasting its beauty

while secreting the question
that falls out of their eyes:
But to whom do we pray?
The caw caw copies
But to whom do we pray?
The drummer gives the question wing
But to whom do we pray?

And the prayer answers
Pray to yourselves.
The vision has carriage,
Pray to yourselves,
You ask the earth for its food
      the river for its song
     the drum for its dance
    the moon for its ritual
   the plant for its seed
What do you ask of yourselves?
You are
the vision,
the song,
the note,
the dance,
the ritual,
the fire,
the seed.

ritual
prayer
moment
go inside
reconstruct
what we ask of ourselves.

Carole Boston Weatherford

FROM THE MOUTH OF THE GXARA

Inkomo luhlanga, zifile luyakufa uhlanga.
Cattle are the race; they being dead, the race dies.
—Xhosa proverb

Though the Xhosa owned the coast,
they cast neither line nor net and launched
no craft upon the waves
that brought the English there.
The seer's niece was chasing birds
from cornfields near the river's mouth
when the current conjured men long dead,
presaging resurrection. She drank
their words as if palm wine. *Return
to the kraal*, they said. *Cease
sowing, kill the cattle, empty the corn bins,
scatter the grain, abandon witchcraft.*
Obedient, the seer slayed one beast daily,
as did the people. When the omen reached
the Paramount Chief, he was bereft
of father, sons and herd. Counting on
Crimeans to prevail, he enlarged the vision,
issued an edict: Spare no beast—
neither hallowed ox nor bride price.
From his Great Place, he looked beyond
the songless twilight, past silent, starving
hordes toward the August moon
when the faithful in white blankets
would watch two rising suns collide
and make the sea a road to damnation,
Englishmen marching down in droves.
Ears to the ground, the people heard
new cattle bellowing inside the earth;

and along the horizon, saw new people
bobbing in the water. But the Day
of Darkness did not arrive. Instead,
hunger became the darkness,
the prophesy soured in gullets empty
as milk sacks; new world built on bones.

Note: In May 1856, a Xhosa girl saw a vision demanding cattle sacrifice
for her tribe's salvation. The Xhosa heeded the prophesy and
awaited the arrival of new people and new herds and the departure of the British
settlers from South Africa. This was perhaps the greatest self-inflicted immolation of
a people in all history.

Doreen Baingana

THE SONG TO COME

I.

The endless curve of sky
cradled a dip of land
carved out of high jagged mountains
creating a lush green sink
full of the Small People.

Their mouths were full of songs
that rang clear as dawn
as they tended their garden valley.

This was a vast place in the mind called Peace.

Nothing ruffled the summer calm
except rainbow birds' feathers
fluttering light.
Nothing moved in time
but song,
high and clear around the crater,
bouncing from tree to tree,
echoing to the skies.

In this flower of life a Word
arose and reverberated among the people.
Their songs were shattered silent
by this strange flat sound,
a word spoken:
"No!"

As tiny ants rustled
among tangerine colored leaves,
in the stealthy scurry of red-black beetles,
the bitter word pierced through:

"No!"

Hoes hung mid-air.
Small groups formed, mingled, broke.
Faces froze in doubt and confusion.
Apprehension. Fear.
No?

A gaunt man stumbled down the slope,
his mouth open; a huge crack of O.
His stick struck the ground in stunned mono-sounds,
his sweat stung old, bitter tales,
his eyes melted colorless,
blinded by the valley's shine.

His mind was lost
in the treacherous 'No'that he spat out
to tear it out of existence.
Instead, he spilt it all over
the valley's green grace.

II.

The innocent ones realigned themselves,
grasping for each other to protect minds
scraped raw by the screeching, howling word.
They thought to shield their children
from the underside of the truth:
what was strange and smothered.

Yes, the small people knew
that deep inside each one
was the Voice of All.

They had learnt to sing as they sat in circles
round the fire of existence
sharing each other.
No one questioned the fire's source or essence:
it was.
No one imagined an ending,
all they lived, tasted, was renewal.

They had heard birds compose anthems
to an audience of clouds
with their wings:
flapping, floating, sinking deep
into the blind comfort of hanging air.

Wild quivering tunes
borne by the hopeful wind
that sprayed gentle heat
on their startlingly fresh faces.

Families beaded verses into multicolored strings of songs;
lullabies, love songs, choruses for work, for marches,
for naming the brother animals and sister plants,
tunes telling of the wonderful never-ending
meandering of the imagination;
the ringing of gratitude bells.

The small ones sang the comforts of fire,
the redness of life,
of blood that richly soaked the ground
when a new one joined their garden choir.

The innocent moaned with dogs in dark blue nights,
trying to touch the moon;
crying in wonder to the brushing wind
that escaped to seek out new places;
showering scent, then leaving.

Thus, "No" was dreadfully strange.
It hinted vaguely at bitter possibilities,
of the unknown;
of unresponsive, jarring replies.
No sounded the opposite of opposite,
the other side of beyond,
the hard grasp of nothing.

The man's mouth was stuck painfully open.
A wide "O" of emptiness.
A lacking.

The younger children, curious
yet innocent of fear, came up to him.
He stumbled helplessly toward them.
They did what they had been taught:
they blessed him with his own song.

He did not, he would not understand.

Lush women
heavy with health and fruitfulness,
with henna-red hair wrapped
mightily towards heaven,
slapped their thighs with pity,
clasped hands over ears
to shut out, to halt his eerie hollowness.

The women pleaded in high notes to the open sky
to juice this dry apparition
the image of flatness,
the unreflecting.

Men reached for the stranger's face
to mold 'No' out of his mouth.
They massaged his throat
to coax out smooth sound: a song.
"No!"

He was blocked
by an utterable blankness.
"No!" he said.
"No!" was all he could say.
His voice cracked like a whip on skin.

Where was this dead branch torn from?
What bleak tree?
Who was this mistake of creation?
This tear?

III.

In that blank moment,
a long wail spiraled up the crater slopes
from a closeting circle of thorn trees
that was home to the Mother of Mothers.
Out crawled a ball of bones and flesh,
layers of fat and smiles,
wrinkles counting years of wisdom,
deep chuckles of song.

Out flowed their Time Keeper, their Flower Head,
The Big Child who was ever, yet never
child, woman or bird,
but a sliver of the Source;
the Eternal Anthem.

She was the Black Sweetness of Song,
the Seed held warm in their hands,
their hopes alive
and bounding from yesterday's story;
She was the old breath of memory.

The carrier of the smoke of dreams,
summer grain for long winters.
She opened the sky's curtain each dawn
and sang the sunset to sleep at night.

Motherlove called the children to her folding flesh,
and painted rainbow songs on their soft bellies.
She held heat safe
and made love out of laughter
for the future of her people.

The Small Ones
parted a highway in the dust for her.
She moved in, as a dream,
sprinkling the dry confusion
with lavender drops of peace.

She spoke.

She had journeyed out of the crater, across time,
visited the mountains of the dead,
and come back to her children.
She knew 'No', had fought with it.
She could see the stranger's birthplace,
how treacherous his desert.

Only she could wrest with sorrow
and teach him how to sing,
while still holding her people within her.

IV.

She gathered the small ones close
and then melodiously, powerfully let lose the legend
of the visitation of words and their meaning.

Transforming song into separate syllables,
She painfully birthed a new story.

She sang of how, with garlands of words,
they could pass on the secrets of their blood
stored from hand to hand held tight,
to be ripely exposed to the sunlight
of new days, new ways, new notes of expression.

She would teach them to bear
the weight of words spoken,
to slowly savor the strange stutter of tongues
that captured syllables and clenched accents,
letting all loose in resounding vowels
consonantly.

They would wind up sentences with elastic pauses,
cut down, chop up, and grind words
into nuanced meaning.
Save the letters that fell out in protest
to weave bead necklaces of flowing saga
fermented in longing and loneliness.

Aaaahh but what blues and terror "No"
could let loose, would let loose,

if flung around like hard hailstones
in an abused season!
This "No" in bitter bubbles
would burst into bloodfalls of lies,
of theft, banal tears, mad hungers.

Motherlove cried against the negative clamor for gain,
of the harsh numbers to follow this one man,
tracing his lineage down trails of loss
forming ice-worlds of planned anarchy.

She bellowed out the need to stand ready.
To fight speech sometimes, staying supple,
to close the fist tight to hide old birthsongs.

Sweet Mother ordered the capture of 'No',
They must boldly break down its stony stanza,
unsnarl "No," then embrace it.
Decipher it.

To continue the dance of clarity
between sky and earth, whirling.

Later, much later, the no longer innocent would question
and turn away from verses grown mouldy
and tired with doubt.
They would cautiously, painfully
pull out a new 'No'
from keen ears, strong bellies, brave eyes,
laboring virgin brews of fiery contention.

This open quest would test anchored elders
but feed the redwood trees of knowledge,
spewing new ballads
entwining dance, mud, rich talk, the void
into open theater, children's play.

V.

The children, overwhelmed, sobbed fear.
Innocence scattered into black holes of danger.

528

They saw their people with the No-man's blindness
and struck, hid raw faces
from the harsh, skewing light.
Their minds, still soft, little flowerbuds,
opened to sensations of refusal
that courted cursed poison bees of retaliation.

Wild women shook loose vibrant rivers of hair,
coughed down choked tears.
Men hammered anger into cracking ground,
shocking up clouds of shrieking birds.

The stranger was struck flat by the wild alarm.
Motherlove wrapped him in her sagging folds,
sucked him under.

The valley became one anguished shout of thunder.
Great Mother answered with swords of lightening,
her stinging chants cutting through the chaos.
It sank to limpid heaves, stifled sniffs;
a slow death of sound.

The Grand Mother faced her people,
who stood stiff and watching.
She reached out both arms wide,
flung her fierce face to the sky
calling to the mystery magnificent:

> "We shall venture ceaselessly
> beyond this virgin cradle
> singing, seeking out every sign
> of the Word—

"Listen, listen!"

Lori Tsang

lunching

the abiku-child,
ernesto, is still
talking about going back
to his roots. but the workshop
is over: we've floated
down frank o'hara's stream
of consciousness; explained
to brian that the "adams"
in brandon's poem is ansel,
not sam; now, it's already three
o'clock and none of us have
eaten yet. joel says he's
hungry as a motherfucker—
even though he just
scarfed down three
donuts and a bag of chips
ahoy cookies—
and so am i.

everybody starts talking
about food: ben's
chili-cheeseburgers washed
down with grape nehi; greens
from muhammad ali's; new, upscale
joints like b. smith's
and georgia brown's; smothered
ribs, macaroni and cheese,
fried chicken, real
mashed potatoes — food
their grandma's
used to fix.

so now i'm wanting
those falling-off-the-bone
kind of ribs like i used
to get at the florida
avenue grill before
they got busted
for running a fencing
operation. fat curls
of macaroni that're baked,
not the kind you make
out of a box. they all want
to go eat at daddy
grace over at seventh
and m, and i am so
hungry, when we get there,
i want to devour everything,
the way i gobbled
up james baldwin and toni
morrison long before i knew
about maxine hong
kingston or frank
chin.

our food comes,
and i start shoveling
stuff into my mouth.
everything tastes
so good –– they have
the smoky, peppery
kind of greens i like,
and the cornbread is sweet,
but not too sweet,
the way some of those
southern folks like it.
then, i start thinking
about chicken and waffles
at the vietnamese
chinese joint on tenth
and f, fried fish
on fridays, no — flounder

steamed with ginger
and scallions at li ho's
in chinatown, won ton mein
at full kee, see yau
gai — homefood
i never grew up with,
but learned to crave watching
other chinese eat, practiced
forming my mouth around
the sounds, but never getting
the tones right.

scooping rice
from a twenty-five
pound sack, sucking
the scent through lungs
into my bloodstream, lifting
the lid of the rice cooker — sweet
smell of rice, fragrant
rice, filling the house — i finally
understand. but when i was little,
i always wanted to eat mashed
potatoes with our meatloaf
like everybody else,
not rice, always
rice. and now i want rice
and peas, like my mom's
sisters fix, with coconut
milk and fatback, curry
goat, oxtail, fricassee
chicken, stew peas
and rice.

but daddy grace
ain't got no curry
goat, just a pile
of sucked-off rib
bones sitting
on my plate
next to a little
puddle of pot

liquor to soak
up with my last
bite of cornbread.
and i am full,
so full, but still
so hungry. sweet
potato pie, peach
cobbler, coffee
hot and black, like
bo lay cha, i want
it all, and i am still eating
and eating ——
i can never
get enough.

E.Juaquina Watkins-Cothran

THE BELOVED ONES

yours is a journey everlasting
for the soles of your feet
have touched upon the soul of history
your dreams are
in tune with psalms
spirituals and talking drums
those gone before you
embodied a free spirit
one often tested
but never enslaved
they suffered displacement
now the future foretold
begins again
in each renewed breath
of the dream.

swinging doors of knocking-wood cowards

8

for us

for us who sometimes fly in dreams,
speaking a dialect of eye language.
sustained thought, a reflective neck,
caught in the curve of time. a road,
not starting nor stopping. who is
witness to this whole? i know you
don't always remember when it's
me in the morning with the sun and
the purple, knocking, knocking,
knocking. me in the morning saying
prayers for the flyers who remain
in dreams speaking, speaking eye.

Gigi Maria Ross

AT THE THRESHOLD OF THE MOON

We think of you before dawn.
We know you are there
on that farther side of longing, light.
We dive into the depths that lead
to your night, aim for your air,
eat nothing, float on nothing.
On the fourth day, we surface, breathe,
bathe our bodies in your sands.
Silent, in cold dark, we stand.
Here, for the first time,
we lift our heads and wonder.

Amitiyah Elayne Hyman

SURRENDER

Come to me God
I surrender.

Pull me under You.
Slip Your arms
Beneath my back
Stretch me out
On sheets of faith.
Pillow my turned up head
In thoughts of You.
Split my legs
In wide openess
Let me writhe,
Squirm,
Sweat
Ooze
Your overdue entrance.

Come to me God.
I surrender.

Have Your way with me.
Take off my gown of doubt
Ride my resistance
Tangle my hair
Rear up on my shoulders
Push into me
Bear down on me
Soft squeeze me
Into Your image.
Smooth circle Your hands
Over my belly
Seed me with Your will.

E. Ethelbert Miller

MORNING BUDDHISM

In the yard
dead leaves
from last night's winds

I sweep small twigs
and branches into a pile

in the house
everyone is sleeping

on a table a cup filled
with tea and honey

the newspaper sections
scattered across the
floor

POEMS BY TITLE

Title	Last Name	First Name	Page
'7-30-96	Kelly	Erren Geraud	155
(1/vacant)	Bomani	Nadir Lasana	395
100 Million	Watley	Matthew	478
100 Times	Kemp	Arnold J.	187
1619. Virginia	Jackson	Gale P.	17
1691. Tituba of Salem	Jackson	Gale P.	18
1st Lt. John R. Fox: Rain of Fire	Asim	Jabari	293
1st Lt. Vernon J. Baker: Hero on the Hill	Asim	Jabari	287
a black soldier	Moore	Lenard D.	304
A Debt is Paid	Jordan	A. Van	80
A Guard	Frazier	John	285
a song for serpents	Brown	Kysha N.	505
A Streetwalker Trying to Speak{....}	Upton	Elaine Maria	484
A Thousand Marionettes	March	Sydney	243
A White Man and the Judge	Simmonds	Kevin	257
African Morning	okantah	mwatabu s.	492
African Sunrunner	Winbush-David	Wanda	48
After an All Day Skirmish with the Clouds	Goodwin	Eli	143
After the 200th White Person Locks Her Car{....}	Jacobs	Bruce A.	3
Alley Games 6/the ascension	Jones	Ira B.	253
American Sonnet (46)	Coleman	Wanda	124
An Irresistible Light	Phaire	Dorothy	168
Anacaona	Georges	Danielle Legros	495
And all the sisters said...	Hisle	Janeya K.	336
And the Birds Sing of Life	Wright	Stephen Caldwell	455
angry sisters	Nickelson	Christopher	337
Annuals and Perennials	Hodges	Janice W.	109
another day	King	Rosamond S.	69
Another Ode to Salt	Georges	Danielle Legros	498
April 19, 19—: A Sonnet	Clarke	George Elliott	170
As Dancers	Teasley	Lisa	220
As from a Quiver of Arrows	Phillips	Carl	463
Ashy Gal	Lukata	Baba	360
Astrology?	Jean	Valerie	194
At Five	Oktavi		65
At the Jackson Pollock Retrospective in L.A.	Johnson	Harold L.	298
At the Threshold of the Moon	Ross	Gigi Maria	536
Audre's Son	Frazier	John	164
back road	Keita	Nzadi Zimele	329
Back to the Blues	Barnes	S. Brandi	406
Baltimore	Weaver	Afaa Michael S.	145
Barrage	Garnett	Ruth-Miriam	12

541

Title	Last Name	First Name	Page
Beaches	Robbins	Zak	106
Bird	Cherry	James E.	223
Black Drag Queen	Jordan	A. Van	89
Black on Black	Jacobs	Bruce A.	125
black tax	Keita	Nzadi Zimele	282
Black Women with Jewish Names	Coleman	James	428
Blackbottom	Derricotte	Toi	144
Blood	Radden	Viki	434
Blue	Phillips	Carl	56
Born	Glover	Yao (Hoke S. III)	8
Bound	Norton	Odetta D.	15
Boy at the Paterson Falls	Derricotte	Toi	81
Brother is a Star	Harding	Rachel E.	156
Brown Bomber	Cornish	Sam	450
Bruised Children	Hodges	Janice W.	171
Burn Rubber On Me	X	Derrick (Goldie Williams)	238
Call and Response	Renegade	D. J.	157
Can We Talk?	Mataka	Laini	370
charleston, south carolina	Nickelson	Christopher	132
Child in the New Delhi Sun	McDowell	Garrett	148
Chittlin's	Eady	Cornelius	228
Christmas Eve: My Mother Dressing	Derricotte	Toi	95
Circumcising Pandora	Jean-Giles	Mirlande	24
City in You	Hill	Michael	119
Color-Struck	Weaver	Afaa Michael S.	323
Come and See My Little Toys	Shephard	S.P.	306
coming to the net	Gilmore	Brian	442
Concerning Violence	Garnett	Ruth-Miriam	251
Confession	Goodwin	Eli	456
Control	Hodges	Janice W.	418
cornbread blues	Woodward	Vincent	368
Cross Burning Black	Howard, Jr.	Willie Abraham	210
Crushin	StacyLynn		420
Cycles	Keita	Nzadi Zimele	349
Daniel's Hands	Williams	Niama Leslie	367
December 12th	Robbins	Zak	255
dedicated to the domestics	Keita	Nzadi Zimele	192
defensive driving	singleton	giovanni	30
Deposed	Frazier	John	392
Dirt	StacyLynn		142
Dr. Jack	Stanley	Thomas	245
Dream of mango	Preston	Rohan B.	28
Drifter	Nelson	Marilyn	75

Title	Last Name	First Name	Page
Examination	StacyLynn		256
Exits from Elmina Castle: Cape Coast, Ghana	Derricotte	Toi	4
Ezili Impending	Harding	Rachel E.	473
Fallen Bodies	Ferebee	Gideon	327
Father and Son	Renegade	D. J.	183
father country	jess	tyehimba	185
father's shoes	jess	tyehimba	184
Finished Poem	Greene	Michelle Calhoun	377
Fire/Water Blues	Stover	Darrell	375
fisher king	Tolliver	Imani	374
For Brothas That Like to Holla	Carroll	Kenneth	503
For Fatma and her Co-wives	Hisle	Janeya K.	340
for lester	Timpson	Reggie	222
for my 27th birthday	singleton	giovanni	78
For My D.C. Girlfriends	Greene	Michelle Calhoun	378
For My Mother	Ferebee	Gideon	326
For My Mother	Harris	Duriel E.	324
For the Man I Met on Georgia Ave.	Watley	Matthew	176
Four and Twenty Soldiers	Shephard	S.P.	305
Friendly Skies	Jacobs	Bruce A.	335
From the Mouth of the Gxara	Weatherford	Carole Boston	520
From the Spirit of Phillis Wheatley {....}	Williams	Karen	19
fruitbowl 1	Wilson	Imani e.	90
Funeral	Lilley	Gary	275
Gale Sayers	Coates	Ta-Nehisi	448
Generation Gap	Pertillar	Tammy Lynn	273
Gentleman at the Barbershop	Barnes	S. Brandi	87
Girlfriend	Tsang	Lori	316
Glass Box Puzzle No. 1	Baldwin	André J.	254
Going Home	Burwell	Toneka N. Bonitto	130
Gone	Forbes	Calvin	21
Grand Canyon	Farley	Estelle E.	365
Grand Diva	Shiphrah	Thandiwe	330
Grandma	Shiphrah	Thandiwe	332
Gullah Women	Lewis	Melvin E.	136
H E L P	King	Rosamond S.	67
Haiku	Brinson	C. Yaphet	36
haiku # 135	Ya Salaam	Kalamu	364
Haiku for My Brothers	Jones	Ira B.	468
Hands	Shannon	Angela	352
Harvest	Wright	Stephen Caldwell	27
Hazing	Gilmore	Brian	181
Hearts	Lewis	Melvin E.	384

Title	Last Name	First Name	Page
High School	Derricotte	Toi	207
history of the quilt{....}	Wilson	Carletta	512
Home Cookin	Farley	Estelle E.	366
Homeless Vets	Shephard	S.P.	307
How to Build a Prayer	Sharp	S. Pearl	514
How to Make It	Jackson	Yvonne A.	161
Hues of Electric Blue	Morgenstern	Felicia L.	427
I Am a Creature of the Obvious	Mason	Keith Antar	41
i am open	datcher	michael	474
I know I Aint Hip No More	Harris	Peter J.	91
I Love You, Though You're Unemployed	Hannaham	Dawn L.	259
I watched	Williams	Kimmika L.H.	396
If Harriet Tubman Were Alive Today	Lights	Verneda (Rikki)	22
If there's no sugar	Hannaham	Dawn L.	260
Imani's Song	Morris	Alison	419
Imperialism - The Dancing Do Not Die	Stanley	Thomas	268
In Oklahoma	Lightfoot	Toni Asante	281
In Search of Aunt Jemima	Williams	Crystal	97
In This, the Fifth World	Vest	Jennifer Lisa	383
Integration	Shannon	Angela	141
Interpretations	Lukata	Baba	371
Invisibles	Braxton	Joanne M.	10
It's a Dog's Life	Jacobs	Bruce A.	165
Jamaica, October 18, 1972	McCallum	Shara	499
jesus'song	louise	esther	436
John Birks Gillespie: an appreciation {....}	Goodwin	Everett	225
JoNelle	Shannon	Angela	138
Just Asking	Rux	Carl Hancock	457
Just Say No Blues	Morris	Tracie	388
Keep a Good Thought	Keller	Bernard	470
kiss her that she don't know how	Wilson	Carletta	372
Land of the Lost	Porter	Charles	118
Landmarks	Wilkinson	Claude	77
Leaving Winston-Salem	Burwell	Toneka N. Bonitto	131
Legacy	March	Sydney	46
lessons in lying	Keita	Nzadi Zimele	413
Letter from Kuwait	Moore	Lenard D.	303
Licorice	Mataka	Laini	369
Lights of the Bigtop	McDowell	Garrett	309
Lines	Weaver	Afaa Michael S.	358
Locks	Dawson	Joy	32
lookin good	StacyLynn		460
Lost	Jacobs	Bruce A.	147

Title	Last Name	First Name	Page
Love Song of a Red Cap	Cornish	Sam	76
Lover's Total Recall	Morris	Tracie	387
Loving	Jackson	Angela	429
Lunching	Tsang	Lori	530
market day	okantah	mwatabu s.	493
Mary, Don't You Weep	Jeffers	Honoree F.	483
Matisse, Cut Outs	Johnson	Trasi	199
Meditations I	Harris	Duriel E.	52
Meetin the Conjure Woman	Lilley	Gary	350
Memorial	Gill	Charmaine A.	37
Memorial Drive	Howard, Jr.	Willie Abraham	127
Memory of Wings	Asim	Jabari	38
Meridian Hill Terrace	Walters	Wendy S.	153
Michele	Weaver	Afaa Michael S.	64
Midnight	Hayes	Terrance	359
Midnight in Mississippi	Hamilton	M. Eliza	175
Mississippi on the Doorstep	Cornish	Sam	111
Mississippi: Bell Zone 1	Ward, Jr.	Jerry W.	501
Mom Used to Listen to Erroll Garner	Goodwin	Everett	224
Moment	Jackson	Angela	437
Monk	Neal	Gaston	230
Monk's Misterioso	March	Sydney	231
Moon Daughters	White	Artress Bethany	195
Moons...tides	Baldwin	André J.	45
More Than Anything	Baingana	Doreen	416
Morning Buddhism	Miller	E. Ethelbert	538
Mother's Day at McDonald's	Elam	Patricia	178
My Family	Miller	Nyere-Gibran	177
My Mother	Lewis	Melvin E.	133
my sleeping husband	Keita	Nzadi Zimele	397
Negroes	Watley	Matthew	445
Nice Sister-Scholars Need Loving, Too	Jackson	David Earl	424
Noon Talk at Georgia's Coffee Shop	Joseph	Allison	236
Nuclear Peril	Lane	Pinkie Gordon	510
Obessions are Important	St. John	Primus	421
Objects of Desire	Love	Monifa A.	59
October 7th	Robbins	Zak	467
october death	Leeke	Kiamsha Madelyn	465
One Million Men Marching II.	Keller	Bernard	469
One More Once	jackson	reuben	417
Our Mothers	Hope	Melanie	319
Our Second Night	Radden	Viki	300
Paralyzed	Howard, Jr.	Willie Abraham	189

545

Title	Last Name	First Name	Page
Passing	Phillips	Carl	196
Passing through This House	Glover	Yao (Hoke S. III)	57
Peace Be Still	Iverem	Esther	120
Perspective	Pegram	Lisa	379
Photo by Ron Carter, playing his bass	Eady	Cornelius	239
Poem # 3	Roberts	Sybil J.	398
Poem for the Purchase of a First Bra	Joseph	Allison	62
Port Townsend Poems	Lane	Pinkie Gordon	33
Praise the Daughter	Hope	Melanie	472
Praisesong: From Son to Mother	Moore	Lenard D.	26
Prelude to a Kiss	Morris	Tracie	389
Pretty White Girls	Cherry	James E.	86
Private Thoughts	Wray	Clyde A.	356
Rain Making	Gilkes	Dana	202
Raindrop Women	Tallie	Mariahadessa	99
Refugee	Ferebee	Gideon	44
Rehersal	Lukata	Baba	252
Returning the Water	Shannon	Angela	40
Revolutionary Thoughts	Williams	Crystal	93
Ride Me Baby, Ride Me	Morgenstern	Felicia L.	426
Rising	Keita	Nzadi Zimele	348
Roots	Bomani	mawiyah kai el-jamah	88
roots I: {....}	Floyd-Miller	Cherryl	410
roots II: the conjure woman replies	Floyd-Miller	Cherryl	411
Saints	Williams	Lana C.	160
Saudades	Johnson	Jacqueline Joan	500
Savannah Brass	Lights	Verneda (Rikki)	240
Say Something: a Change Is Gonna Come	Umoja	Mbali	277
Sea Shells	Lowe	Lorna	477
Senegal Sestina	Norton	Odetta D.	49
Set Piece	Baker, Jr.	Houston A.	242
Sex	Radden	Viki	430
Sextet	Brinson	C. Yaphet	404
Shame of the Writers' Conference	Joseph	Allison	447
she kneels at the wailing wall	Floyd-Miller	Cherryl	321
She-Ghosts of Tiresias	Hand	Monica A.	211
Sin, 1969	Weaver	Afaa Michael S.	357
Smile	jackson	reuben	113
Snapshot: West Philly	Williams	Kimmika L.H.	158
Soledad	Glover	Yao (Hoke S. III)	152
Some Solace, Some Yearning	Lewis	William Henry	280
Something Terrible Something	Cornish	Sam	85
Sorrow Song	Frazier	John	286

Title	Last Name	First Name	Page
Soul Roots	Morgenstern	Felicia L.	16
Space	Lights	Verneda (Rikki)	204
Spirit of the Dancer	Johnson	Lisa Elaine	219
Staff. Sgt. Edward A. Carter, Jr.{....}	Asim	Jabari	290
Sterling Brown	Palmer	Ronald D.	198
Stevie Wonder	Chapman	Lyn'elle Patrice	234
Storm	Johnson	Brandon D.	481
Stranger	Bryant	Tisa	415
Stranger at Home	Lee	James R.	494
Stranger in the Village	Williams	Lorelei	200
Stringbeans	Lindsey	Kay	354
Suicides and Fools	Shephard	S.P.	308
Sunday	Shannon	Angela	129
Surrender	Hyman	Amitiyah Elayne	537
swinging doors of knocking-wood{....}	louise	esther	535
taboo	Floyd-Miller	Cherryl	412
Tattoo, or Henna	Norton	Odetta D.	51
Tattooed Girl	Hand	Monica A.	209
Temple of Your Familiar	Morgenstern	Felicia L.	425
The Artifice of War	Johnson	Brandon D.	272
The Beelzebub Chronicles	White	Artress Bethany	353
The Beloved Ones	Watkins-Cothran	E. Juaguina	534
The Bible Buckle	Caldwell	Rozell	159
the black experience	okantah	mwatabu s.	486
The Edge	Jamal	Paul	261
The Fitting Room	Jackson	Angela	116
The Fourth Supreme	Joseph	Allison	232
The Good Ole Days	Washington	Harriet Wilkes	258
The Knockout	March	Sydney	451
The Lock and Key	Asservero	Vicki-Ann	215
The Long Walk Home	Fleming	Robert	328
The Love of Travellers	Jackson	Angela	112
The Major	Keller	Bernard	180
The Mighty Blood	Vessup	A. Anthony	235
The Museum Cashier	Harvey	Yona Camille	190
The Names of Summer: A War Memory	Johnson	Harold L.	295
The New Sestina	Simmonds	Kevin	381
The Next Malcolm Poem	Harris	Peter J.	446
The Plea	Forbes	Calvin	315
The Prayer of Miss Budd	Nelson	Marilyn	73
The Science of Forgetting	Glover	Yao (Hoke S. III)	213
The Song to Come	Baingana	Doreen	522
The Star	Wray	Clyde A.	355

Title	Last Name	First Name	Page
The Tar Baby on the Soapbox	Weatherford	Carole Boston	105
The Woman Who Jumped	Hamilton	M. Eliza	14
Thelonius	Weaver	Afaa Michael S.	229
thermometer	singleton	giovanni	29
They Do Not Have to Nest in Your Hair	Joyner	Carolyn	201
Things No One Told Me	Adisa	Opal Palmer	139
this mortal coil	Fleming	Robert	311
those I love are sometimes white	Tolliver	Imani	188
Thoughts from a 747	Gilkes	Dana	203
three men	Nickelson	Christopher	338
Threnody	Ya Salaam	Kalamu	149
To a Flasher	Hannaham	Dawn L.	376
to adam	Shiphrah	Thandiwe	331
To Keep from Shouting Something	Jeffers	Honoree F.	317
To the People of a Small Town in Ohio...	Lewis	William Henry	103
Trying to Sleep After Studying Color Photos{....}	Love	Monifa A.	9
Untitled	Arrington	Lauren Anita	394
Untitled	Goodwin	Eli	122
Untitled	Nickelson	Christopher	339
Untitled One	Booth	Kwan	444
verbal gun shots	Timpson	Reggie	244
Vipers, Flies, and Women of the Cloth	Coleman	James	249
Visiting Hours	Frazier	John	250
Vivian, Take 57	Jacobs	Bruce A.	107
Voudou Mama	Bomani	mawiyah kai el-jamah	409
Walking On: A Declaration of Wholeness	Khali	Saddi	82
Washboard Wizard	Nelson	Marilyn	70
We	Hisle	Janeya K.	134
Wet Oak	Shannon	Angela	351
what does a man do	jess	tyehimba	361
What I Am	Hayes	Terrance	101
what is left	Keita	Nzadi Zimele	283
What is There for Us?	Johnson	Jacqueline Joan	341
What My Mother Taught Me	McCallum	Shara	471
When Africa Speaks	Okpala	Jude Chudi	47
When I Leave My Body	Preston	Rohan B.	462
when you say no	Murphy	Merilene M.	408
When you Talk that Talk	Radden	Viki	432
While Communing with a Tree {....}	Hamilton	M. Eliza	333
white	Wilson	Ronaldo V.	54
Who Sez Thunderbirds Can't Fly	Lilley	Gary	266
Why I Don't Leave the Apartment{....}	Ya Salaam	Kalamu	362
Why I Won't Wear a Tatoo	Morris	Tracie	386

Title	Last Name	First Name	Page
Work to be Done	Cornish	Sam	115
Worry All the Time	Morris	Alison	172
Yellow is Me, But all The Same Are We	Adams	Joan	167
yet another epiphany	Pegram	Lisa	390
Yu no send. Me no come.	McCallum	Shara	508
Zoning	Braxton	Joanne M.	441

POEMS BY AUTHOR

Last Name	First Name	Title	Page
Adams	Joan	Yellow is Me, But all The Same Are We	167
Adisa	Opal Palmer	Things No One Told Me	139
Arrington	Lauren Anita	Untitled	394
Asim	Jabari	1st Lt. John R. Fox: Rain of Fire	293
Asim	Jabari	1st Lt. Vernon J. Baker: Hero on the Hill	287
Asim	Jabari	Memory of Wings	38
Asim	Jabari	Staff. Sgt. Edward A. Carter, Jr.{....}	290
Asservero	Vicki-Ann	The Lock and Key	215
Baingana	Doreen	More Than Anything	416
Baingana	Doreen	The Song to Come	522
Baker, Jr.	Houston A.	Set Piece	242
Baldwin	André J.	Glass Box Puzzle No. 1	254
Baldwin	André J.	Moons...tides	45
bandele	asha	the subtle art of breathing	262
Barnes	S. Brandi	Back to the Blues	406
Barnes	S. Brandi	Gentleman at the Barbershop	87
Bell	Eddie D.	Help is a Discotheque	221
Bomani	Nadir Lasana	(1/vacant)	395
Bomani	mawiyah kai el-jamah	Roots	88
Bomani	mawiyah kai el-jamah	Voudou Mama	409
Booth	Kwan	Untitled One	444
Braxton	Joanne M.	Invisibles	10
Braxton	Charlie R.	Word/Life	402
Braxton	Joanne M.	Zoning	441
Brinson	C. Yaphet	Haiku	36
Brinson	C. Yaphet	Sextet	404
Brown	Kysha N.	a song for serpents	505
Bryant	Tisa	Stranger	415
Burwell	Toneka N. Bonitto	Going Home	130
Burwell	Toneka N. Bonitto	Leaving Winston-Salem	131
Caldwell	Rozell	The Bible Buckle	159
Carroll	Kenneth	For Brothas That Like to Holla	503
Chapman	Lyn'elle Patrice	Stevie Wonder	234
Cherry	James E.	Bird	223
Cherry	James E.	Pretty White Girls	86
Clarke	George Elliott	April 19, 19—: A Sonnet	170
Coates	Ta-Nehisi	Gale Sayers	448
Coleman	Wanda	American Sonnet (46)	124
Coleman	James	Black Women with Jewish Names	428
Coleman	James	Vipers, Flies, and Women of the Cloth	249
Cornish	Sam	Brown Bomber	450
Cornish	Sam	Love Song of a Red Cap	76
Cornish	Sam	Mississippi on the Doorstep	111
Cornish	Sam	Something Terrible Something	85

Last Name	First Name	Title	Page
Cornish	Sam	Work to be Done	115
datcher	michael	i am open	474
datcher	michael	soul gestures in spring	400
Dawson	Joy	Locks	32
Derricotte	Toi	Blackbottom	144
Derricotte	Toi	Boy at the Paterson Falls	81
Derricotte	Toi	Christmas Eve: My Mother Dressing	95
Derricotte	Toi	Exits from Elmina Castle: Cape Coast, Ghana	4
Derricotte	Toi	High School	207
Eady	Cornelius	Chittlin's	228
Eady	Cornelius	Photo by Ron Carter, playing his bass	239
Elam	Patricia	Mother's Day at McDonald's	178
Farley	Estelle E.	Grand Canyon	365
Farley	Estelle E.	Home Cookin	366
Ferebee	Gideon	Fallen Bodies	327
Ferebee	Gideon	For My Mother	326
Ferebee	Gideon	Refugee	44
Fleming	Robert	The Long Walk Home	328
Fleming	Robert	this mortal coil	311
Floyd-Miller	Cherryl	roots I: {....}	410
Floyd-Miller	Cherryl	roots II: the conjure woman replies	411
Floyd-Miller	Cherryl	she kneels at the wailing wall	321
Floyd-Miller	Cherryl	taboo	412
Forbes	Calvin	Gone	21
Forbes	Calvin	The Plea	315
Frazier	John	A Guard	285
Frazier	John	Audre's Son	164
Frazier	John	Deposed	392
Frazier	John	Sorrow Song	286
Frazier	John	Visiting Hours	250
Garnett	Ruth-Miriam	Barrage	12
Garnett	Ruth-Miriam	Concerning Violence	251
Georges	Danielle Legros	Anacaona	495
Georges	Danielle Legros	Another Ode to Salt	498
Gilkes	Dana	Rain Making	202
Gilkes	Dana	Thoughts from a 747	203
Gill	Charmaine A.	Memorial	37
Gilmore	Brian	coming to the net	442
Gilmore	Brian	Hazing	181
Glover	Yao (Hoke S. III)	Born	8
Glover	Yao (Hoke S. III)	Passing through This House	57
Glover	Yao (Hoke S. III)	Soledad	152
Glover	Yao (Hoke S. III)	The Science of Forgetting	213
Goodwin	Eli	After an All Day Skirmish with the Clouds	143
Goodwin	Eli	Confession	456
Goodwin	Everett	John Birks Gillespie: an appreciation {....}	225

Last Name	First Name	Title	Page
Goodwin	Everett	Mom Used to Listen to Erroll Garner	224
Goodwin	Eli	Untitled	122
Greene	Michelle Calhoun	Finished Poem	377
Greene	Michelle Calhoun	For My D.C. Girlfriends	378
Hamilton	M. Eliza	Midnight in Mississippi	175
Hamilton	M. Eliza	The Woman Who Jumped	14
Hamilton	M. Eliza	While Communing with a Tree {....}	333
Hand	Monica A.	She-Ghosts of Tiresias	211
Hand	Monica A.	Tattooed Girl	209
Hannaham	Dawn L.	I Love You, Though You're Unemployed	259
Hannaham	Dawn L.	If there's no sugar	260
Hannaham	Dawn L.	To a Flasher	376
Harding	Rachel E.	Brother is a Star	156
Harding	Rachel E.	Ezili Impending	473
Harris	Duriel E.	For My Mother	324
Harris	Peter J.	I know I Aint Hip No More	91
Harris	Duriel E.	Meditations I	52
Harris	Peter J.	The Next Malcolm Poem	446
Harvey	Yona Camille	The Museum Cashier	190
Hayes	Terrance	Midnight	359
Hayes	Terrance	What I Am	101
Hill	Michael	City in You	119
Hisle	Janeya K.	And all the sisters said...	336
Hisle	Janeya K.	For Fatma and her Co-wives	340
Hisle	Janeya K.	We	134
Hodges	Janice W.	Annuals and Perennials	109
Hodges	Janice W.	Bruised Children	171
Hodges	Janice W.	Control	418
Hope	Melanie	Our Mothers	319
Hope	Melanie	Praise the Daughter	472
Howard, Jr.	Willie Abraham	Cross Burning Black	210
Howard, Jr.	Willie Abraham	Memorial Drive	127
Howard, Jr.	Willie Abraham	Paralyzed	189
Hyman	Amitiyah Elayne	Surrender	537
Iverem	Esther	Peace Be Still	120
Jackson	Gale P.	1619. Virginia	17
Jackson	Gale P.	1691. Tituba of Salem	18
Jackson	Yvonne A.	How to Make It	161
jackson	reuben	Love # 49	399
Jackson	Angela	Loving	429
Jackson	Angela	Moment	437
Jackson	David Earl	Nice Sister-Scholars Need Loving, Too	424
jackson	reuben	One More Once	417
jackson	reuben	Smile	113
Jackson	Angela	The Fitting Room	116
Jackson	Angela	The Love of Travellers	112

Last Name	First Name	Title	Page
Jacobs	Bruce A.	After the 200th White Person Locks Her Car{....}	3
Jacobs	Bruce A.	Black on Black	125
Jacobs	Bruce A.	Friendly Skies	335
Jacobs	Bruce A.	It's a Dog's Life	165
Jacobs	Bruce A.	Lost	147
Jacobs	Bruce A.	Vivian, Take 57	107
Jamal	Paul	The Edge	261
Jean	Valerie	Astrology?	194
Jean-Giles	Mirlande	Circumcising Pandora	24
Jeffers	Honoree F.	Mary, Don't You Weep	483
Jeffers	Honoree F.	To Keep from Shouting Something	317
jess	tyehimba	father country	185
jess	tyehimba	father's shoes	184
jess	tyehimba	what does a man do	361
Johnson	Harold L.	At the Jackson Pollock Retrospective in L.A.	298
Johnson	Trasi	Matisse, Cut Outs	199
Johnson	Jacqueline Joan	Saudades	500
Johnson	Lisa Elaine	Spirit of the Dancer	219
Johnson	Brandon D.	Storm	481
Johnson	Brandon D.	The Artifice of War	272
Johnson	Harold L.	The Names of Summer: A War Memory	295
Johnson	Jacqueline Joan	What is There for Us?	341
Jones	Ira B.	Alley Games 6/the ascension	253
Jones	Ira B.	Haiku for My Brothers	468
Jordan	A. Van	A Debt is Paid	80
Jordan	A. Van	Black Drag Queen	89
Joseph	Allison	Noon Talk at Georgia's Coffee Shop	236
Joseph	Allison	Poem for the Purchase of a First Bra	62
Joseph	Allison	Shame of the Writers' Conference	447
Joseph	Allison	The Fourth Supreme	232
Joyner	Carolyn	They Do Not Have to Nest in Your Hair	201
Keita	Nzadi Zimele	back road	329
Keita	Nzadi Zimele	black tax	282
Keita	Nzadi Zimele	Cycles	349
Keita	Nzadi Zimele	dedicated to the domestics	192
Keita	Nzadi Zimele	lessons in lying	413
Keita	Nzadi Zimele	my sleeping husband	397
Keita	Nzadi Zimele	Rising	348
Keita	Nzadi Zimele	what is left	283
Keller	Bernard	Keep a Good Thought	470
Keller	Bernard	One Million Men Marching II.	469
Keller	Bernard	The Major	180
Kelly	Erren Geraud	'7-30-96	155
Kemp	Arnold J.	100 Times	187
Khali	Saddi	Walking On: A Declaration of Wholeness	82
King	Rosamond S.	another day	69

Last Name	First Name	Title	Page
King	Rosamond S.	H E L P	67
Lane	Pinkie Gordon	Nuclear Peril	510
Lane	Pinkie Gordon	Port Townsend Poems	33
Lee	James R.	Stranger at Home	494
Leeke	Kiamsha Madelyn	october death	465
Lewis	Melvin E.	Gullah Women	136
Lewis	Melvin E.	Hearts	384
Lewis	Melvin E.	My Mother	133
Lewis	William Henry	Some Solace, Some Yearning	280
Lewis	William Henry	To the People of a Small Town in Ohio...	103
Lightfoot	Toni Asante	In Oklahoma	281
Lights	Verneda (Rikki)	If Harriet Tubman Were Alive Today	22
Lights	Verneda (Rikki)	Savannah Brass	240
Lights	Verneda (Rikki)	Space	204
Lilley	Gary	Funeral	275
Lilley	Gary	Meetin the Conjure Woman	350
Lilley	Gary	Who Sez Thunderbirds Can't Fly	266
Lindsey	Kay	Stringbeans	354
louise	esther	jesus'song	436
louise	esther	swinging doors of knocking-wood{....}	535
Love	Monifa A.	Objects of Desire	59
Love	Monifa A.	Trying to Sleep After Studying Color Photos{....}	9
Lowe	Lorna	Sea Shells	477
Lukata	Baba	Ashy Gal	360
Lukata	Baba	Interpretations	371
Lukata	Baba	Rehersal	252
March	Sydney	A Thousand Marionettes	243
March	Sydney	Legacy	46
March	Sydney	Monk's Misterioso	231
March	Sydney	The Knockout	451
Mason	Keith Antar	I Am a Creature of the Obvious	41
Mataka	Laini	Can We Talk?	370
Mataka	Laini	Licorice	369
McCallum	Shara	Jamaica, October 18, 1972	499
McCallum	Shara	What My Mother Taught Me	471
McCallum	Shara	Yu no send. Me no come.	508
McDowell	Garrett	Child in the New Delhi Sun	148
McDowell	Garrett	Lights of the Bigtop	309
Miller	E. Ethelbert	Morning Buddhism	538
Miller	Nyere-Gibran	My Family	177
Moore	Lenard D.	a black soldier	304
Moore	Lenard D.	Letter from Kuwait	303
Moore	Lenard D.	Praisesong: From Son to Mother	26
Morgenstern	Felicia L.	Hues of Electric Blue	427
Morgenstern	Felicia L.	Ride Me Baby, Ride Me	426
Morgenstern	Felicia L.	Soul Roots	16

Last Name	First Name	Title	Page
Morgenstern	Felicia L.	Temple of Your Familiar	425
Morris	Alison	Imani's Song	419
Morris	Tracie	Just Say No Blues	388
Morris	Tracie	Lover's Total Recall	387
Morris	Tracie	Prelude to a Kiss	389
Morris	Tracie	Why I Won't Wear a Tatoo	386
Morris	Alison	Worry All the Time	172
Murphy	Merilene M.	park mole	270
Murphy	Merilene M.	when you say no	408
Neal	Gaston	Monk	230
Nelson	Marilyn	Drifter	75
Nelson	Marilyn	The Prayer of Miss Budd	73
Nelson	Marilyn	Washboard Wizard	70
Nickelson	Christopher	angry sisters	337
Nickelson	Christopher	charleston, south carolina	132
Nickelson	Christopher	three men	338
Nickelson	Christopher	Untitled	339
Norton	Odetta D.	Bound	15
Norton	Odetta D.	Senegal Sestina	49
Norton	Odetta D.	Tattoo, or Henna	51
okantah	mwatabu s.	African Morning	492
okantah	mwatabu s.	market day	493
okantah	mwatabu s.	the black experience	486
Okpala	Jude Chudi	When Africa Speaks	47
Oktavi		At Five	65
Palmer	Ronald D.	Sterling Brown	198
Pegram	Lisa	Perspective	379
Pegram	Lisa	yet another epiphany	390
Pertillar	Tammy Lynn	Generation Gap	273
Phaire	Dorothy	An Irresistible Light	168
Phillips	Carl	As from a Quiver of Arrows	463
Phillips	Carl	Blue	56
Phillips	Carl	Passing	196
Porter	Charles	Land of the Lost	118
Preston	Rohan B.	Dream of mango	28
Preston	Rohan B.	When I Leave My Body	462
Radden	Viki	Blood	434
Radden	Viki	Our Second Night	300
Radden	Viki	Sex	430
Radden	Viki	When you Talk that Talk	432
Renegade	D. J.	Call and Response	157
Renegade	D. J.	Father and Son	183
Robbins	Zak	Beaches	106
Robbins	Zak	December 12th	255
Robbins	Zak	October 7th	467
Roberts	Sybil J.	Poem # 3	398

Last Name	First Name	Title	Page
Ross	Gigi Maria	At the Threshold of the Moon	536
Russell	Pat	Be Careful When You Go Looking{....}	344
Rux	Carl Hancock	Just Asking	457
Shannon	Angela	Hands	352
Shannon	Angela	Integration	141
Shannon	Angela	JoNelle	138
Shannon	Angela	Returning the Water	40
Shannon	Angela	Sunday	129
Shannon	Angela	Wet Oak	351
Sharp	S. Pearl	How to Build a Prayer	514
Shephard	S.P.	Come and See My Little Toys	306
Shephard	S.P.	Four and Twenty Soldiers	305
Shephard	S.P.	Homeless Vets	307
Shephard	S.P.	Suicides and Fools	308
Shiphrah	Thandiwe	Grand Diva	330
Shiphrah	Thandiwe	Grandma	332
Shiphrah	Thandiwe	to adam	331
Simmonds	Kevin	A White Man and the Judge	257
Simmonds	Kevin	The New Sestina	381
singleton	giovanni	defensive driving	30
singleton	giovanni	for my 27th birthday	78
singleton	giovanni	thermometer	29
St. John	Primus	Obessions are Important	421
StacyLynn		Crushin	420
StacyLynn		Dirt	142
StacyLynn		Examination	256
StacyLynn		lookin good	460
Stanley	Thomas	Dr. Jack	245
Stanley	Thomas	Imperialism - The Dancing Do Not Die	268
Stover	Darrell	Fire/Water Blues	375
Tallie	Mariahadessa	Raindrop Women	99
Teasley	Lisa	As Dancers	220
Timpson	Reggie	for lester	222
Timpson	Reggie	verbal gun shots	244
Tolliver	Imani	fisher king	374
Tolliver	Imani	those I love are sometimes white	188
Tsang	Lori	Girlfriend	316
Tsang	Lori	Lunching	530
Umoja	Mbali	Say Something: a Change Is Gonna Come	277
Upton	Elaine Maria	A Streetwalker Trying to Speak{....}	484
Vessup	A. Anthony	The Mighty Blood	235
Vest	Jennifer Lisa	In This, the Fifth World	383
Walters	Wendy S.	Meridian Hill Terrace	153
Ward, Jr.	Jerry W.	Mississippi: Bell Zone 1	501
Washington	Harriet Wilkes	The Good Ole Days	258
Watkins-Cothran	E. Juaguina	The Beloved Ones	534

Last Name	First Name	Title	Page
Watley	Matthew	100 Million	478
Watley	Matthew	For the Man I Met on Georgia Ave.	176
Watley	Matthew	Negroes	445
Weatherford	Carole Boston	From the Mouth of the Gxara	520
Weatherford	Carole Boston	The Tar Baby on the Soapbox	105
Weaver	Afaa Michael S.	Baltimore	145
Weaver	Afaa Michael S.	Color-Struck	323
Weaver	Afaa Michael S.	Lines	358
Weaver	Afaa Michael S.	Michele	64
Weaver	Afaa Michael S.	Sin, 1969	357
Weaver	Afaa Michael S.	Thelonius	229
White	Artress Bethany	Moon Daughters	195
White	Artress Bethany	The Beelzebub Chronicles	353
Wilkinson	Claude	Landmarks	77
Williams	Niama Leslie	Daniel's Hands	367
Williams	Karen	From the Spirit of Phillis Wheatley {....}	19
Williams	Kimmika L.H.	I watched	396
Williams	Crystal	In Search of Aunt Jemima	97
Williams	Crystal	Revolutionary Thoughts	93
Williams	Lana C.	Saints	160
Williams	Kimmika L.H.	Snapshot: West Philly	158
Williams	Lorelei	Stranger in the Village	200
Wilson	Ronaldo V.	dungle sublime	166
Wilson	Imani e.	fruitbowl 1	90
Wilson	Carletta	history of the quilt{....}	512
Wilson	Carletta	kiss her that she don't know how	372
Wilson	Ronaldo V.	white	54
Winbush-David	Wanda	African Sunrunner	48
Woodward	Vincent	cornbread blues	368
Wray	Clyde A.	Private Thoughts	356
Wray	Clyde A.	The Star	355
Wright	Stephen Caldwell	And the Birds Sing of Life	455
Wright	Stephen Caldwell	Harvest	27
X	Derrick (Goldie Williams)	Burn Rubber On Me	238
Ya Salaam	Kalamu	haiku # 135	364
Ya Salaam	Kalamu	Threnody	149
Ya Salaam	Kalamu	Why I Don't Leave the Apartment{....}	362

CONTRIBUTORS

Joan Adams is an Administrative Assistant in a Baltimore law firm and a part-time student concentrating in professional writing. She has written three short stories, one screen play and over one hundred poems.

Opal Palmer Adisa is a writer, storyteller and mother of three. Her published works, include *It Begins With Tears* (1997), *Tamarind and Mango Women* (1992), *Traveling Women* (with Devorah Major, 1989), *Bake-Face and Other Guava Stories* (1986) and *Pina, the Many-Eyed Fruit* (1995).

Lauren Anita Arrington lives and writes in Silver Spring, Maryland. Jabari Asim is the author of *Not Guilty: Twelve Black Men Speak Out on Law, Justice, and Life*.

Vicki-Ann Assevero lives and writes in Trinidad.

Doreen Baingana was born in Uganda. Her fiction and poetry has been published in *Brochu's*, *The American Literary*, *The Dexter Review*, and *The New Vision* –Uganda's leading English language newspaper.

Houston A. Baker, Jr is a professor of English at Duke University. He is the author of *Modernism and The Harlem Renaissance, Workings of The Spirit* and *Afro-American Poetics*. He is the former director of the Center for the Study of Black Literature and Culture at the University of Pennsylvania.

Andrew J. Baldwin was a Lannan poetry fellow with the Folger Shakespeare Library from 1997-1999.

asha bandele is the author of a collection of poems, *Absence in the Palms of My Hands*, and a memoir, *The Prisoner's Wife*. She lives and writes in Brooklyn, New York and is a member of the Malcolm X Grassroot Movement.

S. Brandi Barnes has literary work in anthologies such as *Nommo-2, Remembering Ourselves Whole*, the 1991 Anthology of Chicago Writers. Chicago Writers. *Nommo: A Literary Legacy of Black Chicago*, and *The Woman that I Am: Literature by Women of Color*. She is a former member of the OBAC Writers founded by Hoyt Fuller.

Eddie D. Bell is a writer, educator, consultant and photographer. He resides in New Paltz, New York.

Nadir Lasana Bomani was born in New Orleans in 1972. He is a graduate of Southern University at New Orleans. His work is included in *Fertile Ground*.

Mawiyah Kai El-Jamah Bomani has work in *Freeform Magazine, Dark Eros* and *Fertile Ground*.

Kwan Booth was born in Richmond, Virginia. He has been writing since 1996.

Charlie R. Braxton is a poet, playwright and journalist from Mississippi. His poems, essays and criticism has appeared in *Black American Literature Forum, The Black Nation, Catalyst* and *The Minnesota Review*.

Joanne M. Braxton is a poet and assistant professor of English, American Studies and Afro-American Studies at the College of William and Mary in Williamsburg, Virginia. She is the author of *Black Women Writing Autobiography*.

C. Yaphet Brinson was born and raised in the New York City area. His work has appeared in *Long Shot, A Gathering of the Tribes*. He died in 1999.

Kysha N. Brown lives in New Orleans. She is the co-editor of *Fertile Ground*.

Tisa Bryant is a San Francisco-based writer and curator. Her work has recently appeared in *Clamour, Children of the Dream: Our Own Stories of Growing Up Black in America*. A novel, *Letters toRegret* will be published by Leroy Press.

Toneka N. Bonitto Burwell lives and writes in Corona, New York.

Rozell Caldwell was born in 1948 in Trenton, Tennessee and grew up in Cairo, Illinois. He received his B.A. from Lane College in 1971. He is the author of *Things as They Seem* and *Tales of the Griot*.

Kenneth Carroll is a native Washingtonian. He is the author of *So What!* He is the Site Coordinator for WritersCorps, an arts and social-service program founded by the NEA and Americorps.

Lyn'elle Patrice Chapman lives and writes in New Orleans.

James E. Cherry is a poet/fiction writer and a native Tennessean. He states that one of his major objectives is to write the way Coltrane, Monk, Dizzy and others of a similar vein, played a form of music that is the exemplification of intelligence and freedom. Cherry's work has been featured in *Callaloo, African American Review, Crab Orchard Review, Illuminations* and *Stolen Island Review*. He is currently working on a new a novel.

George Elliott Clarke received the Governor General Literary Award for Poetry in 2001 for his newest collection *Execution Poems*. He teaches English Literature at the University of Toronto.

Ta-Nehisi Coates was born in Baltimore, Maryland and now lives in Brooklyn, New York where he is a freelance writer.

James Coleman lives in Washington, D.C. He appeared on a number of the early Ascension Poetry Reading programs.

Wanda Coleman was born and raised in Los Angeles. She is the author of several collection of poems published by Black Sparrow Press. Her last book *Bath Water Wine* was released in 1998.

Sam Cornish lives in Massachusetts. He is the author of *Songs of Jubilee, Generations, Sam's World* and *1935*.

Michael Datcher was born in Chicago and raised on the Eastside of Long Beach, California. He is a graduate of the University of California and is the editor of *My Brothers Keeper* published in 1992. He is the author of *Raising Fences: A Black Man's Love Story*.

Joy Dawson is a graduate of Howard University. During the 1997-1998 school year, she was a Lannan poetry fellow with the Folger Shakespeare Library.

Toi Derricotte teaches at the University of Pittsburgh. Her memoir, *The Black Notebooks* won the Black Caucus of the American Library Association Award for non-fiction, the Annisfied-Wolf Award for non-fiction from the Cleveland Foundation, and was nominated for the PEN Martha Albrand Award.

Cornelius Eady is the author of *Kartunes, Victims of the Latest Dance Craze, The Gathering of My Name* and *You Don't Miss Your Water*. His last book is *Brutal Imagination*.

Patricia Elam is a fiction and non-fiction writer. Her work has been published by *The Washington Post, Essence,* and *Emerge.* Her commentaries have been heard on National Public Radio (NPR). Her novel *Breathing Room* was published by Pocketbooks in Spring 2000.

Estelle Elizabeth Farley is a member of the Carolina African American Collective. She was born in Berkeley, California and graduated from Fisk University.

Gideon Ferebee is a poet, singer, filmmaker, and civil rights director for the EPA. He is the author of *Out! To Lead.*

Robert Fleming is a freelance journalist, and formerly worked as a reporter for the New York Daily News. His articles have appeared in *Essence, Black Enterprise, The New York Times* and *Omni.* He is the author of *The Wisdom of the Elders* and *The African American Writer's Handbook.*

Cherryl Floyd-Miller is a Cave Canem Fellow and a 1994-1995 Indiana Arts Commission Associate Fellow for Literature. She lives and works in North Carolina.

Calvin Forbes was born in Newark, New Jersey. He teaches at the School of the Art Institute of Chicago. He is the author of *Blue Monday, From the Book of Shine,* and *The Shine Poems.*

John Alexander Frazier, Jr. has written three collections of poetry: *Natasha and the Wolf, Real Sugar* and *Husk.* His work has appeared in many journals and anthologies including *The Massachusetts Review, Revolutionary Voices, Testimony* and *Presence Africaine.* He teaches rhetoric, literature and creative writing at Georgetown Day School in Washington, D.C.

Ruth-Miriam Garnett is the editor of Harlem Arts Journal and author of *A Move Further South.*

Danielle Legros Georges is a poet and translator. She is the author of *Maroon.* Her awards for writing, include a MacDowell residency, a Caribbean Writers' Summer Institute Scholarship and the Fannie Lou Hamer Award.

Charmaine A. Gill lives and writes in Barbados.

Dana Gilkes lives and writes in St.Michael, Barbados.

Brian Gilmore was born and raised in Washington, D.C. He is the author of *elvis presley is alive and well and living in harlem, jungle nights and soda fountain rags.*

Bro. Yao (Hoke S. Glover III) is a poet living in the Washington Metropolitan Area, and a graduate of the M.F.A. program at the University of Maryland College Park. His work has appeared in *Obsidian III, African American Review, Crab Orchard Review* and other journals.

Eli Goodwin lives in Cambridge, Massachusetts. He is the brother of the poet Everett Goodwin.

Everett Goodwin is a poet and playwright.

Michelle Calhoun Greene is a longtime resident of the Washington, D.C. area. She attended Howard University. She is a credit union manager by profession and is employed by the Navy Federal Credit Union

M. Eliza Hamilton is of Fulani (Guinea), Jamaican, Grenadian, and Carib Indian ancestry. She has a self-published chapbook *What is Now Unanswerable.*

Monica A. Hand is a poet and book artist living in working class Maryland with her two children. A Maryland State Arts Council grantee and Cave Canem Fellow, she has been writing since she was ten.

Dawn L. Hannaham was born and raised in the New York metropolitan area, attended NYU and Georgetown University. She writes in English, Russian and Spanish. Her work has appeared in *Brownstone* and *the Journal of Downward Mobility*.

Rachel E. Harding is a native of Atlanta, Georgia. She presently writes and teaches in Denver, Colorado. Her poems have appeared in several journals and anthologies, including *My Soul Is a Witness: African American Women's Spirituality*.

Duriel Harris is a native of Chicago. She is a co-founder of The Language Art Collective. She lives in New York and teaches at the Dalton School.

Peter J. Harris is a graduate of Howard University. He is the founding publisher and editor of the magazines, *The Drummin Between Us: Black Love & Erotic Poetry* and *Genetic Dancers*. He is the author of *Hand Me My Griot Clothes: The Autobiography of Junior Baby* which won the 1993 PEN Oakland Josephine Miles Award for literary excellence.

Yona Camille Harvey is a graduate of Howard University and a former member of the Washington, D.C. Writers Corps. She has facilitated creative writing workshops in undeserved communities and taught English in southern Japan. She currently lives in Pittsburgh with her husband, poet Terrance Hayes and their daughter.

Terrance Hayes lives in Pittsburgh. He is the author of *Muscular Music*. His poems have appeared in *Poet Lore* and *The Shooting Star Review*. In 1995 he won an Academy of American Poets Prize.

Michael Hill is a graduate of Howard University. Hill lives in Alexandria, Virginia.

Janeya K. Hisle is a graduate of Howard University. Hisle lives in Jedda, Kingdom of Saudi Arabia.

Janice W. Hodges is co-founder of La Jan Productions, Inc. a writer's consortium that promotes works by African American artists. She is a charter member of the Carolina African American Writer's Collective.

Melanie Hope is a lesbian poet of African heritage. Her writing has appeared in *The Caribbean Writer and Sinister Wisdom, The Key to Everything, The Arc of Love* and *Afrekete*.

Willie Abraham Howard, Jr. lives in Decatur, Georgia. This anthology would not have been possible without his encouragement.

Amitiyah Elayne Hyman is a minister living in Washington, D.C.

Esther Iverem is an essayist, cultural critic and poet. She is the author of *The Time: Portrait of a Journey Home* published by Africa World Press in 1994. She lives in Washington, D.C. With her son.

Angela Jackson is the author of *And All These Roads Be Luminous: Poems Selected and New*. She has won numerous awards from the Illinois Arts Council and a National Endowment for the Arts Creative Writing for Fiction in 1980.

David Jackson was a Southern-born (Chattanooga, TN.) poet and journalist, who died in 2001. As a poem crazy cultural worker in the 1970s, he sponsored readings by most of the leading black poets at the original location of the Studio Museum in Harlem. Jackson was the 1998 Legacy Award winner presented by the Arts and Entertainment Task Force of the National Black Journalists Association.

Gale P. Jackson is currently serving as assistant professor and resident storyteller on the faculties of CUNY and the Hayground School. Her books include *Khoisan Tale* and *Bridge Suite: Narrative Poems Based on the Lives of African and African American Women in the Early History of These Black Nations.*

reuben jackson lives in Washington, D.C. where he works as an archivist with the Smithsonian Insitituion's Duke Ellington Collection. His first book of poems *Fingering the Keys* won the 1992 Columbia Book Award. His work has been published in *Gargoyle, Indiana Review, Chelsea,* and *Word Wrights.*

Yvonne A. Jackson is a graduate of Yale University. Her work experience runs the gamut – janitorial, foodservice, secretarial, publishing, and computer consulting. She received a Masters of Fine Arts in Fiction from the University of Alabama in 1995.

Bruce A. Jacobs' first book of poems, *Speaking Through My Skin* won the Naomi Long Madgett Poetry Award and was published by Michigan State University Press in 1997.

Paul Jamal's contributed poem was submitted by Dorothy Hazell who lives in Brooklyn, New York.

Mirlande Jean-Gilles is a graduate of Bernard Baruch College. She is an assistant fiction editor at *African Voices Magazine.*

Valerie Jean received her MFA from the University of Maryland in 1989. Her work has been published in *Spirit and Fire,* and *Double Stitch.*

Honoree F. Jeffers is a graduate of Talladega College. She received her MFA in Creative Writing from the University of Alabama.

tyehimba jess lives in Chicago. He is a Cave Canem graduate. He won an Illinois Arts Council Artist Fellowship in Poetry for 2000 – 2001, the 2001 *Chicago Sun Times* Poetry Award, and the 2001 Gwendolyn Brooks Open Mic Poetry Awards. He is the author of *when niggas love Revolution like they love the bulls.*

Brandon D. Johnson is originally from Gary, Indiana, but now lives in Washington, D.C. He is a founding member of the poetry and performance collective, The Modern Urban Griots. He is the author of *Man Burns Ant.*

Harold L. Johnson was born in 1933 in Portland, Oregon. He is the author of one chapbook *Dry Boats* and has published often regionally. He is an Africa-USA fellow of the Ragdale Foundation of Lake Forest, Illinois, and co-editor of the poetry quarterly *Fireweed: Poetry of Western Oregon.*

Jacqueline J. Johnson is a multi-disciplined writer. A native of Philadelphia, she is the author of *Stokely Carmichael: The Story of Black Power.* Ms. Johnson reviews books for *Upscale* magazine.

Lisa Elaine Johnson is a graduate of the Ellington School of the Arts and the Howard University Drama Department. She teaches at Paul Junior High School in Washington, D.C.

Trasi Johnson lives and writes in France.

Ira B. Jones lives and writes in St. Louis Missouri.

A. Van Jordan was born and raised in Akron, Ohio. He attended Wittenberg University, Howard University and Warren College. He worked for two years with the WritersCorp branch of the AmeriCorps program in Washington, D.C. In 1995, he was awarded a D.C. Commission on the Arts Literary Fellowship. He is the author of *Rise*.

Allison Joseph is the author of three books of poems: *What Keep Us Here, Soul Train* and *In Every Seam*. She teaches at Southern Illinois University in Carbondale, Illinois.

Carolyn Joyner is a member of the DC-based sisterhood of poets, Collective Voices. She performs her poetry in the metropolitan area and with the collective, performed at the 1998 Women's Weekend Conference in London, England. Her work has appeared in *360'A Revolution of Black* Poets and *The Edge of Twilight*. She is currently pursuing an M.A. in writing in the John Hopkins University part-time graduate degree program.

Nzadi Zimele Keita writes poetry, fiction and non-fiction. She is the author of *Birthmarks*. She has been nominated for a Pushcart Prize and her work has appeared in numerous publications, including: *In Defense of Mumia, Confirmations: An Anthology of African American Women*. She lives in Philadelphia.

Bernard J. Keller is an educational consultant living in New York.

Erren Geraud Kelly is a poet based in Baton Rouge, Louisiana.

Arnold J. Kemp is a writer of Afro Caribbean decent. His poetry has been published in *Callaloo, Agni Review, River Styx, Three Rivers Poetry Journal* and *Mirage Periodical*.

Saddi Khali lives in New Orleans. His work appears in *Fertile Ground*.

Rosamond S. King is a founding member of BlaWoWow-Black Women Who Write. She has published poems in *Poet Lore, Obsidian II*, and *Onionhead*. She lives in Brooklyn, New York.

Pinkie Gordon Lane is the author of four volumes of poetry and the editor of two anthologies of poems by African American poets. She served as the first African American poet laureate of the state of Louisiana from 1989-1992.

James R. Lee graduated from Lincoln University and attended Howard and American Universities for graduate studies. His work appears in *Drumming Between Us, The Journal of African Travel Writing, The Arkansas Review, Obsidian II* and *Dialogue*.

Kiamsha Madelyn Leeke is an online minister, mixed media artist, poet, writer, online legal columnist, lawyer, motivational speaker, and entrepreneur who lives and works in Washington, D.C.

Melvin E. Lewis has work published in *Shooting Star Review, Pen International* and the anthology *The Poetry Connection: Dial-A-Poem Chicago! Tenth Anniversary 1981-1991*.

William Henry Lewis is the author of *In the Arms of our Elders*, a collection of stories published by Carolina Wren Press.

Toni Asante Lightfoot is the author of *Let Pharoah Go*. She has performed her "jazzoetry" throughout the United States and the Caribbean. She has been an avid supporter of writers throughout the diaspora.

Vernada (Rikki) Sagay-Lights is a medical doctor living in Philadelphia. She is the author of *Dog Moon*.

Gary Lilley is a poet and playwright from North Carolina. He is a former member of the DC Writers Corps and a 1996 recipient of the D.C. Commission on the Arts Fellowship in Poetry. He has published a book of short fiction with Renee Stout, entitled *Hoodoo You Love?*

Kay Lindsay...is hopefully alive and well and writing more wonderful poems. Please contact the editor. We would love to hear from you.

Esther Louise lives and writes in Brooklyn, New York.

Monifa A. Love is the author of *Provisions* and *Freedom in the Dismal*. She lives in Tallahassee, Florida.

Baba Lukata (Louis Anderson) is a native of Powhatan, Virginia. A longtime activist and counselor, Lukata has developed the Madaadi Rites of Passage program for youth.

Shara McCallum was born in Kingston, Jamaica and emigrated to the United States at the age of nine. She completed her MFA at the University of Maryland and her Ph.D in English at SUNY-Binghamton. She lives in Memphis, Tennessee. She is the author of *Water Between Us*.

Garrett McDowell grew up in California and now lives and writes in Washington, D.C. His publications include short fiction in *Streetlights* and essays in *the Encyclopedia of African American Education*.

Keith Antar Mason is a poet, playwright, artist, community activist, and creator of the Hittite Empire, an African American male performance-art collective that has performed throughout the world.

Sydney March was born in Jamaica and educated in the UK and the USA. He is a poet, musician, and folklorist. A WritersCorps member 1996-98, Jenny Moore Fellow in 1993. He is the author of *Stealing Mangoes*.

Laini Mataka was born, raised and miseducated in Baltimore, Maryland. She is the author of *Black Rhythms for Fancy Dancers*, *Never As Strangers* and *Restoring the Queen*.

E. Ethelbert Miller is the author of *Fathering Words: The Making of an African American Writer*. He is the editor of *In Search of Color Everywhere*, which was awarded the 1994 PEN Oakland Josephine Miles Award. The anthology was also a Book of the Month Club selection. Mr. Miller can be reached at emiller698@aol.com. His website is: www.eethelbertmiller.com.

Nyere-Gibran Miller is a student at the Edmund Burke School in Washington, D.C. He is the son of E. Ethelbert Miller.

Kimberly Williams Moore was born in Monroe, Louisiana. She attended the University of North Carolina at Chapel Hill and received an M.A. in Creative Writing from North Carolina State University. She lives in Durham, North Carolina and owns ComSolutions, Inc., a public relations firm.

Felicia L. Morgenstern is a globetrotting teacher and writer. She is the author of *The Night Mother Earth Told Father Sky She Was Tired of the Missionary Position* by Compass Rose Press.

Lenard D. Moore is a poet, playwright, essayist, book reviewer and fiction writer. He is the author of *Forever Home*, and *Desert Storm: A Brief History*. He is the founder and executive director of the Carolina African American Writers'Collective.

Alison Morris is a graduate of Howard University and Long Island University. She is a free-lance writer and lives in Brooklyn, New York with her son.

Tracie Morris has performed her work in England, Switzerland, Germany, Denmark, Korea, and Japan. Her work is included in *The United States Of Poetry*, *Rock She Wrote: Women Write about Rock, Pop and Rap*, *In Defense of Mumia*, and *Voices from the Nuyorican Poets Cafe*. She is the author of *Chap-T-her Won* and *Intermission*.

Merilene M. Murphy is the poet author of *Under Peace Rising*. She is the founder of Telepoetics, a global poetry forum formed in 1994. She lives in Los Angeles, California.

Gaston Neal died in 1999. His work appeared in the classic anthology *Black Fire*. He was the author of *The Poetry of Gaston Neal, a Sampler*.

Marilyn Nelson is the author of *The Fields of Praise: New and Selected Poems*. Her book *Homeplace* was a finalist for the National Book Award. She is a recipient of the Annisfield-Wolf Award. She is professor of English at the University of Connecticut at Storrs.

Christopher Nickelson lives in Brooklyn. He is a graduate student at the New School in New York.

Odetta D. Norton was born in Halifax, Nova Scotia and raised in Syracuse, New York. She lived and worked in Senegal as the recipient of a Fulbright fellowship in 1993-94. She is a doctoral student in the Visual and Cultural Studies program at the University of Rochester.

Mwatabu S. Okantah lives in Kent, Ohio. He is the author of *Afreeka Brass*.

Jude Chudi Okpala is an emerging Nigerian writer. He is the author of the novel *The Visible Man*.

Oktavi is a member of the Carolina African American Writers Collective. She is the author of *Restoration*.

Ronald D. Palmer was Ambassador to Togo (1976-1978), Ambassador to Malaysia (1981-1983) and Ambassador to Mauritius (1986-1989). He is Professor of the Practice of International Affairs at George Washington University.

Lisa Pegram is currently an active member of the performance collective Generation 2000. She is a poet, teacher and human rights advocate.

Tammy Lynn Pertillar is a scholar of African American and Brazilian history. She live in Washington, D.C.

Dorothy Phaire writes contemporary fiction, poetry and personal experience essays. She is the author of *Almost Out of Love*.

Carl Phillips teaches at Washington University, St. Louis, where he also directs the Creative Writing Program. His collections, include *Cortege*, nominated for the 1995 National Book Critics Circle Award, and *From the Devotions*.

Charles Porter was born in New Jersey. He is a graduate of Howard University.

Rohan B. Preston is the winner of the 1997 Henry Blakely, Jr. Poetry Prize and the recipient of a 1996 fellowship from the Illinois Arts Council. He is the author of *Dreams in Soy Sauce*. His poems have appeared in *The Atlanta Review*, *The Crab Orchard Review*, *Eyeball*, *Hammers*, *Ploughshares*, *River Styx*, and *TriQuarterly*.

Viki Radden is the author of *Trapped Behind Glass*. She lives in Woodacre, CA.

D.J. Renegade was born in Pittsburgh, PA. A former nightclub disk jockey, he has lived in Washington, D.C. for the last 16 years. He works in the WritersCorps program teaching poetry workshops in underserved areas. A runner-up in the 1997 National Poetry Slam, he appears in the movie *Slam*.

Zachary Scott Robbins currently teaches high school English in Montgomery County, Maryland and Washington, D.C.

Sybil Roberts is a playwright and teaches Drama at Howard University.

Gigi Maria Ross lives and writes in Washington, D.C.

Pat Russell lives in Seattle. She is the director of the Goodwill Learning Center.

Carl Hancock Rux is the author of *Pagan Operetta*. He appeared in the PBS 1997 documentary, *Shattering the Silence*. His CD *Rux Revue* (Sony 550 Music) was co-produced by the Dust Brothers. His forthcoming novel is entitled *Asphalt*.

Kalamu Ya Salaam lives in New Orleans. He is the founder and director of Nommo Literary Society, a Black writers' workshop. He is also the leader of WordBand, a poetry performance ensemble. He can be reached via email: kalamu@aol.com.

Angela Shannon is the winner of the 1997 Willow Review Poetry Prize as well as a 1996 poetry award from Illinois Arts Council. She is a member of the Chicago-based Blue Ellipsis Collective. Her work has been published in *The Crab Orchard Review*, *Jackleg*, *Ploughshares* and *TriQuarterly*.

S. Pearl Sharp is a producer, writer and director. She is the author of four volumes of poetry, the stageplay; *The Sistuhs*, the non-fiction work; *Black Women for Beginners* and a spoken word album; *On the Sharp Side*.

S.P. Shephard is a 1981 graduate of Howard University with a degree in Elementary Education. She writes poetry and children stories.

Kevin Simmonds studied at Vanderbilt University, Mills College, and Middle Tennessee State University. His writings have appeared in *Black Arts Quarterly*, *Black Bear Review*, *Haight-Ashbury Literary Journal* and *Folio: A Literary Journal*.

giovanni singleton is a native of Richmond, Virginia. She received an MFA in Creative Writing and Poetics from The New College of California. She lives in the San Francisco Bay Area. Her work has been published in *Five Fingers Review* and *Superflux*. She is the editor of *nocturnes* magazine.

StacyLynn lives and writes in Laurel, Maryland.

Primus St. John is the author of *Communion, Poems 1976-1998*. He has taught literature and creative writing at Portland State University in Oregon for the past twenty-six years. He is a winner of the Oregon Book Award for Poetry.

Thomas Stanley was born in Cincinnati, Ohio. He lives in Mechanicsville, Maryland. His poetry is included in *Erotique Noire: An Anthology of Black Erotica.*

Darrell Stover is Program Director for St.Joseph's Historic Foundation/Hayti Heritage Center. He directed The Spoken Word Performance Poetry Ensemble in Washington, D.C. He has an MA in Writing from John Hopkins University. He co-hosts the nationally broadcasted examination of southern literature, "Storylines Southeast."

Mariahadessa Ekere Tallie is the co-founder of Words and Waistbeads, a five-woman ensemble. She is the senior writer with *African Voices.*

Kim Taylor (Thandiwe Shiphrah) is a poet, writer and orator who uses the written and spoken word to effect personal healing and transformation. Her work has been published in *The Potomac Review* and *The Journal of Applied Poetry.* Taylor's work also appears in the anthology *Fast Talk, Full Volume: An Anthology of Contemporary African American Poetry.*

Lisa Teasley has fiction and poetry in the anthologies *In The Tradition: An Anthology of Young Black Writers* and *Women For All Seasons.* A native of Los Angeles, she is a also a painter and exhibits extensively throughout the country. She is the author of *Glow in the Dark.*

Reggie Timpson is the author of *Verbal Gunshots.* He lives in Baltimore, Maryland.

Imani Tolliver was born in West Los Angles. She is a 1997 graduate of Howard University. She was a writing instructor for WritersCorps. Her poems have appeared in *The Drumming Between Us* and *Janus.*

Lori Tsang was raised by a Chinese Jamaican mother and an "American" Chinese father in Connecticut and Indiana. She received the 1997 Mayor's Arts Award for Outstanding Emerging Artist. She produced and directed the award-winning film *Chinaman's Choice.*

Mbali Umoja lives in St.Lucy, Barbados.

Elaine Upton is the author of *Children of Apartness.* It was a co-winner of the 1993 Columbia Book Award and finalist for the Paterson Poetry Prize. She resides in Lenox, Massachusetts.

A. Anthony Vessup's performance and publication awards, include the Australian Peace Day Medallion, the National Library of Poetry, the International Society of Poets and the American Poetry Association.

Jennifer Lisa Vest is a graduate of Hampshire College and Howard University. She received her Masters Degree in History from Howard in 1992.

Jerry W. Ward, Jr. is the Lawrence Durgin Professor of Literature at Tougaloo College. He is the co-editor of the *Richard Wright Newsletter.* He is the editor of *Trouble the Water: 250 Years of African American Poetry.*

Matthew Watley lives and writes in Hyattsville, Maryland.

Harriet Wilkes Washington is a graduate of Michigan State University. She has been an editor and feature writer for the *National Society of Black Engineers* magazine and *Pride* magazine.

Wendy S. Walters has poetry in *Obsidian II* and *Hues* magazine. She is completing a PhD from Cornell Univesiy.

Eunice Juaguina Watkins-Cothran is assistant to the director of the Advanced Education Program in general dentistry at Howard University.

Carole Boston Weatherford has authored 13 books, including *The Sound That Jazz Makes*. Her poetry is collected in *The Tan Chanteuse* and *The Tar Baby on the Soapbox*. Her children's poetry titles, include *Remember the bridge: Poems of a People*; *Sidewalk Chalk: Poems of the City*; and *Princeville: The 500-Year Flood*. Weatherford is a columnist for the *Greensboro News & Record*.

Afaa Michael S. Weaver is the author of several collections of poems. The most recent collection is *Multitudes: Poems Selected and New*.

Artress Bethany White's fiction, poetry and prose have appeared in *Callaloo*, *River Styx*, *Ark/angel Review*, *A Gathering of the Tribes*, *Quarterly Black Review of Books* and the *Village Voice*.

Paula White-Jackson is a member of the Carolina African Writers Collective. In 1990 she received an Emerging Artist Fellowship from the Winston-Salem Arts Council. She graduated from Upsala College, East Orange, New Jersey.

Claude H. Wilkinson has taught in the English Departments of a number of colleges and universities. His poetry has won awards from the Arkansas Writers' Conference, the Mississippi Poetry Society and the Poetry Society of Tennessee.

Crystal Williams began her career at the Nuyorican Poets Cafe. She was captain of the 1995 New York Slam Team. She is the author of *Here and Reachin'*.

Derrick "Goldie" Williams is a poet and actor from Oakland, California. He is a member of the Anansi Writers' Workshop at the World Stage in Los Angeles.

Karen Williams is a poet, essayist and freelance editor/writer. She is also a health administrator in metro Detroit. She is a member of the Detroit Black Writers' Guild. Her work has been published in *Spirit and Flame: A Contemporary Anthology of African American Poetry*.

Kimmika L. H. Williams is the author of six books of poetry. The most recent is *Epic Memory; Places and Spaces I've Been*. She teaches in the Theater Department at Temple University.

Lana C. Williams is a staff writer for the *Independent Weekly* and has published her poetry in the *African American Review*.

Lorelei Williams was born and raised in the South Bronx and Harlem. In 1992, she attended the Breadloaf Young Writers Workshop and in 1996 she joined Cave Canem. A graduate of Yale University in 1998, she is currently working as an analyst with Andersen Consulting in New York.

Niama Leslie Williams is a writer, scholar and adjunct professor at Temple University.

Wanda Winbush-David lives and writes in Ft. Washington, Maryland.

Carletta Wilson has poetry in *The Raven Chronicles*, and *Prism International*. She publishes for children under the pseudonym Sundaira Morninghouse. She works for the Seattle Public Library in the Fine and Performing Arts Department.

Imani e. Wilson lives and in Laurelton, New York.

Ronaldo V. Wilson is a graduate of New York University's Creative Writing Program and the University of California at Berkeley. He is a Cave Canem fellow and has held residencies at Squaw Valley and the Provincetown Fine Arts Work Center. His poems have been published in Provincetown Arts.

Clyde A. Wray lives and writes in Van Nuys, California.

Vincent Woodard is presently living in Austin, Texas. He is working towards a doctorate degree in English Literature.

Stephen Caldwell Wright is Founder and President of the Gwendolyn Brooks Writers Association of Florida and the editor of *Revelry*. He teaches English and Creative Writing at Seminole Community College. His poems have appeared in *the Colorado Review, The Carolina Quarterly* and *Phylon*. He recently edited *On Gwendolyn Brooks: Reliant Contemplation*.